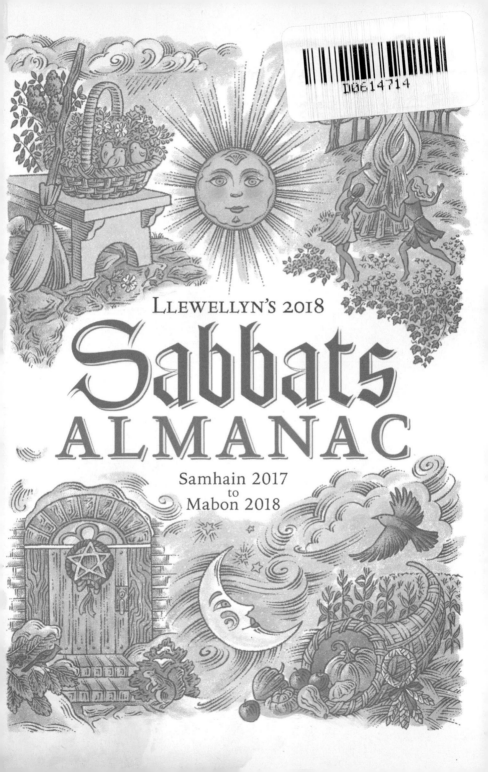

LLEWELLYN'S 2018

Sabbats

ALMANAC

Samhain 2017
to
Mabon 2018

Llewellyn's Sabbats Almanac:
Samhain 2017 to Mabon 2018

Cover art © Carolyn Vibbert
Cover design by Ellen Lawson
Editing by Aaron Lawrence
Interior Art: © Carolyn Vibbert, excluding illustrations on pages 37, 38, 76, 78, 113, 114, 146, 180, 216, 257, 292, and 294, which are © Wen Hsu

You can order annuals and books from *New Worlds*, Llewellyn's catalog. To request a free copy call toll free: 1-877-NEW WRLD, or order online by visiting our website at http://subscriptions.llewellyn.com.

ISBN: 978-0-7387-3771-3

Llewellyn Worldwide Ltd.
2143 Wooddale Drive
Woodbury, MN 55125-2989
www.llewellyn.com

Printed in the United States of America

2017

JANUARY
S	M	T	W	T	F	S
1	2	3	4	5	6	7
8	9	10	11	12	13	14
15	16	17	18	19	20	21
22	23	24	25	26	27	28
29	30	31				

FEBRUARY
S	M	T	W	T	F	S
			1	2	3	4
5	6	7	8	9	10	11
12	13	14	15	16	17	18
19	20	21	22	23	24	25
26	27	28	29			

MARCH
S	M	T	W	T	F	S
			1	2	3	4
5	6	7	8	9	10	11
12	13	14	15	16	17	18
19	20	21	22	23	24	25
26	27	28	29	30	31	

APRIL
S	M	T	W	T	F	S
						1
2	3	4	5	6	7	8
9	10	11	12	13	14	15
16	17	18	19	20	21	22
23	24	25	26	27	28	29
30						

MAY
S	M	T	W	T	F	S
	1	2	3	4	5	6
7	8	9	10	11	12	13
14	15	16	17	18	19	20
21	22	23	24	25	26	27
28	29	30	31			

JUNE
S	M	T	W	T	F	S
				1	2	3
4	5	6	7	8	9	10
11	12	13	14	15	16	17
18	19	20	21	22	23	24
25	26	27	28	29	30	

JULY
S	M	T	W	T	F	S
						1
2	3	4	5	6	7	8
9	10	11	12	13	14	15
16	17	18	19	20	21	22
23	24	25	26	27	28	29
30	31					

AUGUST
S	M	T	W	T	F	S
		1	2	3	4	5
6	7	8	9	10	11	12
13	14	15	16	17	18	19
20	21	22	23	24	25	26
27	28	29	30	31		

SEPTEMBER
S	M	T	W	T	F	S
					1	2	3
4	5	6	7	8	9	10
11	12	13	14	15	16	17
18	19	20	21	22	23	24
25	26	27	28	29	30	

OCTOBER
S	M	T	W	T	F	S
1	2	3	4	5	6	7
8	9	10	11	12	13	14
15	16	17	18	19	20	21
22	23	24	25	26	27	28
29	30	31				

NOVEMBER
S	M	T	W	T	F	S
			1	2	3	4
5	6	7	8	9	10	11
12	13	14	15	16	17	18
19	20	21	22	23	24	25
26	27	28	29	30		

DECEMBER
S	M	T	W	T	F	S
					1	2
3	4	5	6	7	8	9
10	11	12	13	14	15	16
17	18	19	20	21	22	23
24	25	26	27	28	29	30
31						

2018

JANUARY
S	M	T	W	T	F	S
	1	2	3	4	5	6
7	8	9	10	11	12	13
14	15	16	17	18	19	20
21	22	23	24	25	26	27
28	29	30	31			

FEBRUARY
S	M	T	W	T	F	S
				1	2	3
4	5	6	7	8	9	10
11	12	13	14	15	16	17
18	19	20	21	22	23	24
25	26	27	28			

MARCH
S	M	T	W	T	F	S
				1	2	3
4	5	6	7	8	9	10
11	12	13	14	15	16	17
18	19	20	21	22	23	24
25	26	27	28	29	30	31

APRIL
S	M	T	W	T	F	S
1	2	3	4	5	6	7
8	9	10	11	12	13	14
15	16	17	18	19	20	21
22	23	24	25	26	27	28
29	30					

MAY
S	M	T	W	T	F	S
		1	2	3	4	5
6	7	8	9	10	11	12
13	14	15	16	17	18	19
20	21	22	23	24	25	26
27	28	29	30	31		

JUNE
S	M	T	W	T	F	S
					1	2
3	4	5	6	7	8	9
10	11	12	13	14	15	16
17	18	19	20	21	22	23
24	25	26	27	28	29	30

JULY
S	M	T	W	T	F	S
1	2	3	4	5	6	7
8	9	10	11	12	13	14
15	16	17	18	19	20	21
22	23	24	25	26	27	28
29	30	31				

AUGUST
S	M	T	W	T	F	S
			1	2	3	4
5	6	7	8	9	10	11
12	13	14	15	16	17	18
19	20	21	22	23	24	25
26	27	28	29	30	31	

SEPTEMBER
S	M	T	W	T	F	S
						1
2	3	4	5	6	7	8
9	10	11	12	13	14	15
16	17	18	19	20	21	22
23	24	25	26	27	28	29
30						

OCTOBER
S	M	T	W	T	F	S
	1	2	3	4	5	6
7	8	9	10	11	12	13
14	15	16	17	18	19	20
21	22	23	24	25	26	27
28	29	30	31			

NOVEMBER
S	M	T	W	T	F	S
				1	2	3
4	5	6	7	8	9	10
11	12	13	14	15	16	17
18	19	20	21	22	23	24
25	26	27	28	29	30	

DECEMBER
S	M	T	W	T	F	S
						1
2	3	4	5	6	7	8
9	10	11	12	13	14	15
16	17	18	19	20	21	22
23	24	25	26	27	28	29
30	31					

Contents

Ostara

Beltane

Litha

Lammas

Contents

Introduction

NEARLY EVERYONE HAS A favorite sabbat. There are numerous ways to observe any tradition. This edition of the *Sabbats Almanac* provides a wealth of lore, celebrations, creative projects, and recipes to enhance your holiday.

For this edition, a mix of writers—Melanie Marquis, Kristoffer Hughes, Susan Pesznecker, Michael Furie, Dallas Jennifer Cobb, Suzanne Ress, Blake Octavian Blair, and Stacy Porter—share their ideas and wisdom. These include a variety of paths, such as a traditional wheat harvest and the baking of bread for Lammas, as well as the authors' personal approaches to each sabbat. Each chapter closes with an extended ritual, which may be adapted for both solitary practitioners and covens.

In addition to these insights and rituals, specialists in astrology, history, cooking, crafts, and family impart their expertise throughout.

Corrine Kenner gives an overview of planetary influences most relevant for each sabbat season and provides details and a short ritual for selected events, including New and Full Moons, retrograde motion, planetary positions, and more.

Natalie Zaman explores the realm of old-world Pagans, with a focus on traditional gravestone symbols we often associate with Samhain, as well as some unique sabbat festivals tied to the Nordic culture.

Laurel Reufner conjures up a feast for each festival that includes an appetizer, entrée, dessert, and beverage.

Linda Raedisch offers instructions on DIY crafts that will leave your home full of color and personality for each and every sabbat.

Charlie Rainbow Wolf dissects a range of sabbat-specific plants and their usefulness in rituals and ceremonies.

About the Authors

Blake Octavian Blair is an eclectic Pagan, ordained minister, shamanic practitioner, writer, Usui Reiki Master-Teacher, tarot reader, and musical artist. Blake blends various mystical traditions from both the East and West along with a reverence for the natural world into his own brand of modern Paganism and magick. Blake holds a degree in English and Religion from the University of Florida. He is an avid reader, knitter, crafter, and practicing pescatarian. He loves communing with nature and exploring its beauty whether it is within the city or hiking in the woods. Blake lives in the New England region of the USA with his beloved husband. Visit him on the web at www.blakeoctavianblair.com or write him at blake@blakeoctavianblair.com.

Deborah Castellano writes for many of Llewellyn's annuals and writes a blog on PaganSquare about unsolicited opinions on glamour, the muse, and the occult. *Glamour Magic: The Witchcraft Revolution for Getting What You Want* (Llewellyn Publications) is available for preorder on Amazon. Her shop, the Mermaid and the Crow, specializes in handmade goods. She resides in New Jersey with her husband, Jow, and two cats. She has a terrible reality television habit she can't shake and likes St. Germain liqueur, record players, and typewriters. Visit her at www.deborahmcastellano.com.

Dallas Jennifer Cobb practices gratitude magic, giving thanks for personal happiness, health, and prosperity; meaningful, flexible, and rewarding work; and a deliciously joyful life. She is accomplishing her deepest desires. She lives in paradise with her daughter in a waterfront village in rural Ontario, where she regularly swims and runs, chanting: "Thank you, thank you, thank you." Contact her at jennifer.cobb@live.com or visit www.magicalliving.ca.

Michael Furie (Northern California) is the author of *Spellcasting for Beginners, Supermarket Magic,* and *Spellcasting: Beyond the Basics* published by Llewellyn Worldwide. Furie has been a practicing Witch for over twenty years. An American Witch, he practices in the Irish tradition and is a priest of the Cailleach. You can find him online at www.michaelfurie.com.

Kristoffer Hughes is the founder and Chief of the Anglesey Druid Order in North Wales, UK. He is an award-winning author and a frequent speaker and workshop leader throughout the United Kingdom and the United States. He works professionally for Her Majesty's Coroner. He has studied with the Order of Bards, Ovates and Druids, and is its 13th Mount Haemus Scholar. He is a native Welsh speaker, born to a Welsh family in the mountains of Snowdonia. He resides on the Isle of Anglesey.

Corrine Kenner specializes in bringing metaphysical subjects down to earth. She is the author of more than two dozen books, including *Astrology for Writers* and *Tarot for Writers.* She lives in Florida with her husband, two cats, and a dog who can sing.

Melanie Marquis is a lifelong practitioner of magick, the founder of United Witches global coven, and a local coordinator for the Pagan Pride Project in Denver, Colorado, where she currently resides. Melanie is the author of numerous articles and several books, including *The Witch's Bag of Tricks, A Witch's World of Magick, Beltane,* and *Lughnasadh,* and she's written for many national and international Pagan publications. She is the co-author of *Witchy Mama* and the co-creator of the Modern Spellcaster's Tarot. An avid crafter, cook, folk artist, and tarot reader, she offers a line of customized magickal housewares as well as private tarot consultations by appointment. Connect with her online at www.melaniemarquis.com or facebook.com/melaniemarquisauthor.

Susan Pesznecker is a writer, English teacher, nurse, practicing herbalist, and hearth Pagan living in Oregon. Sue holds an MS in professional writing and loves to read, watch the stars, camp, and garden. Sue has authored *Yule: Rituals, Recipes, & Lore for the Winter Solstice* (Llewellyn 2015), *The Magickal Retreat* (Llewellyn 2012), *Crafting Magick with Pen and Ink* (Llewellyn, 2009), and contributes to the Llewellyn Annuals.

Stacy Porter is a Sea Witch. She has survived a Russian winter, studied politics in Africa, sampled the best gelato in Italy, and saved sea turtles in Nicaragua. Stacy holds a degree in International Studies with an emphasis in politics from Juniata College. She is a second-degree Priestess in the Ravenmyst Tradition, studying under Dorothy Morrison, Maggie Shayne, and Gail Wood. She is a certified yoga instructor, meditation guide, writer, and passionate advocate for those who don't have a voice. Stacy travels the world, as a mermaid and on two legs, teaching yoga, spreading magic, and daring the world to believe in their dreams. She lives by a lake on the east coast with her Jack Russell terrier, Mackenzie. Her writings regularly appear in *Elephant Journal* and you can follow her adventures on her website www.theavalonapothecary.com

Linda Raedisch is a papercrafter, house cleaner, and professional organizer who has somehow managed to find the time to write two books: *Night of the Witches: Folklore, Traditions and Recipes for Celebrating Walpurgis Night* (Llewellyn 2011) and *The Old Magic of Christmas: Yuletide Traditions for the Darkest Days of the Year* (Llewellyn 2015). Since 2011, she has been a regular contributor to the Llewellyn annuals. Linda lives in northern New Jersey, but enjoys the odd vacation on the west Baltic coast. She has eaten Danish hot dogs beside a fjord.

Laurel Reufner loves writing about all sorts of topics. Developing, adapting, and testing all of these recipes was a lot of fun, not only for her, but also for the friends and family who volunteered as taste-testers, although Yule cooking in August does have its own set of challenges. Rowan, her eldest daughter, deserves a shout-out for not only helping develop the menus, but for also providing one of the recipes. Laurel lives in beautiful southeastern Ohio with her husband and two rapidly growing teenage daughters, who both continue her Wild Child legacy. Drop in and visit her on Facebook at Laurel Reufner.

Suzanne Ress has been practicing Wicca for about twelve years as the leader of a small coven, but she has been aware of having a special connection to nature and animal spirits since she was a young child. She has been writing creatively most of her life—short stories, novels, and nonfiction articles for a variety of publications—and finds it to be an important outlet for her considerable creative powers. Other outlets she regularly makes use of are metalsmithing, mosaic works, painting, and all kinds of dance. She is also a professional aromatic herb grower and beekeeper. Although she is an American of Welsh ancestry by birth, she has lived in northern Italy for nearly twenty years. She recently discovered that the small mountain in the pre-alpine hills that she inhabits with her family and animals was once the site of an ancient Insubrian Celtic sacred place. Not surprisingly, the top of the mountain has remained a fulcrum of sacredness throughout the millennia, and this grounding in blessedness makes Suzanne's everyday life especially magical.

Natalie Zaman is a regular contributor to various Llewellyn annuals. She is the author of the upcoming *Color and Conjure: Rituals and Magic Spells to Color* (Llewellyn, 2017), *Magical Destinations of the Northeast* (October 2016), and writes the recurring feature "Wandering Witch" for *Witches & Pagans* magazine. Her work has also appeared in *FATE*, *SageWoman*, and *newWitch* magazines. When she's not on the road, she's chasing free-range hens in her self-sufficient and Pagan-friendly back garden. Find Natalie online at http://nataliezaman.blogspot.com.

Samhain

Days of the Dead

Kristoffer Hughes

Tis the night, the night, of ghouls' delight,
When cauldrons boil o'er ghostly light,
By Punkie's glow, a Souling we'll go,
To greet the dead who rot below.
Three nights that brings the ancestors near,
Through veils so thin they gather here.
No rules, nor neither slight nor sin,
Shall spoil our joyous Hallowe'en din.

HALLOWEEN, SAMHAIN, ALL SOUL'S Night, Dia de los Muertos, to name but a few of the myriad of names that decorate the end of October. There is perhaps no other festival during the cycle of the seasons that has exhibited more endurance, steadfastness, and the ability to spark human imagination as Halloween. In this short article, I will explore some of its roots and history, its expression through the centuries, its relevance to Pagans and non-Pagans alike, and attempt to unearth answers that may explain why millions of people are compelled, intrigued, and fall in love with the Halloween season.

The Wheel of the Year turns on its axis, moving us subtly yet powerfully from one season to another, from one time to another, from one state of consciousness to another. As the wheel turns toward late October, we may become conscious of what we reaped during the second harvest of the year—the growing season is done, what we sowed and grew have come to fruit, the harvest is in. The nights draw in, mornings are darker, dew and mists sing songs of mystery to the land. And as the last leaf sighs and falls from weary branches, and the tomb of winter draws ever nearer, something incredible happens within the imagination of mankind. The dead draw near, and ghouls and spirits of all kinds mingle with the mortal realms. It is the season of magic and enchantment as the veils between the worlds thin—Samhain is upon us.

Ever since I was a small child growing up in a village deep in the mountains of North Wales, I have long been fascinated and drawn by the feast of Halloween, or *Calan Gaeaf,* as we say in the Welsh language, meaning the Calends of Winter, a title that refers to both the secular feast of Halloween and the sublime festival known as Samhain in neo-Paganism. It is a festival of contradictions and paradox, nothing is entirely as it seems, normal rules are suspended, ancestors are venerated, lines of gender and conformity blur. Its ability to spark my imagination has had a profound and lasting effect on the rest of my life—its associations with the death and the dead continues to bleed into my everyday life as I chose a career with the coroner where I work with the dead on a daily basis.

Echoes of the Old World

Whilst the roots of Samhain reach far into the distant past, its current expression cannot be pinpointed to a particular time, peoples, or tradition. What makes this festival so unique and special is its fusion of numerous paths. It is a melting pot, a cauldron of Pagan, indigenous folk harvest, and pre-winter celebrations, Celtic and Christian traditions, and secular expression.

Anything that has relevance to society will endure; anything that brings people together will inevitably survive, at times against all the odds. What drives this function is a mystery, one that adds to the intrigue of the holiday. The popular festival of Halloween has endured against all odds; it combines elements of the old and new world in a delicious fusion that transcends religious identity and is so compelling that hundreds of thousands of people are openly addicted to the festival.

In a sometimes frightful world where terror has such a real and tangible component, it is no great surprise that as a people we turn to its antithesis, the creation of conjectured terror for the sake of entertainment. Something within this pretend terror enables us to assimilate the risk of real horror in a way that is cathartic, non-threatening, and perhaps even healing.

The old folk practices and rites of Halloween and the Irish Samhain were slowly adopted by the Christian church, and by papal decree the feasts of All Souls and All Saints were attached to Halloween. The migration of people initiated the fusion of ideas and traditions. And as the Celts moved across the Atlantic Ocean in search of new opportunities, the Old World was to meet the new.

The Land of Hope and Gory

The United States of America has never claimed ownership of the roots of Halloween, its partly Celtic and Christian origins have never been disputed, but the worldwide communal expression of Halloween is inspired by American popular culture. The fact that many British folk to this day believe that Halloween is an American import serves only to display ignorance for a cultural tradition that has its roots in their own history. America on the other hand took the various community based traditions, and over the space of around two hundred years transformed what would have been locally specific traditions into a national obsession.

Every single culture that arrived on the shores of America brought with them their traditions, magic, and customs. These were not necessarily aspects of their religious practice but rather traditions that were applicable to the people, to the land, and to the cultures that arose there. Consequently, Halloween is a feast that can be practiced by anyone regardless of their religious persuasion. The unique American environment and the declining influence of the puritans ensured that by the end of the 19th century, Halloween was indeed becoming a part of annual traditions. This cultural stew pot also ensured that the ancient practices of spell casting, divination, and communication with the dead continued to be an integral part of Halloween, and this survives to this day.

Various circumstances inspired a new expression of Halloween in the USA, with the arrival of German, Polish, Eastern European British, and African immigrants and the uniqueness of their respective cultures. The potato famine in Ireland forced over one and a half million people into the USA, each individual bringing family practices and traditions from the Celtic motherlands. Perhaps the greatest contributor to the modern Halloween is the American spirit of celebrating freedom, community, integrity, dreams, hopes, and ambitions that make seasonal festivals a vital and vibrant part of its culture. From Thanksgiving to Labor Day, Columbus Day to Halloween, this spirit of celebration enabled a nation to grasp old traditions and make them applicable to the New World.

America spawned an industry that embraced tradition and celebration, and by the beginning of the 20th century, manufacturers were making and importing party products specifically designed for the Halloween feast, which by now had become a national holiday. Costumes, decorations, and special effects were widely available as the years progressed. The practice of trick or treat, influenced by the Celtic world, soon became a firm tradition of the American Halloween. Its reach was not restricted to the lands of America; it soon made its way back across the ocean from where it had originated, to a land that had forgotten its own customs.

Halloween will always be seen as heavily American, and it has every right to claim responsibility for successfully preserving it. The influence of the States cannot be ignored in the modern sense; they deserve a pat on the back for doing a job well done. They have succeeded in combining the magic of Samhain, the mystery of All

Souls and the frivolity and frights of Halloween in a manner that is positive, inspiring, and creative. Without America, Halloween may well have been lost to the mists of time.

Days of the Dead

The Coligny calendar, made of bronze and dating to the second century of the Common Era, records a festival called Trinoxtion Samonii, or the three nights of Samhain (summer's end). Whilst we cannot be certain that this title refers to what we now call Halloween or Samhain, it does indicate that their feasting may have lasted for more than one night. With gleeful delight I take this as ancestral permission to extend the Samhain festivities to cover three wondrous nights.

In my tradition Samhain is a time to remember; for three divine days we stop and think of our dead. This may sound a rather maudlin affair, but on the contrary, it provides a sense of focus and structure to remembering the dead. Halloween offers an opportune period at the end of the harvest that combines the secular frivolity of the holiday in all its commercial glory, the sublime aspects of the Celtic Samhain, and the colorful influence of the Mexican celebration of Dia de los Muertos. With the rise of modern Paganism, these traditions are deliciously blending together in the cauldron of inspiration, and the result—a new and vibrant tradition that not only sings of the Old World and the Old Ways, but is relevant and applicable to those who practice it today. It is rapidly becoming the perfect blend of frivolous partying and somber honoring of the dead.

So what can we do over the three nights of Samhain? Perhaps the best course of action here is to briefly describe my own traditions in the hope that they will inspire yours.

On the first day we host a dumb supper; the table is strewn with flowers and photographs of our dead. No electric lights are used, candles are lit in the windows to welcome the dead, and the meal is served in reverse order, starting with dessert, and consumed in utter silence. The effect is rather peculiar. Eating is such a social affair ordinarily. In this case, what one is focused upon is the dead.

The second day of Samhain has two aspects to it. During the day I journey around my locality visiting the graves of my loved ones. The graves are tended and cleaned and flowers left and small cakes offered to the dead. It is a poignant time for I tend to do this alone; it's just me and the memories of those I loved.

The evening of the second day sees our annual Samhain ritual; this year the first half is undertaken at an ancient burial chamber to honor the ancient dead. The second half focuses on the recent dead. It is a moving, touching, and deeply humbling ritual where the dead are called by name and candles lit in their memories. As the ritual gives way to socializing and feasting, we are continuously reminded of the dead by the burning of candles upon the altar dedicated to their memory.

Day three of Samhain I set aside to remember my animal companions and also to recall and acknowledge the fallen dead, those who have died in or as a result of conflict or its collateral damage.

When we are forgotten we cease to exist—people only truly die when we forget them. Samhain offers us the space and a time to remember. This year I encourage you in true Celtic fashion to celebrate over three glorious nights, to create new traditions and new practices that fuse the old and the new. Samhain is not necessarily about what we believe, but rather what we do...

What will you do this year?

Cosmic Sway

Corrine Kenner

THE SABBAT HOLIDAYS ARE astrological milestones that mark the Earth's journey around the Sun. On a symbolic level, the Sun's movement through the zodiac parallels the mysteries of existence, just like the Moon's cycle of waxing and waning reflects the cycle of life and death.

Samhain, on October 31, marks the end of the harvest season and the start of a new year. It's celebrated as the Sun moves through watery Scorpio, at the halfway point between the autumn equinox and the winter solstice.

Samhain, like Halloween, celebrates the dark mysteries of life and death. It marks the time when the veil between this world and the next is at its thinnest, and spirits of the dead return to visit the land of the living. That's why we light our walks with lanterns carved from harvest vegetables, and offer sweets to haunts that come trick-or-treating at our homes.

Mythic Astrology: Pluto, Lord of the Dead

At Samhain, the Sun's passage through Scorpio marks the true significance of the holiday. Scorpio is fixated by the dark mysteries of life and death—and it's ruled by Pluto, the lord of the dead.

In ancient Greece, Pluto was the god of the Underworld. He was one of a triumvirate of power: his brother Jupiter ruled the heavens, and his brother Neptune ruled the seas. Pluto has a shadowy partnership with Saturn, the god of time.

Pluto's ensign of power was a staff, which he used to drive the souls of the dead into their new life in Hades. Once they were safely ensconced in the realm of the dead, spirits were shadows of their former selves. They would pass their time brooding over all that they had loved and lost. Most were only semiconscious. They could only be awakened by drinking the blood of sacrifices offered by their living friends.

Some storytellers did describe the Afterlife as a happier place, where Pluto would simply bid a warm welcome to the newly departed as they made their way to the Elysian Fields. It was a heavenly place with balmy winds, fragrant breezes, rippling brooks, smiling meadows, fields of flowers, and wooded groves filled with the songs of birds. Everything the dead loved in life would be waiting for them in death, too. Warriors would find their horses, musicians would find their lyres, and hunters would find their quivers and bows.

For the most part, however, Pluto was fierce and inexorable, and he was hated by mortal men. Somber priests in black robes sacrificed black sheep to appease him—but whoever actually offered the sacrifice had to turn his face away.

Pluto did have one redeeming quality, as far as the ancients were concerned: as king of the lower world, he was the giver of all the blessings that came from earth, including precious gems and metals.

In astrology, Pluto symbolizes death and resurrection, forgiveness and release. It's the planet of endings, death, and unavoidable change. Pluto compels us to release anything that's no longer living up to our needs or expectations, so we can recycle and reuse that energy in better ways. In a horoscope chart, Pluto's placement indicates areas of testing and challenge, power struggles, and resistance.

Pluto also teaches us that endings are merely part of the cycle of regeneration and rebirth, which inevitably lead to a second chance at a new life.

Pluto also rules the eighth house of the horoscope, where astrologers look for information about partnerships, shared resources, and your most intimate associations.

The glyph for Pluto "♇" looks like someone rising from the dead; technically, it's a coin and a chalice, symbols of payment for everlasting life. An alternate version of the glyph combines the letters "P" and "L," which also happen to be the initials of the planet's discoverer, Percival Lowell.

Reading the Signs

This year, Samhain is marked by a close conjunction between the Sun and Jupiter in watery Scorpio, the sign of cosmic mystery. They're standing side by side, working in partnership to deliver a bountiful harvest holiday—which means that costumed ghosts and goblins could well enjoy the most bountiful yield of their young lives. Jupiter has been in Scorpio since October 10, and it will stay in the watery sign until November 2018.

The Sun and Neptune are in a harmonious trine that emphasizes glamour and illusion—an aspect that perfectly illustrates the effect of costumes at holiday celebrations.

Planetary Positions

- Sun in Scorpio
- Moon in Pisces
- Mercury in Scorpio
- Venus in Libra
- Mars in Libra

- Jupiter in Scorpio
- Saturn in Sagittarius
- Uranus ℞ in Aries
- Neptune ℞ in Pisces
- Pluto in Capricorn

The Moon is in watery Pisces, the sign of hidden mysteries and mystic secrets. It's in an easy, flowing trine with Mercury in watery Scorpio. The aspect will be short-lived, because the Moon and Mercury both move at breakneck speeds. Even so, it should be fun while it lasts. Keep your journal handy, because the trine could lead to amazing psychic revelations while you sleep tonight.

The Moon is also in a far less comfortable square with Saturn, the ringed planet of boundaries, limitations, and restrictions. If you don't have your dream journal on your nightstand, Saturn will wipe your dreams from your memory before you get out of bed.

Those dreams could include visits from the spirit world. The Moon in Pisces is sextile Pluto, the planet of death and resurrection.

Saturn, in Sagittarius, is in a harmonious trine with Uranus in Aries, fueling a cosmic quest for wisdom from offbeat sources. Saturn is normally a dour planet, but in the optimistic sign of the archer, it can focus on personal growth, and apply itself to learning and thinking on a grand scale.

Venus—the romantic planet of beauty and attraction—is sextile Saturn. The aspect suggests a happy interlude with an older man or woman, or praise from an authority figure. That exchange will probably be completely unexpected. Venus is on the receiving end of crazy Uranus energy, because Uranus is staring at Venus from Aries, on the other side of the zodiac.

Venus is also in an uncomfortable square with Pluto, the planet of death and resurrection.

Venus has been in its own sign, Libra, since October 14. Libra is the airy realm of social grace and balance, and it will be in its home sign until November 7, when it moves into Scorpio.

Mars is also in airy Libra—which means the god of war is moving toward a passionate encounter with the goddess of love. Mars moved into Libra on October 22.

Mercury has been in Scorpio since October 17. It will move into Sagittarius on November 5. The messenger planet is the smallest, fastest planet, with the closest orbit to the Sun, and it moves through all twelve signs of the zodiac in just 88 days. (Earth, by comparison, takes 365 days to circle the Sun.)

Generational Planets

The three outermost planets are so far from the Sun that they take years to move through each sign of the zodiac.

Uranus, the rebel planet of the unusual and the unexpected, is currently moving backward through fiery Aries, where it's been hovering since 2011. It won't start moving forward again until May 15, 2018, when it enters Taurus—but then it will go retrograde again and head back into fiery Aries from November 6 to March 6, 2018. Whenever Uranus passes through fiery Aries, the impulsive planet's focus on freedom and individualism is heightened and focused. When it finally moves into earthy Taurus for the long term, its focus will shift toward Taurean matters of property and prosperity.

Neptune is in watery Pisces, also moving retrograde. Neptune is comfortable in watery Pisces, because it's the ruler of the sign. Its dreamlike transits marks this as a period that can be wistful at best—or, at worst, marked by deceptions on a cosmic scale. Neptune will be in watery Pisces until 2025.

Pluto has been in Capricorn since 2008, and it will stay in the earthy sign until 2023. In Capricorn, Pluto fights to maintain traditional standards of behavior, along with conventional standards of personal responsibility and self-discipline.

Phases of the Moon

On October 5, the last full Moon in fiery Aries was completely illuminated by the Sun, on the other side of the zodiac in Libra. When the Moon is full in fiery Aries, it takes on many of the qualities we associate with the sign: a commanding sense of leadership, impulsiveness, and a yearning for independence.

On October 19, the New Moon in airy Libra marked a conjunction between the Sun and the Moon, as the Moon moved directly between the Earth and the Sun.

The next Full Moon will occur on November 4 in earthy Taurus. It will be completely illuminated by the Sun, 180 degrees away in watery Scorpio. The Moon represents emotional well-being, and it's exalted in Taurus, the sign of comfort and security.

On November 18, the New Moon in watery Scorpio will usher in a night of intense emotions, with an undercurrent of sexual desire.

On December 3, the Full Moon in airy Gemini will be illuminated by the Sun in Sagittarius. The energy of a Gemini Moon makes small talk and conversation easier.

Practical Astrology

Aspects describe the planets' geometric relationships with each other as they orbit around the Sun. They're easy to spot when you see the planets plotted on an astrological chart. Commonly used aspects include the conjunction, sextile (60° of separation), square (90°), trine (120°), and opposition (180°).

The effects of planetary aspects are usually fairly generalized, but they can be intense if they happen to mirror key points in your own birth chart.

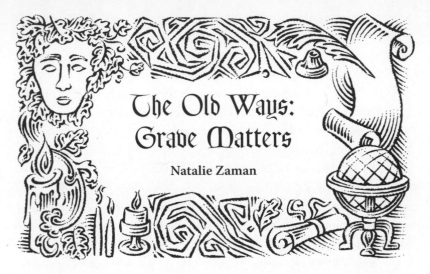

The Old Ways: Grave Matters

Natalie Zaman

SAMHAIN IS A DAY for honoring ancestors, and cemeteries are sacred sites designed for this very purpose. Step into a cemetery and you'll find religious symbols (or lack thereof), as well as flowers and trees—living and carved in stone. Obelisks soar into the sky, mysterious vaults, some decorated and capped with ornate metalwork or fitted with stained glass are silent and mysterious chapels. Here and there, angels pray with clasped hands or outstretched arms, their faces drawn in eternal expressions of grief. Each has a story to tell, mostly through imagery, and sometimes, in verse:

> *Lasting only and divine*
> *Is an innocence like thine[1]*

The language of the graveyard is largely, though not wholly, symbolic and expresses the spirit of Samhain—a knowledge and acceptance of our shared mortality, whatever the faith or path of the deceased. Alongside names and dates are images with histories that can date back thousands of years and over time have acquired new layers of meaning.

---

1 Poem on a headstone in the Old Presbyterian Burying Ground, Bound Brook, NJ

The human skull, or an entire skeleton—sometimes accompanied by the Latin phrase *Memento Mori*, meaning "remember death"—is the ultimate symbol of mortality. This image of the last vestige of human remains—popular in the Middle Ages throughout Europe in the form of transi tombs, elaborate bunk tombs consisting of an idealized effigy above and a realistic cadaver below—expressed the notion that whatever station or status one held in life, we all, in the end, share the same fate. But there's hope. Winged skulls (death heads) and skeletons were reminders that whatever the fate of the body, the soul is immortal.

In the eighteenth century, winged skulls and skeletons evolved into something softer and rounder. Unlike their decidedly scarier predecessors, putti-like soul effigies expressed a more positive outlook on the afterlife. Pouting, smiling, scowling—some, perhaps, portraits of the deceased with individualistic expressions—conveyed the idea that while the nature of the afterlife is uncertain, we hope to retain that which makes us who we are. Soul effigies are often mistaken for angels who appear on later tombs and are separate entities who acted as mourners, intercessors, and guardians.

Cemeteries are filled with trees both living and rendered in stone. Each tree carries its own message: The oak symbolizes strength and longevity, but broken or cut down, the end of life. A watery tree, the willow is connected to emotions, and so a fitting mourning image. Willows are associated with the Moon and feminine divinity, specifically Hecate the goddess of the crossroads and Persephone, Queen of the Underworld. Passing through the veil of the willow's boughs is a metaphoric passing to the next life. The willow is also a symbol of renewal; a cut willow will always grow again.

People have been placing flowers on graves since ancient times. As an offering of beauty for ancestors (whose spirits were believed to inhabit tombs), flowers were also used to mask the smell of death. Living or carved in stone, every flower has unique symbolic value. Roses represent love; rosebuds could mark the grave of a child. Lilies, a flower of spring and the renewal of life, suggest hope in grief.

Forget-me-nots invoke remembrance, and since the early twentieth century, poppies have become associated with the military. Wilted flowers or flowers with a broken stem express grief or the end of life.

For thousands of years, urns held both mortal remains (internal organs or ashes) as well as "grave goods," material possessions the deceased would need for his or her stint in the afterlife. Sometimes urns are depicted partially draped, the cloth denoting the veil through which we pass. The hidden part of the urn expresses the thought that we do not, and perhaps cannot, know or see all.

The sun is a symbol of deity, the power around which all life turns. Often depicted on the horizon—rising or setting—it is a statement of the end of one life and the beginning of another. Sometimes accompanied by stars and the Moon, the Sun represented the life cycle and the vastness of the universe—a universal tenet.

The use of birds on tombs dates back to ancient Egypt where they represented the soul. The most prevalent cemetery bird in the United States is the dove. In Christian iconography, doves symbolize the Holy Spirit, but they could also represent the flight of the soul from this earth and the peace one achieves in the hereafter.

Hourglasses represent not only the passage of time, but the finite nature of mortal creatures. An hourglass depicted on its side denotes that time has stopped for the deceased. Wings added to an hourglass express the sentiment *tempus fugit*—time flies. As when they appear on skulls and soul effigies, wings are a reminder of the eternal and unlimited nature of the soul.

The most expressive appendage on the human body, hands in various gestures are a common funerary image. A finger pointing upwards directs the gaze heavenward, to the afterlife or perhaps a higher power. Held palm outward, a single hand reminds the visitor to pause and reflect. Clasped hands express universal brotherhood, or eternal love. Look closely at the sleeves that border each hand. If one is distinctly feminine and the other masculine, it represents a spouse welcoming his or her partner into heaven.

Circles symbolize the never-ending nature of eternity. Interestingly, circles on tombstones are sometimes rendered as snakes. This misunderstood and often misrepresented creature is honored in the cemetery when carved in a circle; because he cyclically sheds his skin, the snake is a symbol of renewal and rebirth—one who dies only to be reborn.

Graveyards are publicly accessible spaces that are garden and museum, historical record and house of worship. Most importantly, they are ancestor altars on a grand scale. Learn the language of this sacred space and speak to the mighty dead.

Blessed Samhain!

Additional Resources

Keister, Douglas. *Stories in Stone: A Field Guide to Cemetery Symbolism and Iconography*. Layton: Gibbs Smith, 2004.

The Association for Gravestone Studies (www.ags.org)

Find a Grave (www.findagrave.com)

Zaman, Natalie and Clark, Katharine. *Graven Images Oracle*. Woodbury: Galde Press, 2007.

Feasts and Treats

Laurel Reufner

AND SO WE COME to the end of the year and the last of the harvest festivals. Samhain comes just as farmers have finished up the year's butchering, storing the meat away with a variety of preserving techniques. I wonder if this is part of the reason they saw it as the ending of the current seasonal life cycle and the beginning of a new year.

Apple Cider Pork Roast

This menu will easily feed 4, maybe 5. This roast is ever so tasty. If you use a lesser cut of meat for the roast, simply let it bake longer. The combination of the time, heat, and apple cider will help tenderize the roast.

Prep time: 10
Cook time: 70–100 minutes
Servings: 12

3 pounds center cut loin roast
1 tablespoon or so garlic minced
1 to 1½ tablespoon rosemary
Salt and pepper to taste
2 cups apple cider

Start your oven heating to 375 degrees F. Place the pork in a roasting pan and top with the garlic, rosemary, salt, and pepper. Take a moment to rub it in, then flip the roast and rub the seasonings into the other side as well. (Use the bits of rosemary and garlic that fell off to the sides.) Gently pour the apple cider into the pan, letting some drizzle over the top.

Place in the oven on a center rack and set the timer for 30 minutes. When the timer goes off, carefully flip the roast over and reset the timer for another 40 minutes. If you have the time, go ahead and set the timer to 30 minutes, flip once more, and then let it cook until as tender as you want. The rule of thumb is 20 minutes per pound.

Once the roast is done to desired tenderness, pull it out and let it rest a minimum of 10 minutes before cutting. If you want to make it look all fancy, garnish with a sprig of fresh rosemary.

Garlic Green Beans with Tomatoes and Almonds

I'm going to be completely honest here and tell you up front that we use jarred, chopped garlic in our house. It's convenient, stores well, and is super easy to grab when cooking in a hurry. If you use fresh garlic cloves for this green bean recipe, you may want to sauté it a little before adding to the green beans.

Prep time: 10 minutes
Cook time: 10–15 minutes
Servings: 6

1 pound green beans, fresh
4 ounces cherry or grape tomatoes
1 tablespoon garlic
¼ cup chopped almonds
Balsamic vinegar

Clean the green beans and tomatoes. You'll want to halve the tomatoes and possibly quarter them if they're very big. Add the beans and garlic to a pan of lightly salted water, bring to a boil and cook until they are tender-crisp.

Drain and move them to a serving dish. Gently stir in tomatoes, almonds, and a splash of the vinegar. Serve.

Roasted Root Veggies

This next dish was created just for the *Almanac*, and it was a total hit at our house. Amazingly there weren't any vegetables that anyone disliked. I really hope that you enjoy it as much as we all did.

Prep time: 30 minutes
Cook time: 45 minutes
Servings: 6

3 cups sweet potatoes (all measurements are approximate for the vegetables chopped)
2 cups parsnips
1 cup carrots
1 cup daikon radish
2 cups turnips
1 cup beets
1 cup kohlrabi
About ⅓ cup olive oil
1 tablespoon garlic
1 tablespoon fresh rosemary, snipped smaller
1 tablespoon summer savory

Preheat oven to 400 degrees F and line a rimmed baking sheet with aluminum foil. Wash and scrub veggies, peeling the turnips, beets, and kohlrabi. You'll want to cut all of them up into approximately 1-inch pieces. As you finish with each root veggie, toss it into a large bowl.

In a smaller bowl, mix your olive oil and the herbs. Now pour the oil mixture over your veggies and either use a sturdy spoon or your hands to mix it all around, making sure to completely coat the veggies. Once coated, pour them on the baking sheet and spread out into a single layer.

Pop the sheet into the oven and set your timer for 15 minutes. At the 15 minute mark, pull them out enough to give them a good stir, then pop them back in and set the timer for another 15 minutes. Repeat the stirring and roasting process one more time. (They should roast for a total of 45 minutes.)

If you'd like, sprinkle with a little salt to finish, although they honestly don't need it. Transfer to a bowl when ready to serve.

When making this menu, I cooked the roasted veggies first, then popped them back in the oven for the last 10 minutes of the roast's cooking time. That way they were nice and hot when they hit the table.

Soul Cakes

A medieval British tradition, it would seem that there were even more variations of soul cake recipes than there are variations on the "Soul Cakes" folk song. This might be part of the reason the tradition eventually died out. It seems high time to bring it back!

Prep time: 30 minutes
Cook time: 11–30 minutes
Servings: 1–2 dozen

3¾ cups flour
1 cup butter, fairly cold
2 cups sugar
1 teaspoon cinnamon
1 teaspoon ginger
1 teaspoon allspice
¼ teaspoon nutmeg
2 eggs
1 tablespoon apple cider vinegar
3 tablespoons milk

Put your flour into a large bowl and cut in the butter using a pastry blender, a large fork, or—the preferred method—your hands. Get the two ingredients well integrated together before adding the sugar and spices. Blend together well.

In a small bowl, beat together the eggs, vinegar, and milk. Combine with the flour mixture and continue mixing until you have a stiff dough. Turn out onto a lightly floured surface and knead well. Once you're sure everything is worked together and the dough is nice and pliable, roll it out to about a quarter inch thick. (I worked with about half of the dough at a time due to my available surface area.)

I used pumpkin-shaped cookie cutters to cut out my cookies, which yielded about 5 dozen. Bake at 350 degrees F for about 11 minutes or until lightly browned. These cookies don't really rise or spread out, so you can cluster them fairly close together on the cookie sheet.

Store in an airtight container. Makes between one and two dozen cookies, depending on your cutter size.

Crafty Crafts

Linda Raedisch

THIS YEAR'S CRAFTY CRAFTS are all made either exclusively of paper or with paper as the main component. We're going to fold, cut, glue, and roll it. Paper has long been my preferred artistic medium. For a time, I was known locally as the "other origami lady" (long story!) but while the crafts in these pages are not origami projects, strictly speaking, it would not hurt to dust off your grade-school paper-folding skills.

As much as I love paper, I hate to measure. If you take care to line up your edges neatly and make sharp creases, you'll almost never have to measure; the folds will do it for you. Fold a sheet of paper in quarters to find the center point. To turn a rectangular sheet into a square, fold a triangle at one end and cut along the bottom edge. When cutting a pattern though several layers of paper at once, spread your fingers wide so the layers don't shift. Treat the paper with respect and it will be your friend.

Some of these projects call for specialty papers which can be quite expensive. Keep in mind that I made almost all of the prototypes with plain old white printer paper, and they looked fine. Also, I've put asterisks after supplies that are used in more than one craft, so what looks at first like a long shopping list will get shorter as you craft your way around the Wheel of the Year. And then again, you might like to mix it up. Swap orange and black for red and green, or substitute pink for gold, red for blue, etc. Many of these crafts will do double or even triple duty at your Sabbat celebrations. There are no rules (except for tidy folds).

Black and Orange Basketwork Star

Our first craft is based on a type of Christmas star I have seen in Germany and at Scandinavian craft fairs. I have seen them made of wood strips and of red and white paper. There is even a plastic version with a little light inside. Because Samhain is coming, we're going to make them in black and orange.

I must say I am not pleased with the current trend toward using purple at Halloween, especially those horrible purple bat costumes you can buy for children. Bats are not purple; they come in brown, gray, and, in the case of fruit bats, a rusty orange. (Besides, purple is for Michaelmas—more about that later.) If you make these stars in purple, you can expect me to come knocking on your door to complain. You do, however, have my full blessing to make them in black and green for Walpurgis Night.

Time frittered: Each star takes about 10 minutes, but, of course, you'll want to make lots of them.

Cost: About $8.00 if you use quilling paper (and if you don't have any glue in the house), cheaper if you cut your own paper strips.

Supplies

¼" wide quilling paper in black and orange (Quilling paper usually comes in 24" strips which you can cut in half to make 12" strips. If you are using another kind of paper, make sure your strips are at least 10" long.)

White all-purpose glue*

Black or orange thread

For each star, you will need 6 black and 6 orange strips of paper. Begin by weaving your strips together as if you are making the bot-

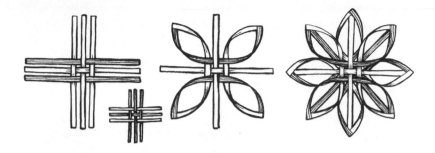

tom of a square basket. Hold on! Don't start yet! You are going to weave two separate basket bottoms: one with 4 orange strips interwoven with 2 black, the other with 4 black strips interwoven with 2 orange. Remember that place mat you wove out of construction paper strips in first grade? It's the same basic technique, except that this is openwork weaving, so you are going to leave about ¼" (or one strip width) between each strip. When the strips are properly positioned, fix them in place with tiny dabs of glue.

Observe one of your finished basket bottoms. Notice how at each corner there is an orange strip adjacent to a black strip. Give each of these strips a half twist then glue their ends together in the shape of a pen nib or candle flame. Do this at the other three corners to make three more candle flames. Repeat the whole process with the other basket bottom.

Now comes the fun part: joining the two basket bottoms together into a hauntingly beautiful Samhain star. See those straight strips sticking out between each candle flame? You thought they had nowhere to go? Wrong! Those strips are the key to assembling your star.

Lay one basket bottom over the other so the center squares are at 45 degree angles to each other, i.e., one positioned like a square, the other like a diamond. Also, the basket bottoms should be convex-side out so they are bulging away from each other. If they are kissing, turn them over!

Once the two halves of your star are positioned correctly, you will be able to easily glue the tip of each candle flame to the strip that's sticking out of the other half star. Once all the point and strips are glued, trim off the projecting ends and you're done!

Make lots and lots of them, hang them from threads and put them in the window for the duration of the season.

Tip: For a more intricate star, weave your basket bottoms using ten strips of paper each instead of six. (The star will still have only eight points.)

Wispy Greeting Card

I love to send cards at Halloween—all those pumpkin-colored envelopes flying off across the country and the ocean to distant relatives who might not even be thinking of black cats and witches' hats until my card arrives. If you're reading this, there's a good chance you like to send cards at this time of year too. The will-o'-the-wisp is my favorite symbol of the season. What's that you say? Wispy is not an official Halloween creature? Let's change that right now! Whether you call it Halloween or Samhain, this is a holiday centered on children, for it's through them that we pay our respects to the ancestors. Will-o'-the-wisps are children too: they're the ghosts of babies who died abandoned and unchristened. Are these little Pagans of long ago not deserving of our special attention?

Time frittered: About 15 minutes, more if you get involved with the collage elements.

Cost: About $15.00 if you don't already have any of the supplies listed below. But $15.00 will set you up to make many cards, not just one.

Supplies

For each card: one 8½" × 11" sheet white drawing paper or other fairly heavy paper*

Hole puncher*

Tape*

Gold acrylic paint*

Broad paint brush*

Collage elements (optional)

Fold your drawing paper in half like a book and cut along the crease. Fold each half in half again to make two cards. Sketch the shape of your will-o'-the wisp on one half. Remember, a will-o'-the-wisp is part ghost and part wavering flame. Make him big enough to fill the space nicely, leaving plenty of room around him to "glow." Cut him out and use the hole puncher to make his eyes and mouth. This is your template.

Place the template over the plain card and stick it temporarily in place with a small roll of tape. (Here's a trick I learned at art school: before applying the tape roll, tap it lightly against your clothes. It will pick up some lint and be easier to remove later.)

Now paint over your template in broad strokes of gold paint, making sure to get into the mouth and eye holes. Don't load the

brush with too much paint; you want the brush strokes to show. Peel off the template carefully and there he is, your very own will-o'-the-wisp, looking like he simply materialized in the midst of some random brushstrokes.

You can use your (now gold) template to paint more cards. If it starts to get tired, simply make a new one.

You can quit here or add some collage elements. I like my Wispy with horns, which I might make with tiny, glittered twigs or snippets of millet from an old broom. Why the horns? Because Wispy is a kind of "spook," a word that, along with the devilish Old Norse *puki*, springs from an ancient root denoting a horned, mischievous spirit. I also like to give my Wispy a pair of tiny hands cut from black paper. These symbolize the marsh mud, which is his natural environment.

I know what you're thinking, and the answer is yes: a Wispy card is just as appropriate at Yuletide as it is at Halloween.

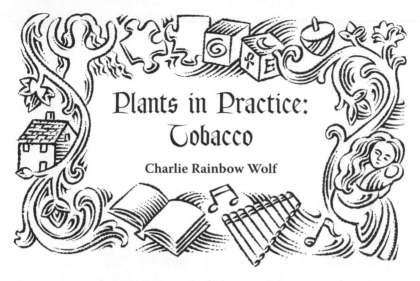

Plants in Practice: Tobacco

Charlie Rainbow Wolf

TOBACCO IS PROBABLY ONE of the most misunderstood—and perhaps misused—herbs of today. Like all herbs, it has its place in healing, folklore, and even the herb garden, although the latter could surprise some of you. It's actually not that hard to grow, and although it's a regulated herb, you are allowed to grow a certain amount of it for personal use (check the laws for your location if you'd like to give it a try).

Like other herbs, there are many different types of tobacco. They're all a member of the *Nicotiana* genus, and they're all loosely related to tomatoes, potatoes, and other nightshades. The most commonly grown varieties are *N. tabacum* and *N. rustica*, which is slightly stronger. The active stimulant in tobacco is nicotine, which is what makes it addictive. The dried leaves are used in cigarettes, cigars, chewing tobacco (or dip), pipe tobacco, and snuff. Tobacco gets a bad reputation as it's linked with many diseases, but, used correctly, it too has beneficial qualities.

Tobacco is easier to raise than you'd think. It's very hardy and will grow just about anywhere, although it does like well-drained soil and warm air. It takes about four months from seedling to harvest, and a mature plant often reaches over three feet in height. The harvest period needs to be dry for the crop to be successful. The seeds are small, so it's best to start them indoors and then harden them off prior to transplanting outside. This way your seedlings are recognizable when you're weeding your garden!

Apart from water when it's young, and regular doses of fish emulsion or other good fertilizer, tobacco pretty much takes care of itself when it's growing. Don't let it flower (although saving some aside to do just that is interesting as they make a very attractive plants when blooming); nip the buds off as soon as they appear so that all the nutrients stay in the leaves—the part of the plant that is most commonly used. Remove any side "suckers" that appear too, for the same reason. You want one strong, healthy, foliage plant.

Tobacco doesn't offer a lot in the way of being a good garden companion with other plants. Treat it like any other member of the nightshade family and keep it separate from tomatoes and potatoes, as they draw the same kind of garden pests. It does well planted in with cabbage and members of the *brassica* family: beans, marigolds, and nasturtiums. Gophers and moles don't seem to like it, so it might act as a deterrent for them. A spray made from tobacco leaf "tea" is a powerful natural insecticide, particularly for aphids and centipedes.

Tobacco is harvested as a plant, and then the leaves are dried in pairs. This curing process is vital to the smoothness, flavor, and scent of the finished product. The leaves should be hung in a hot, humid, and well-ventilated place without touching one another, where they are left to age (we hung ours on the rafters of our attic one year, and it worked well). The smoothest tobacco is sometimes aged for up to five years, which is why you'll need a climate controlled area if you're really going to get into this seriously. There's a fine art between keeping the leaves moist enough to age, but not so humid that they start to rot.

In folk medicine, tobacco was used as a pain reliever both internally and as a poultice. Chewing on a leaf relieved toothache, and sometimes tobacco was made into a paste for cleaning the teeth.

Chewed leaves were applied to the skin as a treatment for snake bites or insect stings. It was smoked to clear out bronchial and nasal passages.

Magically, tobacco is a very powerful ally when it comes to divination and knowledge. It helps when folding or stretching time. It's easy to alter your perception of yourself and see what's stopping you from succeeding and what changes you need to make in order to manifest your bliss. It encourages dreams and visions. Some cultures believe that when used as a sacred smoke, tobacco lifts up our prayers and carries them to the ancestors and spirit helpers. It's widely used in ceremonies of many cultures because of its link with mysticism.

A Samhain Ritual to Appease the Spirits

Samhain is the time of year when the veil between our reality and that of the spirits is the thinnest, and that makes it easier to communicate with them. You'll need a pipe and some tobacco, or a cigar. (Some of you could already have a pipe that you use just for ceremonies.) Photos of your ancestors, deceased family, and friends—or even representations of your totems, spirit guides, or gods and goddesses will add to the observance, but they aren't necessary. You'll also want something heatproof to catch ashes and a lighter or a box of matches.

The best time for the ceremony is just after sunset when the sun has dipped below the horizon but there's still some light in the sky. This can be done inside or outside, but there's just something very primitive and connected about doing it outside around a fire. If you cast a circle, then do so to start the ceremony. Light your pipe or cut the end off your cigar and light it. Lift your pipe skyward, and as you do so, offer your prayer to the ancestors. Speak this aloud; you may improvise or write something beforehand, or you can say something like this:

> *I summon those beyond the veil*
> *To hear my prayer, I shall not fail*

> *To speak to helpers far and wide*
> *To thank the spirits at my side*
> *To know with you my life is blessed*
> *When I'm awake and when I rest*
> *My sacred smoke, I now send high*
> *My words to carry through the sky*
> *And summon those beyond the veil*
> *To hear my prayer, I shall not fail.*

Now put your pipe to your lips and take in the smoke. Slowly exhale, and as you do, turn the stem of the pipe (or the mouth end of your cigar) clockwise, so that it passes through all four directions. Raise the pipe to the heavens once again, and repeat your verse.

If you're doing this with others, pass the pipe around, and while everyone else is offering their prayers, reach out with your energy and feel the presence of your spirit helpers as they come be stand with you on this night of acknowledgment and homage. If you're working solitary, put the pipe (or cigar) down on the heatproof surface and spend some time in quiet contemplation of your relationship with your ancestors. When your ceremony is finished, dismiss any circle that you have cast. Leave the pipe alone, or place it (or the cigar butt) in front of any images you included in your ceremony until All Souls' Day, on November 2. At that time, pipes should be emptied or the cigar crumbled, and the tobacco remains scattered on the ground—preferably where you had your ritual space or fire, or in another spot of significance.

Tobacco always demands respect, and it teaches you to finish what you start, take nothing for granted, and not to abuse or trivialize anything that you have been given. You only have to look at the side effects of habitual smoking to see what a harsh teacher tobacco will be when it is treated with disdain. However, if you pay the proper attention to tobacco and work with it as an ally, it can be a very loyal and powerful companion as a spiritual smoke, a herbal totem, and more.

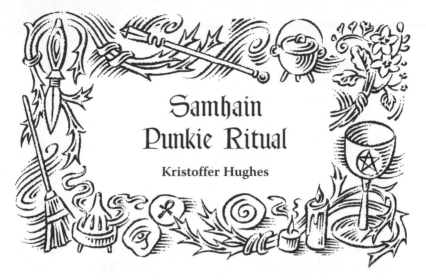

Samhain Punkie Ritual

Kristoffer Hughes

I DON'T BELIEVE THAT the visible and invisible worlds are necessarily aware of each other. For awareness and communication to occur, we must do something that causes the divide between the two worlds to collide and subsequently thin. In Pagan practice we have a name for such a method—ritual. The Wheel of the Year itself can act as a moderator of this function, and within its liminal phases, we are able to work with liminality to bridge the chasm between the seen and unseen, the living and the dead. Samhain is one such liminal time, a time between times. Ritual helps us to psychologically prepare and magically connect with otherworldly forces. Within the practices of secular Halloween we can see elements of this that far exceed the understanding of children and adults in fancy costume and attire. The current Halloween rites embody, albeit on a subconscious level, a sacred exchange between the visible and invisible worlds.

If you are reading these words anywhere other than England and Wales, you may never have heard of the word Punkie. And yet, within that rather peculiar word swims centuries of tradition and practice that is inexorably tied to the Halloween traditions of the secular world and also the Samhain practices of modern Pagans.

The Punkie, or Spunkie, as it was called in some of England's south-west counties, is essentially a jack-o'-lantern, albeit significantly smaller in stature, but what it lacks in grandeur and sheer size it certainly makes up for in character.

Whilst the magnificent pumpkin has become the primary symbol of Halloween in the twentieth and twenty-first centuries, its ancestor is in fact the Punkie, and its history is as colorful as Halloween itself. In olden times the Punkie formed the traditional lantern used by guisers and mummers during the dark nights of Halloween and was carved from a varied selection of native British root vegetables. These ranged from turnips, to swedes (rutabagas) to the peculiar root called a mangel-wurzel! These root vegetables, whilst harder and tougher to carve than the giant pumpkin of North America, were hollowed out and carved with hideous features in the guise of spirits and goblins.

The tradition of Punkie's would see children wander from door to door in their locality whilst singing the following verse:

It's Punkie night, it's Punkie night,
Give us a candle, give us a light,
If 'ee don't, we'll give 'ee a fright.

A sagacious household would offer treats in return for the song, and thus prevent any mischief or tricks being played upon themselves or their homes. Whilst it is tempting to assume a connection, it must be said that the similarity between this tradition and the modern trick-or-treat tradition is tenuous, but who knows—it may have all started with a humble vegetable!

The function of the lanterns were twofold: on one hand they represented shades of the dead, whilst simultaneously acting as protective devices. The necessity for protection during the dark part of the year may be somewhat alien to us in our brightly lit, heated homes, with supermarket shelves busting with year-round produce, but to our ancestors the winter posed a real threat. Not only did they fear recompense from the shades of the dead, they feared for their own lives and well-being during the harsh winter months.

This simple ritual will connect you to the ages-old practice of the Punkie lantern, whilst simultaneously honor the dead and protect your home from negativity during the 3 nights of Samhain.

Items Needed

3 tall black dinner or taper candles
3 suitable candle holders
1 circle made of card
1 large rutabaga (also called a swede or a turnip in commonwealth countries)
Tea light candles
Permanent marker pen
1 sharp knife
Strong ice cream scoop
Pencil

If you are able, try and perform the following ritual in one session. Have all the tools and equipment listed above in the same room. Create or delineate sacred space as you would ordinarily do.

Identify a suitable windowsill in your home that can be cleared of all items and redecorated for this ritual. Prepare the sill by decorating it with fabric and other seasonal accoutrements, leaving enough space for the Punkie to take central position with three candles around it: one to its left, another to its right, and one behind it. Be sensible with your decor, there will be a living flame on the sill!

Take a piece of stiff black card and cut it into a circle approximately 8 inches in diameter; personally I use a slate coaster of the same size I found in a market. You could also use a slice of wood, or anything else that you may have about your possessions.

Take three deep breaths, one with the land, one with the sky, and one with the seas that surround you, and bring to mind the gorse bush or furze; this small evergreen shrub covered in yellow flowers that has a distinctive coconut aroma is sacred in Celtic traditions for its protective qualities.

To aid your visualization, use a search engine to find an image of the shrub. Now draw the symbol on your card or whatever other material you have chosen to use. The symbol can be as large or small as you fancy and as elaborately or as simply drawn as your abilities and skills dictate. Consider protective qualities as you draw, imbuing the symbol with your intent and will. Position the card centrally on the windowsill. This will form a base upon which your Punkie will stand.

Now take the rutabaga and consider it closely, find its potential countenance, and with a pencil draw a face that you will subsequently carve. With your knife, slice the root end of the rutabaga to form a flat surface on which it will stand. Now take your knife to the opposite end and cut off a lid, as you would with a pumpkin. The next bit is tricky, for the rutabaga is significantly harder to carve, but who said that magic is easy? With your knife, cut crisscross lines into the body of the root, and scoop out the flesh with your ice cream scoop. You must do this slowly and methodically, avoiding going to close to the edge. Go as deep as you can to create enough of a space to hold a tea light candle and to illuminate the design of your Punkie's features.

Once hollowed to your satisfaction, carve out the Punkie's features. Your Punkie is now almost ready to serve as a protective device and to honor the dead with its ghostly light. But first you must inform it of its duty. Take another three deep breaths and kneel or position yourself as close to the Punkie's open lid as you can. Say these words:

Breath of my breath, warm thy breath

Take a deep breath and exhale loudly into the Punkie's innards, visualizing as you do the vitality of your expression flowing into the Punkie and out through its mouth. Repeat this three times.

Now take the Punkie and hold it in front of you, face-to-face, consider it, does it have a name, what personality traits can you glean from its features? As you look at each other repeat these words:

Root from deep within the earth,
Arise now, come to me and serve,
Keep me and mine from harm and strife,
Root of earth now to come to life!

Place the Punkie on the card on the windowsill, and whilst turning it round three times repeat the above spell again. Sit or position yourself so that you can once again be face-to-face, and place the candle into your Punkie and repeat the spell above for a third and final time before lighting the tea light candle. Carefully place the Punkie's lid back onto its body, but be aware that you may need cocktail sticks to secure it firmly. What you will notice is that the flame will slightly cook the lid and create the most delicious smell. If the rutabaga is small, you may need to create a chimney in the lid to allow heat to escape.

Position the candle sticks on the windowsill in a wide triangular formation, with the center candle being nearest the window and behind the Punkie.

Take another three deep breaths and light the candle to the left whilst considering the recent dead. Say these or similar words:

I honor you with glowing light, here upon this Samhain night,
Spirits from the other-side, cross now the great divide

After a few minutes, light the candle behind the Punkie and consider the ancient dead of your family, tribe, or culture, and repeat the verse above. Minutes later light the last candle and bring to mind your deceased pets and those who have died by effect of war, its collateral damage, or who have died in service to their countries. Repeat the words of the spell, and sit in quiet contemplation whilst gazing at the three candles and the glowing face of the Punkie.

Finally turn your Punkie to face the outside world, visualizing its light destroying any negativity directed at your home, move the central candle so that it is now positioned behind the Punkie.

Repeat the candle lighting sequence for each of the three nights of Samhain, and ensure that your Punkie remains lit and facing outward for the duration. Rather than risk fire, place a battery-operated tea light into the Punkie when you retire to bed. Note that a Punkie will not last as long as a pumpkin lantern. Boil and mash the rutabaga's innards with potato, some milk, and butter and serve during the festivities.

The rite is done. Open your space as you would ordinarily do.

When Samhain is over, thank your Punkie and compost it, telling it that he or she can return next year to keep your home safe over the festive period.

Notes

Notes

Yule

A United Yuletide

Blake Octavian Blair

MANY PEOPLE OFTEN SEE the winter holidays as something that highlights our religious differences. While it is true that there are theological differences among various faiths, there is common ground in our shared humanity and community. We need not think exactly alike to celebrate the joys of the season together. Yuletide is a wonderful season for weaving the magick of unity.

While Yule could be looked at as the Pagan and religious celebration that takes place at the winter solstice, the solstice itself is a glorious shared event. It's a natural wonder... owned by no particular faith and common domain for all. Actually, it's hard to find anything opposable with the occasion, although that doesn't mean some scrooges won't. (Seems there is always at least one!) However, I feel we should all, Pagan and non-Pagan alike, embrace the winter solstice and its accompanying Yuletide cheer and promote and claim it as the unifier it is and can be.

At its most basic, winter solstice is the shortest day and longest night of the year, but the time of year that the Yuletide season saddles includes not only this wonderful astronomical event but a myriad of other spiritual holidays. These holidays, while too numerous to expand upon here, often possess shared themes such as hope, goodwill, charitable giving, time with family and loved ones, and community events, parties, concerts, and pageants.

Spiritual Light and Wisdom

While for many people it is easy to turn entirely inward this time of year, I ask you not to resist the urge totally but to channel it in another direction. Yule is often heralded as a celebration of returning light. After all, once the winter solstice passes, the days begin to lengthen. The Sun, being the great spiritual being and spirit that it is to us magickal folks, is a good reminder of divine spiritual light and wisdom. Spiritual light and wisdom, just like the natural wonders of winter solstice, are shared among us all, tradition regardless. This is a wonderful time to use that spirit to shine light not only onto the Pagan faith for others (in a nonintrusive way) but also to learn about other faiths that we may not know or understand well. If you have friends or community members who have a faith differing from yours but are friendly, respectful, and understanding of your beliefs as well, don't be afraid to accept an invitation to join their seasonal and holiday celebrations. Don't be afraid to attend a Christmas Eve service with a friend or family member, or a Hanukkah dinner for example. Notice I was careful to caveat that they are respectful of your beliefs too; I'm not encouraging anyone to embark on what they know is a mission to convert them against their will to another religion. We all avoid that! I'm aware that as members of what is often termed a "minority religion," we often feel a bit ignored or persecuted, especially since only one dominant religion gets a majority of the public attention on TV and in advertising and public events. However, while I feel the "War on Christmas" truly does not exist, it's no call for us to feed into the trope that it does. In fact, agreeing to attend an event of a loved one of a differing faith can often lead to them accepting an invitation to respectfully share in your more Pagan celebration. Often times all parties involved gain great value and wisdom from the experience of attending the other faiths' event. It can often serve to, alongside the differences, highlight the common themes. Hope and joy really are the underlying essence of most of the winter holidays, whether it be the birth of the Son, the return of the Sun, the miracle represented by the Hanukkah lights, or the lessons to be learned from Ganesha during Pancha Ganapati.

When my husband and I lived in the Triangle area of North Carolina, we attended a Unitarian Universalist church. My husband was part of the audio-visual team, and although we are happily Pagan, we volunteered to run the sound system for Christmas Eve services. Now, the flavor of a Christmas Eve service at a UU church, even if it mentions the classic Nativity story at times, is not what you would call traditionally Christian flavored … solstice references are interjected whenever convenient! Still, this was a way to support a community with the more Christian oriented members of the congregation. Wouldn't you know it, we enjoyed the service ourselves as well. Other churches may more strongly draw biblical references, but if you attend with loved ones, I encourage you to dig to the essence of the message rather than names or places used in the stories. Most messages at this time of the year are more compassionate than not. In fact, when you change some of the names in many of the stories, it begins to sound a lot like many of our own Pagan mythologies. All of a sudden we are really starting to celebrate much the same things.

Shared Teachings

Sometimes you don't have to stray far from home to find interfaith opportunities for building unity at the holidays. The parents of our godchildren claim membership to different faiths. The mother is a modern witch and shamanic Pagan, and the father is a Buddhist. Naturally these two faiths are actually quite compatible with each other. Still, a conscious effort is made in holidays and celebrations to include traditions from both faiths, which is easy with the shared theological ground. Both their faiths teach compassion for all living beings, respect for others, and to strive to understand those different from yourself. Coincidentally, those teachings are much of the motivation for this article and themes to explore this season.

Mixed faith families are actually not all that uncommon, and they unfairly get a bad rap. Many say they are doomed to failure and yet many are met with wild success. Frankly, I think the successes are due to the fact that, as we've been discussing, we may clothe our faiths in different trappings, stories, and rituals, but we have fundamentally shared values and goals. These successful blended faith families not only find but celebrate the common ground. Many of them also participate in the religion of the others. Mixed-faith couples often raise their children in both faiths, allowing them to choose their beliefs for themselves when they are old enough. I've met several such grown children who in fact decided not to choose one over the other but still maintain ties to both faiths. When I discuss it further with them, the similarities are so strong that they have resolved any conflicts for themselves. I've been to many Pagan open sabbat circles where a non-Pagan spouse has attended with their partner and joyfully participated.

Many of the events of the season aren't attached to any specific faith and can really help bolster the spirit of community and the season. Charity events and drives are a popular mainstay. Charities need help to assist those they care for all year long, but they get a lot of special attention during this season of giving. Most of these groups are happy to receive either time or money, so there is a way for everyone to give. There are many causes, but common examples are assisting the homeless and helping animals both wild and domestic through shelter and rescue organizations or wildlife preservation and defense groups. Educating the public about the unmerited killing of wild animal populations or helping to serve in a soup kitchen for the homeless are both activities quite fitting for this season. Through these acts of service, you will surely find yourself working with people who have different faith backgrounds but hold much the same beliefs, morals, and values as you!

Public light displays are another example. I currently live in the Boston area. Every year Quincy Market in Boston decorates with decadent evergreen garlands, lights wrapped around all the trees, and a central, grand holiday tree. Every evening near sunset there are light shows accompanied by music. The official holiday tree for the city of Boston is in Boston Common. The tree itself is a wonderful example of community and unity, as every year since 1971 the official tree has been a gift to Boston from Nova Scotia. The tree is a gift of thanks for Boston's assistance to the people of Nova Scotia after the tragedy of the Halifax Explosion, in which a French cargo ship carrying explosives exploded in an accidental collision. For those who know the history behind the tree, it serves as a symbol of goodwill and compassion to our neighbors in a time of need. Leading up to New Years, still in the domain of the Yuletide season in my opinion, Boston also has what they call the First Night and First Day celebrations. Among the numerous activities associated with these events are musical performances as well as a citywide display of ice sculptures. Some of them are quite grand in scale. All these events draw people from multiple religious traditions together to celebrate, both consciously and unconsciously, the wonders of winter, community, growing light (literal, spiritual, and metaphorical), hope, goodwill, and new beginnings. You can see people wearing pentacles, crucifixes, nun's habits, Indian saris, hijabs, yarmulkes, and just plain cozy winter knitted goods. One begins to realize, despite our differences, we are not all that different after all.

These seemingly nonreligious events bring people together to celebrate the themes that I have repeatedly mentioned, such as community, joy, hope, and the natural wonders of the season. They of course may not actively think of it that way; however, when we step back, it's easy to see that is partly what is happening. There is a spark within all of us that, regardless of faith, feels the wonder and magick in the first snowfall, the beauty of icicles hanging off the ledge, the comfort of being around a beloved family member you may not have seen all year, or the building of a snowman and warming up afterward in cozy hand-knit socks with a cup of cocoa. There is magick in seeing friends and family sing in seasonal concerts or in receiving a plate of homemade baked goods from a neighbor; these are the acts of a web of unity being weaved. Common experiences and shared connections—these are the fibers that grow the magick of the season strong.

Solstice belongs to us all and we're all on this big blue planet together. It is my hope you can be inspired by the returning light to make it a theme of your celebrations to use your light to shine bright and weave a magickal web of Yuletide unity!

Cosmic Sway

Corrine Kenner

THOUSANDS OF YEARS AGO, when astrologers were first developing the principles of their art, they saw the Sun rise and set against the backdrop of a different constellation each month. Eventually those twelve constellations became the twelve signs of the zodiac, which led to the development of the twelve-month calendar we use to this day.

Even now, the four seasons of the year are based on the Sun's entry into the four cardinal signs—Aries in spring, watery Cancer in summer, airy Libra in fall, and earthy Capricorn in winter.

Yule is celebrated on the winter solstice, which is the longest night of the year. After a long season of darkness, it's time to celebrate the return of the light and the newborn Sun that promises to add fire to our days.

It's no coincidence that the winter solstice also occurs when the Sun moves into earthy Capricorn. In fact, the winter solstice occurs at the moment when the Sun reaches its southernmost position in the sky, directly over the Tropic of Capricorn.

This year, the Sun moves into earthy Capricorn at 12:29 pm Eastern Time.

Mythic Astrology: Apollo, the God of the Sun

On the winter solstice, the Sun is reborn, and the newborn god promises to add light and heat to days that grow increasingly longer.

In mythic astrology, the Sun was Apollo—the god of music, healing, truth, and light. He rode through the sky in a golden chariot drawn by four fire-breathing steeds.

Apollo was the son of Jupiter and Leto, a nymph that Jupiter had seduced in the form of a swan. Jupiter's jealous wife, Juno, had pursued Leto throughout the course of her pregnancy, decreeing that she would never give birth on dry land. As a result, Apollo was born on the floating island of Delos. Knowing that Juno was still pursuing her, the young mother turned Apollo over to Themis, the goddess of justice, and fled for her life.

Themis fed the newborn nectar and ambrosia. As soon as he had eaten, Apollo bounded out of his swaddling clothes and sprang to his feet, fully grown.

"The golden lyre," he announced, "shall be my friend, the bent bow my delight, and in oracles will I foretell the dark future."

Tell fortunes, he did. He established a sacred site at Delphi, where Gaia herself had revealed the future. It was guarded by the Python, a monstrous, man-eating serpent. Apollo killed the Python with his bow and arrow.

Delphi was said to be the center of the earth, because Jupiter had sent two eagles to circumnavigate the globe—one from the east, the other from the west—and they both reached Delphi at the same time.

In astrology, the Sun is the center of our solar system—and, for all intents and purposes, our universe. Astrology is a geocentric pursuit: we chart the planets and stars from our perspective here on earth.

The glyph for the Sun ☉ looks like the Sun at the center of our solar system surrounded by a ring of orbiting planets.

The Sun rules fiery Leo, the sign of the lion. The Sun also rules the fifth house, where astrologers look for information about creativity, recreation, and play.

Because the Sun is so visible in the sky, its placement in an astrological chart can highlight areas of fame, public recognition, and acclaim. It also describes your inner light and the ways in which you shine. It illuminates your sense of purpose, as well as your life's path, and it shows where you'll expend the most energy in pursuit of your goals.

Reading the Signs

The Sun enters Capricorn, the sign of worldly power, at 12:29 pm Eastern Time.

Saturn has just entered Capricorn, too. This is a monumental event: Saturn rules Capricorn, which puts Saturn at home after a long, 29-year journey around the signs of the zodiac.

The Sun and Uranus are in an easy trine, while the eccentric rebel planet moves backward through Aries.

Venus is in a fiery trine with Uranus, too. Venus, the planet of glamour and illusion, moved into adventurous Sagittarius on December 1. It will move into Capricorn on December 25, and then shift its focus to friends and social groups when it moves into Aquarius on January 18.

Planetary Positions

- Sun in Capricorn
- Moon in Aquarius
- Mercury in Sagittarius
- Venus in Sagittarius
- Mars in Scorpio

- Jupiter in Scorpio
- Saturn in Capricorn
- Uranus ℞ in Aries
- Neptune in Pisces
- Pluto in Capricorn

The Moon is already in futuristic Aquarius, in an uncomfortable square with Mars. Be careful with your words—and your actions. If you're with friends, they might be ultra-sensitive.

That's because the warrior planet moved into mysterious Scorpio on December 9. Mars is the traditional ruler of Scorpio, so it's comfortable with the intensity of the sign—but all that energy could leave some people at your holiday gathering feeling like they're being targeted for attack.

Most people won't even realize how their words could be interpreted. Mars and Neptune, the planet of illusion, are combining forces in an easy trine, and hardcore Saturn and crazy Uranus are trine, too.

To make matters worse, Mercury has been retrograde since December 3. On Yule, it's in an uncomfortable square with Neptune, which could lead to misunderstandings with loved ones, despite everyone's best intentions. The messenger planet is stationed in Sagittarius, preparing to go direct on December 22. Mercury is weak in Sagittarius; it's 180 degrees from its own sign in Gemini, so it's forced to function in a land of opposites. Mercury will find its footing again when it moves into Capricorn on January 11, and Aquarius on January 31.

The good news is that Jupiter, the expansive planet of luck and good fortune, is also in its old sign in Scorpio, where it can spread good cheer and good humor. It's in a watery trine with Neptune in its own sign of Pisces, and a comfortable sextile with Pluto in earthy Capricorn.

Phases of the Moon

On December 3, the last Full Moon in Gemini was illuminated by the Sun in the opposite sign of Sagittarius.

On December 18, a New Moon, with the Sun and the Moon conjunct in fiery Sagittarius, probably inspired a recent burst of wanderlust and curiosity. Sagittarius is the sign of long-distance travel, higher education, and philosophy.

On January 2, a Full Moon in watery Cancer, across from the Sun in earthy Capricorn, will illuminate matters of hearth and home. Now's the time to be nurturing and ask for a little extra affection.

On January 17, a New Moon in earthy Capricorn will align itself in a conjunction with the Sun, which is also in earthy Capricorn. It's a great time to start new projects at work. You can shepherd them toward completion as the Moon waxes toward full, tying up any loose ends as the Moon wanes.

On January 31, the second Full Moon of the month—a proverbial Blue Moon—embodies the fiery energy of Leo. Play games, get involved in an athletic competition, or create something beautiful and artistic.

This Full Moon has an added bonus: a lunar eclipse, when the Earth passes between the Sun and the Moon.

Practical Astrology

If you're in North America, Asia, or Australia, you'll be able to see the lunar eclipse—assuming that the sky is clear. (If you're in South America, Europe, Africa, Asia, or Australia, you'll be able to see a lunar eclipse on July 27.)

In astrology, eclipses represent sudden and dramatic change. Lunar eclipses tend to be personal, while solar eclipses generally affect widespread groups. Lunar eclipses are almost always followed by partial solar eclipses.

The Old Ways: Northern Lights

Natalie Zaman

WHEN I DISCOVERED THAT a smidgen of my DNA is Scandinavian, I embarked on a journey to learn about the culture, now my heritage. An endearing aspect—and one that goes far back and persists to this day—is the reverence of mythical beings. A significant number of folks in Nordic countries (particularly Iceland) believe in the existence of gnomes, trolls, and giants—the spirits of the land. Because they can affect day-to-day life (urban planners have taken them into consideration when shaping the landscape), they are just as revered as any deity. While these entities are a presence all year round, it's especially evident at Yuletide when old traditions persist—sometimes with a modern twist.

One of the most beautiful sights of the Nordic Yuletide season are the Lucia pageants held in mid-December. Girls robed in white and crowned with evergreens and candles sing traditional songs and are accompanied by attendants (sometimes dressed as Nisse or Tomtes—more about them later!). Lucia's legend originated in fourth-century Italy. There are several tales about how she achieved martyrdom, but in nearly all of them she loses her eyes. Lucia, the "light bringer," is the patroness of the sight-challenged, but her name also hints at her connection to the winter solstice.

Merchants, missionary monks, and even the Vikings have all been credited with bringing Lucia northward. For over a thousand years her feast day was celebrated at the winter solstice. It's possible that early Norse belief in the sun goddess Alfrödull (whose name translates to "Elf Shine" or "Elf Splendor") melded with Lucia; both "brought back the light." Once the Gregorian calendar was established, Lucia's feast was moved to December 13 and the tradition evolved to a folk custom as well as a spiritual one. On Saint Lucia's Day, the oldest (or in some places, the youngest) daughter of the house would rise at dawn to serve her family a breakfast of saffron buns (one of Lucia's miracles was the deliverance of a boatload of grain to a starving village).

The pageantry of today's Lucia celebrations dates back to the eighteenth century when children dressed as Lucia and her attendants would travel from house to house to sing songs for food and drink. While all Nordic countries revere her in some way, Lucia shines particularly in Sweden where the pageants were commercialized with a beauty contest element in the nineteenth century. To this day, young girls compete for the coveted role of Lucia in community Yuletide celebrations. The goddess always returns and renews.

Not so welcoming as Lucia is the old hag Gryla. So notorious that she gets a mention in Snorri Sturluson's *Prose Edda*, Gryla was an Icelandic giantess who, like the witch in the *Hansel and Gretel* Fairy tale (and perhaps a forerunner) liked to catch, cook, and eat children. She didn't become a Yuletide figure until the seventeenth century. She herself didn't take part, but her cat and her kids did.

Nordic children knew that if they'd been good then they'd get at least one new piece of clothing for Christmas—this was a boon, for a lack of new threads made one a target for Jólakötturinn, the Yule or Christmas Cat. Gryla's ferocious feline only got to eat once a year and went out hunting on Christmas Eve looking for folks wearing old clothes, a sure sign of wickedness—and Jólakötturinn thought they tasted better.

Gryla is said to have had over eighty children with her three husbands, but only thirteen of her sons came to be known as the Yule Lads (Jólasveinar). They emerged in the sixteenth century, at first just like mom, looking for children to eat. As it's wont to do, time softened the personalities and deeds of the Lads, and they became more mischievous than menacing, at least if you go by their names (sparing the Icelandic, these are their English equivalents): Sheep-Cote Clod harassed the sheep, Gully Gawk hid in a gully until the coast was clear for him to steal milk, Stubby and Pot Scraper both raided the leftovers, Stubby being the shorter of the two. Meat Hook was named for his meat-stealing weapon. The remaining Lads' names are self-explanatory—Spoon Licker, Bowl Licker, Door Slammer, Skyr (yogurt) Gobbler, Sausage Swiper, Window Peeper, Doorway Sniffer, and Candle Stealer. The Lads visit houses starting on December 12. Each stays for twelve days to ensure the good behavior of the occupants. Today children still leave out socks and shoes in the hopes of receiving a treat, and not the rotten potato reserved for the naughty.

Not all Nordic fae folk are frightening or out to cause trouble. Norway and Denmark's Nisse (called Tomtes in Sweden) are a combination of house elf and ancestral spirit. Small yet incredibly strong, they sport snowy beards and conical caps which seem seasonal, but for them it's year-round wear. Nisse were and are very personal to a family. They guard homes and barns and bring good luck to all the occupants of a house—unless they're offended. Gifts pacified temperamental Nisse; at Jul (Yule) it was customary to give them pairs of new white boots and bowls of porridge with large pats of butter.

One of the most familiar Nordic Yuletide symbols is a goat crafted from straw and red ribbon. He is a representation of Joulupukki (Finland), or Julbocken (Norway and Denmark), the "Yule Goat." In all probability he's a Pagan import from Germany and an amalgamation of two older goats, Tanngrisnir and Tanngnjóstr, who pulled Thor's chariot across the sky. In her book *The Yule Goat in*

Folklore and Christmas Tradition, Karin Schager suggests that the last sheaf of harvest grain possessed magical properties and was called the Yule Goat.

Crafting goats out of straw as we see them today is derived from a Swedish tradition called Gävlebokken or the Gävele Goat, named for the Swedish town where he was first made in 1966. He's trotted out in early December to celebrate the return of the light (if the Yule Lads don't set him aflame beforehand—he's been tampered with nearly every year since he's gone up).

As Yule approaches, be aware of the Nordic spirits of winter; they are still very much with us. Good Jul!

Additional Reading

Illes, Judika. *The Encyclopedia of Mystics, Saints and Sages: A Guide to Asking for Protection, Wealth, Happiness and Everything Else!* New York: Harper Collins, 2011.

Jacobs, Ryan. "Why So Many Icelanders Believe in Invisible Elves." *The Atlantic*, Oct. 29, 2013. www.theatlantic.com/international /archive/2013/10/why-so-many-icelanders-still-believe-in-invisible-elves/280783/.

Kinsella, Kajsa. *Nordicana: 100 Icons of Scandi Culture and Nordic Cool and Scandi Style*. New York: Cassell Illustrated, 2015.

Kvilhoug, Maria. "The Old Norse Yule Celebration, Myth and Ritual." Dec. 21, 2012. http://freya.theladyofthelabyrinth.com /?page_id=397.

Schager, Karin. *Julbocken i folktro och jultradition* [The Yule goat in folklore and Christmas tradition]. Rabén & Sjögren, 1989.

Feasts and Treats

Laurel Reufner

MERRY MEET AND WELCOME to the first celebration of the new year! What better way to enjoy it than with a hearty and healthy feast. When my test kitchen turned out this meal, we comfortably fed six, who declared it all delicious.

Holiday Roast Beast

Sorry I don't have a vegetarian option for this meal's main dish; however, the side dishes are also pretty filling.

Prep time: 10 minutes
Marinating time: 12 hours
Cook time: 1 hour 40 minutes (plus 15 minutes to rest)
Servings: 6–8

1 cup pomegranate juice
3 tablespoons balsamic or apple cider vinegar
1 tablespoon garlic (approximately)
¼ teaspoon cardamom, ground
¼ teaspoon cinnamon, ground
¼ teaspoon cumin, ground
2–3 pounds beef roast

In a measuring cup or small bowl, mix together everything but the roast. Place the roast in either a plastic bag or plastic container and pour the marinade over it. Place in the refrigerator and allow to marinate for about 12 hours.

Preheat oven to 375 degrees F and place your roast in a baking dish. Pour the marinade over it and cover with aluminum foil, place in the oven, and set your timer for 40 minutes. When the timer goes off, flip the roast over in the pan and reset the timer for about an hour. (It needs to cook at least 20 minutes per pound.) Remove from the oven and let the roast rest for a good 15 minutes before slicing.

Place the remaining pan liquids into a skillet, add a couple of tablespoons of flour or cornstarch and make a thin gravy for serving with the meat. I used the pan I fried the bacon in for the roasted Brussels sprouts, adding that undertone of bacon flavor to the gravy.

Sautéed Asparagus with Potatoes

I don't know where the idea for this dish came from, but it was certainly inspired. And it's definitely a keeper.

Prep time: 15 minutes
Cook time: 20–25 minutes
Servings: 4–6

1 pound smallish potatoes
1 bunch of asparagus, about 1 pound
Butter, for sautéing
Salt and pepper, to taste
½ lemon

Cut the potatoes into largish chunks and precook in boiling water until just barely done. While they are cooking, snip the asparagus into thirds.

Place the butter in a large saucepan and let it melt. Add the asparagus pieces to the pan and allow them to cook for about 5 minutes, stirring around frequently. Add the potatoes and salt and pepper to taste. Give a good squeeze of the lemon over the top of it all, stir well, and allow to cook for another 5 minutes or until the asparagus is firm but cooked through. (When in doubt, pull out a piece and try it.)

Roasted Brussels Sprouts with Cranberries, Bacon, and Pecans

You have my daughter to thank for the bacon in this dish. It certainly adds to the flavor. If you want things to be vegetarian, either leave it out or use soy-based bacon bits.

Prep time: 15 minutes
Cook time: 40 minutes
Servings: 6

1 pound fresh Brussels sprouts
2 strips bacon, fried crisp and crumbled
½ cup dried cranberries
½ cup pecans
Olive oil

Rinse the Brussels sprouts well and then trim the ends before cutting them in half. If they're really large, cut into quarters. Place in a large bowl and toss in the bacon crumbles, cranberries, and pecans. Drizzle lightly with olive oil to help coat the sprouts, then toss it all gently together to coat with your hands.

Preheat oven to 425 degrees F. Line a baking sheet with aluminum foil and place the Brussels sprouts on the baking sheet. There should be very little oil left in the bowl. Bake at 425 degrees F for about 40 minutes. Serve hot.

Pfefferneusse Cookies

I've got two holiday cookie recipes to finish up the meal for you. These would also be great to make and take to any events. I'll warn you the pfefferneusse recipe (German for "pepper nut") makes 30 dozen cookies if they're properly sized. The cookies are small, though, and the baking goes pretty quickly. If you need to, freeze half the dough and finish baking later. And while the prep work involves a good bit of wait time, they are so worth it. Also, both cookie doughs require extended refrigeration, so be sure to plan your time accordingly.

Prep time: 30 minutes
Chill time: overnight
Bake time: approx. 30 minutes
Servings: 30 dozen

1 cup sugar
½ cup dark corn syrup
½ cup honey
1 cup butter
2 eggs
5 cups flour
1 tablespoon baking powder
1 teaspoon cinnamon, ground
1 teaspoon nutmeg, ground
½ teaspoon anise seed
¼ teaspoon baking soda
¼ teaspoon ground black pepper
⅛ teaspoon cloves, ground
Fruit juice

In a heavy-bottomed saucepan, heat the sugar, corn syrup, honey, and butter over low heat until the sugar is dissolved and the butter has melted. Set aside to cool.

While the sugar mixture cools, whisk together all of the dry ingredients in a large mixing bowl. Once the sugars are cool to the touch, stir in one unbeaten egg at a time until blended. Gradually add the liquids to the bowl of dry ingredients, mixing well. Cover with plastic wrap (or use a bowl with a lid on it) and refrigerate overnight.

Now you want to form your dough into thin rolls, about ¼ to ½ inch in diameter. I found making them the length of a cookie sheet made them a good length to work with. Line the sheet with some parchment first so they don't easily stick. Once you have the sheet full of rolled dough, place it back in the refrigerator for another couple of hours. Any remaining dough should also be refrigerated again as well.

Working with the rolls one at a time, slice them with a sharp knife into rounds about ½ inch thick and place on a parchment-lined cookie sheet. Dab each cookie in the middle with a drop of fruit juice. (I like lemon or orange juice, or maybe apple cider.)

Bake at 375 degrees F for 10 to 12 minutes.

Gingerbread Gods

Prep time: 20 minutes
Chill time: 4 hours
Bake time: 10 minutes
Servings: 1–2 cups

3 cups flour
1 teaspoon baking soda
2 teaspoons ginger, ground
1 teaspoon cinnamon, ground
¼ teaspoon nutmeg, ground
¼ teaspoon salt
¾ cup brown sugar, firmly packed
¾ cup butter, softened some (DO NOT let it melt!)
1 egg
½ cup molasses
1 teaspoon vanilla extract

Whisk together the flour, baking soda, spices, and salt in a medium-sized bowl. In a large mixing bowl, beat together the sugar and butter until it becomes very fluffy, and then add the eggs, molasses, and vanilla and mix well. Now you want to add the dry ingredients about a cup at a time, scraping the sides of your bowl and making sure it's all thoroughly mixed together. You want a firm dough when finished.

Shape your dough into a ball and then flatten it down. Wrap in plastic wrap and refrigerate a minimum of four hours.

When you're ready to start baking, take the dough out of the refrigerator and break the dough into two halves. Put one back in the refrigerator to keep cool.

On a floured surface, roll the dough out until it is about ¼ of an inch thick. Be patient and look at a ruler if need be. Once you have it rolled out, carefully use a gingerbread boy (or girl) cutter to make your cookies. I like to use one that's about 6 inches tall as it makes a nice big cookie for decorating. Preheat oven to 350 degrees F.

Place cookies about 1 inch apart on a parchment-lined cookie sheet. Bake at 350 degrees F for about 10 minutes, watching them closely in those last couple of minutes. You want them to just begin turning brown. Cool on a cookie rack and they can then be sealed in an airtight container for about a week. Makes about 1 dozen large or 2 dozen small cookies.

These cookies are great for family celebrations as you can pull out the decorating icing and candies and let everyone have at! Add holly leaves and solar halos to make your very own little sun gods.

Crafty Crafts

Linda Raedisch

IN BRITAIN, WHAT WE call "Christmas lights" are "fairy lights." The following project is one of several techniques I use for softening the lights to make them more appealing to fairies and other ancestral spirits who might like to visit at this time of year.

Seven-Point Star Reflectors

I once received a Christmas card with a five-pointed origami star stuck to it. Couldn't figure out how it was made. Then, lo and behold, I saw another one folded from tracing paper in my cousin Astrid's picture window. Astrid gave me a copy of the wickedly complex instructions. Tears ensued. I have given up on the five-pointed origami star. My 3D seven-pointed star, which looks more like a flower when all is said and done, is easy-peasy. It is not, strictly speaking, origami, because it requires cutting and gluing, but the results are very pretty and you don't have to worry about spotting the paper with tears.

Since they're reflectors, I'd originally planned to make these stars with multicolored metallic origami paper. Then I saw how much packs of multicolored metallic origami paper cost these days. Yowzah. I ended up making mine out of plain white paper, which

made them look like softly glowing snow flowers. You can also use plain origami paper in a variety of colors or cut your own squares out of metallic wrapping paper. Even if you make them out of newspaper squares, they will still look good. And you don't have to put them on the tree; you can hang a string of them in the window, on the mantel, or anywhere around the Yuletide house.

Time frittered: Once the paper is cut, each star takes about ten minutes. You'll need to make thirty.

Cost: About $25.00 if you go for the expensive origami paper, $13.00 or less if you cut your own paper.

Supplies

Origami or other paper (see above) cut into 210 squares no bigger than 1½" and no smaller than 1¼". I know it sounds like a lot, so make some cocoa and get your friends together to help you.

White all-purpose glue*

One 30-bulb light string (the little twinkly ones, not the big old fashioned bulbs)

Position your square of paper like a diamond. Fold in half, tip to tip, into a triangle. Unfold. Fold the two bottom edges of the diamond in to the center crease, colored side out. The result should remind you of a kite. That's one point. Now make 6 more.

Glue the points together, lining up the upper kite edge of each point with the center crease of the point before it so they overlap as in the picture. When all 7 points are glued, slide the seventh point into place halfway under the first point. This will force the star to become concave. Pop it on to your light bulb. Unless you've been overzealous with the glue, a hole will naturally open in the center to let the bulb through.

Continue with the other 29 stars. Happy folding!

Tracing Paper Frost-Ferns

This project is for those of you who don't live far enough north (or south!) to get frost on the window panes or who are simply impatient for the season to reveal itself in all its wintry glory. In a letter he wrote to J. R. R. Tolkien's children in 1926, Father Christmas's sidekick, the North Polar Bear, mentions how their gardener, the Snow Man, can't get anything but snowdrops and frost-ferns to grow at the North Pole. I have the same problem, even though I live in zone 7.

These are the easiest frost-ferns of all to grow. Spend a few hours folding at your kitchen table and your window panes will soon be as beautiful as Father Christmas's back garden. (I know some of you don't really like the word "Christmas," so just think of him as Grandfather Yule's son.)

Time frittered: A 16-frond fern takes about 30 minutes. If you find you can't stop, then there's no telling how much of your weekend this craft will take up.

Cost: About $10.00. (At this writing, $6.99 buys a 50-sheet pad of tracing paper, but if you use the whole pad, you won't be able to see out of your windows.)

Supplies

Tracing paper*
White all-purpose glue*
Double-sided or other transparent tape*

Cut a 9" square from a 9" × 12" sheet of tracing paper. (If your paper is smaller, that's fine. In fact, your ferns will look more delicate, though they'll be a little trickier to fold.) Fold and cut your square into quarters then fold and cut each of those into quarters. Now you have 16 little squares of paper. This may prove to be more than you need, or you may decide you need twice as many. You'll see as you go.

Take your first little square and fold it diagonally in half and in half again to make a center point. Unfold. Fold two opposite corners in to the center point. Now fold the top two edges in to the center crease as if you are making a pointy little hood. Fold the whole piece in half lengthwise. This is your first "frond." Take another little square of paper and fold a second frond. Slide the two fronds together into a "V," securing them with a tiny dab of glue. Keep folding and gluing until you've used up all sixteen.

Use little rolls of tape (or double sided tape) to attach your fronds to the window pane. Start in a lower corner of the window and build your ferns upward and outward in gentle arcs. To look natural, each pair of fronds should "grow" out of the one before it; no free-floating fronds, please! When the sun shines through the layers of folded paper, your ferns will look more complex than they did on your work surface. Your neighbors might even wonder why their own windows are unaffected!

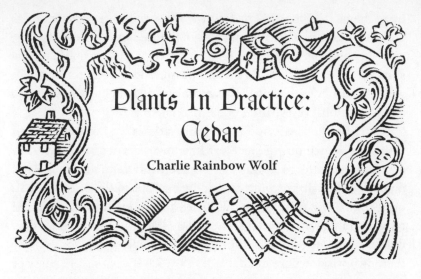

Plants In Practice: Cedar

Charlie Rainbow Wolf

CEDAR IS A WONDERFUL plant ally for the ceremony of Yule because of its evergreen properties and its link with those who no longer walk this Earth. The common cedar (*Cedrus*) is one of the many members of the Pinaceae family, and can be found throughout the world. They're long-lived and can grow anywhere from fifty to one hundred feet tall. Their natural habitat is a moist forest, so they need quite a bit of rainfall to thrive. Cedars are easily recognizable by their unique smell, which is not only pleasing to most people, but it also deters insects and diseases in the tree.

In the US, cedars can be found in most USDA zones 2–9, apart from Texas and Florida. They can be raised from seed, and some grow up to two feet per season. Mostly, though, young trees are obtained through nurseries so you know what type of cedar tree you're getting. They're not hardy as youngsters; the oils aren't strong enough to keep pests and diseases at bay. This is why many cedars have hollow trunks—which makes a most welcome home for local wildlife.

Choose a cedar that is suitable and fairly native to where you want to plant it. They're usually forgiving, but they won't thrive if they're neglected. Because the trees are tall and long-lived, don't plant them where they can grow to entangle overhead lines or where the roots can reach down and impact wells, underground pipes or wires, or septic systems.

As well as going up and down, these giants are going to spread out, so plant them far enough apart that other plants and trees—or other cedars, if you're planting them as a windbreak—have room to grow. It's best to keep them away from fruit trees, too, as they can swap diseases. These huge trees will eventually have equally huge root systems, so don't plant them too near ponds or rivers. The soil could be too wet to provide adequate support for older trees. Young trees need plenty of sunlight, and they need weeds clearing around from the base regularly, so that they get the nutrients in the soil. You may need to protect the saplings from foraging critters, too.

Medicinally, cedar has been used through the ages in a variety of ways, and for even more reasons. It's a preservative—which is why many a young bride's "hope" chest was made from cedar and why grannies used cedar boxes and armoires to store their blankets and bedding. It deterred moths and helped to keep the linens safe. The essence—as in the spirit, rather than the sap—of the tree was used in sympathetic medicine to cure warts, rheumatism, sore throats, and gout. Cedar has to be used with care, though, for it can cause damage to the nervous system if a large dose is used incorrectly.

Magically, cedar is often included in incense and smudge sticks. It's protective and preserving, and it's said that cedar provides a dwelling for the spirits of the dead. There are many stories about the deities and dryads that live in the cedar trees, and Cherokee legend tells us that the heart of the cedar tree is where the ancestors reside. Many cultures have tales of people being turned into cedar trees, so that they can continue to assist their loved ones even after dying. Totem poles and talking sticks—as well as magical wands and staffs—are often made from cedar, and cedar wood is frequently burned in ceremonial fires.

A Yule Ritual to Celebrate the Inner Light

Just as the cedar tree is said to stand tall, live long, and embody the spirits of the ancestors, so do you! The best way that you can honor them is to live your life to the fullest, creating your highest happiness and working toward your greatest success. This ritual will set you up to do just that in the coming year, as the light returns and brings with it another season, another chance for you to manifest your bliss.

You'll need a green taper or pillar candle, a heatproof surface for the candle, and something with which to light it, an athame, knife, other tool to carve the candle, and if you put cloth on your altar or table, choose a dark green one. You'll also need a piece of cheesecloth, or muslin, and a sprig of cedar or cedar wood in some other form (incense, wood disc, sachet, etc.) for everyone in attendance. This—like the other rituals—can be done either solitary or in a group. If you cast the sacred circle, do this before you start the ceremony.

Start by inscribing the candle. Do this inside your circle if you use one. Either carve the word "light" into the candle, or carve a sun or other symbol that means light to you. Dim the lights, light the candle, and say something to honor the flame shining through the darkness. You can write this out beforehand, say something impromptu, or use the following:

> *The light shines as the candle burns*
> *The light through dark and cold returns*
> *To help me learn and watch me grow*
> *And with my inner fire glow*
> *And like the fire that is warm*
> *You shelter me from harm and storm*
> *I will be with you through the night*
> *To welcome you, O' gift of light.*

Pass the cedar through the candle's glow—not through the actual flame, though, you don't want to set it on fire! Work just above the light—and if you're experienced with candle magic, have some fun with this and really get the flame dancing. When you've finished, wrap the cedar up in the piece of cloth. Leave this on your altar or table for now.

If you can stay awake to greet the dawn, so much the better, for then you can let the candle burn so that it eventually extinguishes itself. If this is not possible, then pinch it out with your fingers or use a snuffer. If you've planned a feast, now is the time to dismiss your circle and get busy with the merrymaking. At the end of the festivities, everyone should pick up their cedar bundle from off the altar and take it home with them. Put this in a safe place, somewhere that is personal to you, but somewhere you'll see it often. It doesn't have to be anywhere fancy—a sock drawer will do nicely!

Cedar's lesson is to remind you that you're connected to everything and it's connected to you—the plant kingdom, the animal kingdom, the spirit world, and the realms of your ancestors. You were born with the light within you, and you have the potential to tap into that light and use it to guide you to your fulfillment. Every time you see your Yule bundle, remember that you have the radiance of the whole universe shining through you. Use it to make wise choices!

Sound Salutations for the Sun

Blake Octavian Blair

THE CENTERPIECE OF MOST Yuletide celebrations is a ritual celebration of the astronomical event of winter solstice. Many people the world over celebrate by welcoming the Sun back in one fashion or another. Here I will share my spin on this ritual endeavor flavored with shamanic elements. It can be incredibly casual and low-key or very formal with ornate ceremonial flair. This ritual is easily adaptable to fall anywhere on the spectrum that works for you.

This ritual is short on prescribed words and long on action and adaptability. Where there are verbal parts, you may use the words provided, or you are encouraged to adapt, edit, and create your own as you see fit. Perform it to peak at the deafening noise of twenty drums or the quieter but steady and purposeful ring of a half dozen bells.

I encourage you to perform this ritual at sunrise on the day of the winter solstice. In our home we do it as a prelude to gathering around the Yule tree for gift exchange. While this does mean getting up before sunrise, the scent and allure of hot drinks brewing goes a long way to rousing family members out of bed for the celebration. Gather the items listed below and assemble with your participants in a spot where you can get the best view of the Sun rising over the horizon. A perfect view is not necessary … just do the best you can. This can be either indoors or out.

Items Needed

Altar cloth
Candle
Smudge or incense
Drink for libation
Small pastries, cookies, or other food item
Sacred item for each person for the altar that represents the holiday to them.
Solar/sun symbol
Bells, drums, rattles, etc.
Small watch or clock

Ritual Procedure

Ideally you will want to gather in the ritual space a bit before the actual clock time of the moment of the solstice sunrise (you can check the time of the sunrise in your favorite Pagan calendar or online). Have the participants arrange themselves in a semicircle facing the direction of the view for the sunrise. Place the altar cloth on the floor in the center of the semicircle. Set upon the cloth the solar symbol, the candle, and the smudge or incense.

Proceed to smudge all participants and the ritual space with either your smudge or incense. Next, light the candle on the central altar. You can explain to your participants, in your own paraphrasing, that not only does the candle represent the light and fire that burns within us all, and the power of the Sun, but also that for thousands of years, people have gathered in sacred circles and around sacred fires. The central candle connects us to this time-honored tradition and to our ancestors, who did the same before us, and all those who may doing the same around the world at this very same solstice sunrise.

As ceremonial leader, use a bell, rattle, or drum to call in the spirits of all the directions. (Many shamanic traditions honor six or seven directions, east, south, west, north, below/earth, above/sky, and the seventh is the center. Some honor even more!)

Next, have the participants come forward one at a time, and place the sacred object they brought with them for the altar upon it. Give them the option to say a few short words on what the item is and what it means to them. (It is perfectly fine for them to choose to place their item in silence and pass on sharing as well.) When all participants have placed their items, as ceremonial leader, then bless the altar as you see fit. I like to do so by ringing a bell or rattling over it while praying to the guardians and helping spirits of all present and to the Sun to lend their blessing and empowerment to the altar. Choose a method that resonates with you.

Next, if your participants do not already have their instruments, distribute them and make sure all who wish to use a drum, rattle, bell, etc., have something at the ready. Ideally, for a small family-sized group, the ritual to this point will have likely taken roughly fifteen minutes. You will want to time things so that at this point you have around five or so minutes until the actual moment of sunrise. With just a few moments until the sunrise, begin leading the group in a slow, monotonous beat, rattling and drumming in unison. Start very gentle and soft, and gradually pick up pace as the sky gets brighter and you see the Sun climb higher. By the moment of the official sunrise, you will likely have reached a rousing celebratory fever pitch. After the moment of sunrise and a final crescendo, signal to cease the noisemaking into silence.

Recite an incantation, such as the following:

The Sun has risen on the shortest day of the year. On the shortest day of the year, the light of the Sun still rises and illuminates, just as the fire within us all always burns with life. We honor the growing light that will be marked by this day, we honor the longest night, marked by this day. We honor all those of different spiritual traditions from ours who celebrate light, warmth, family, and goodness during these winter times in their own way. We honor our Ancestors, who also gathered in the past, gather in the present, and will gather in the future in circle, around the sacred fire, with the spirits, in solar celebration. In Gratitude, Blessed Be!

It is now time to share the ritual libation and food. These need not be complicated; it can be hot cocoa from a thermos, orange juice for a breakfast touch with solar symbolism, spiced apple cider, etc. Use the same freedom of choice with your food, although favorite suggestions are Yule cookies and small wrapped chocolates! Ceremonially you should distribute and perform this "cakes and ale" style part of the ritual in any way you wish. However, in contrast to the louder portions of the ritual, I like to simply, silently, or softly bless the libation and food with a bell or rattle and then distribute it to be consumed in silent gratitude. Be sure to leave a serving of the cakes and ale to take out in nature to leave for the spirits, earth, and ancestors.

Release the spirits of the directions, and have a merry Yuletide!

Final Thoughts

Have fun with this ritual's flexibility. Informality does not mean disrespect—it all depends on your approach and intent. If you have just two persons to celebrate together, or you have a dozen, the ritual can be just as meaningful. If you live where you are unable to make a lot of noise, then simply choose softer instruments, or play softer, and simply pick up pace and intent as you play them instead of reaching a high decibel.

Additionally, casual does not by necessity equate to irreverent. My family and I have been known to do solstice sunrise in our pajamas with mugs of hot cocoa or coffee present. While this is a sacred day observance, it is also one of family, coziness, and togetherness. I wish you all the blessings of winter solstice, past, present, and future!

Notes

Imbolc

Imbolc: Reset Yourself

Melanie Marquis

IMBOLC ISN'T THE MOST distinctive of the Pagan holidays, at least not until you dig a little deeper. Marking the start of spring in pre-Christian Europe, Imbolc was celebrated in Ireland, Scotland, and the Isle of Mann. Today, however, Imbolc gets a bit lost between Yule and Ostara. We associate Yule with the returning light and lengthening days of the winter solstice, while we celebrate Ostara and the spring equinox as the true astronomical beginning of spring. Imbolc is stuck right in the middle, and with our modern lifestyles so detached from seasonal changes that hold great significance to agricultural societies, it can be challenging to find a personal connection to this sabbat. I don't raise any crops, and I don't have any fields to start preparing for spring planting—at least not in the literal sense. Metaphorically, however, as spring approaches, I inevitably have a lot of ideas and endeavors that I am hoping to "grow," and there is plenty of preparation and foundational work that must be done before these little thought seeds can begin to take root. By looking honestly at my modern life, I noticed that there are indeed many ways in which my personal experience reflects the changing tides of nature during this special time of year.

For me, Imbolc is a reset, a major reboot. Just as the natural world begins to recover from the ravages of winter in preparation for warmer days ahead, I find myself also in a time of healing and renewal. As the ground warms and softens so that fallow seeds can burst into bloom, I think that my heart warms and softens also. I let my guard down, stripping away defenses that have become less necessary as winter's freeze loses its edge. I open my mind to hopeful thoughts of the future, and suddenly I have found that fresh start that I need.

I'm not very technically inclined, and when something isn't working, my most often used and effective strategy is to turn off the malfunctioning device, wait a few minutes, and turn it back on again. It usually works just fine after that. I like to periodically reset myself in this same way, and I find that Imbolc is a perfect time to do it. I take a few days leading up to Imbolc to completely unwind and shut down, so that when Imbolc arrives, I'm ready to plug myself back in again and start fresh.

I don't do very well with the winter. The Yule holiday season is delightful, but it's also so busy and often stressful! On top of that, I absolutely have no tolerance for the cold, and my body is very sensitive to a lack of sunshine. This all adds up to me typically feeling exhausted, overdrawn, miserable, and anxious for spring long before that spring actually arrives. Taking the time to consciously do a reset during Imbolc helps me to shake off the blues of winter's icy cloak.

It might still be freezing outside, but Imbolc is a reminder that it will, eventually, warm up. Imbolc is to many Pagans what rainbows are to Christians. Christians have a story about a rainbow being God's promise to never again flood the earth. Similarly, Imbolc is the reassurance that the tides of nature are forever flowing, that the stagnation and dormancy of winter was but a passing phase in the blessed illusion we call reality. Celebrating Imbolc restores my hope and rejuvenates my mind, body, and spirit. It might not be a very traditional Imbolc, in the traditional sense of tradition, but for me it feels just right.

I begin my celebration a few days prior to Imbolc with a little purging, letting go of some of the feelings and fears that have been building up throughout the winter, blocking my progress forward. February is a time when we can start cleaning up the physical debris of winter, picking up fallen tree limbs and watching the piles of nasty gray snow sludge begin to disintegrate. I try to mimic this early spring cleaning of sorts in my own life with a ritual involving a jar of salt water.

I begin by pouring a hot bath, adding a handful of sea salt or Epsom salts. I bring with me into the bathroom an empty glass jar with a lid, a notebook that I don't mind getting wet, and a pencil. I place these within my reach at the side of tub, and I settle down into the warm, cleansing water. I think back over the passing winter and I allow myself to experience each feeling that comes up within me. Some of the feelings that come up are inevitably of the unpleasant variety. Sadness, guilt, shame, fear—negative emotions can run the gamut. When something particularly unpleasant comes to my mind, I write about it on a scrap of the notebook paper, then I wad it up and put it in the jar that I've placed tub-side. When I've finished mentally and emotionally rehashing the ups and downs of the past few months, I envision any lingering vestiges of unexpressed emotion flowing out of my body and into the water.

After that, I fill the jar (containing the paper scraps) with water from my bath. I take another pinch of salt in my hand and I think about the purifying, cleansing properties of salt. I envision the strengthening sunlight and I ask this energy to come into the salt. I add the salt to the jar, then I put the lid on tightly.

I take some time to look at the jar, to contemplate all the emotions and obstacles that are now submerged in the salt water solution. I shake the jar gently until the paper softens and begins to disintegrate, then I shake it vigorously until the paper is transformed into a pulpy mush. I get out of the bath and I take the jar outside. I find a spot of dirt in which I'm not planning to grow anything, and here I dump out the jar's contents. I grind the mixture down into the ground with my foot, then I go back inside and wash the jar as well as my hands.

I place the empty jar beside my bed, and I get cozy under the covers. I lay there very still with my eyes closed, and I try to empty my head as completely as possible. I step out of my identity as an individual and enter the flow of all that is. I usually drift off to sleep so that I'm fully unplugged from the mundane world.

When I wake, I fill the jar with clear, fresh water, and if I happen to have any flowers or fresh herbs, I put these in the jar, using it like a flower vase. If I don't have any fresh vegetation, I add a pinch of dried sage, as it has purifying properties. I place the jar on my altar and I anoint myself with the water for the next couple of days. This activity leaves me feeling cleansed and refreshed after being down in the dumps of winter.

I also like to give my house a reset this time of year. Just as the winter has purged the dead vegetation that is no longer needed, so too do I purge my home of anything that no longer serves a purpose. Clothes, papers, knickknacks, all are examined and sorted. If it doesn't make me feel good to look at it and I don't need it, out it goes. This purging ritual usually creates a whole lot of new space—space that I can fill with things that make me happy. Even though it's very wintry this time of year in Colorado, I like to fill my home with symbols of spring to remind me of the warmer days ahead. I hang crystals in the windows to catch the rays of sunlight, I buy myself some fresh flowers that I place on the table along with some yellow or gold candles, and I hang photos of sunny landscapes throughout the house. This brings a fresh, positive energy to my home, and I begin to feel more cheerful and optimistic.

I know that the frozen ground is already beginning to thaw, so I like to embrace that warmer way of being anyway I can. I find that I get a little icy myself in the winter. The stress, the cold, the increased isolation can make me irritable and withdrawn. I go into my shell like a hibernating bear and I often stay there until Imbolc. When Imbolc rolls around, though, I recognize that enough is enough, and I shake off the chill surrounding my heart by making conscious efforts to show the people in my life and the world at large more warmth, love, and compassion. I make small, simple gifts like cookies or herbal sachets, and I give these to friends and neighbors. I charm several dollars with a loving, joyful energy intended to attract good luck, and I go downtown and give the lucky bills to the first person to ask me if I can spare some change. Sometimes I find volunteer opportunities I can help with, and when I can afford it, I like to make a donation to a nonprofit, usually a wildlife protection cause.

It's also important for me to show myself some love, so I try to do something nice just for me. I might make tacos, which is my favorite food, and allow myself to overindulge a bit. I might go out on the town and treat myself to a cheap beer or two. Or I might simply go for a walk by myself, maybe stop by the coffee shop or just sit under a tree somewhere watching the birds and the squirrels. What can I say? I have simple tastes.

After all these personal rituals, I like to do something a little more reverent. I sit quietly under the dark night sky on the evening that Imbolc begins (Celtic holidays run from sundown to sundown) wrapped in a blanket, a single candle burning beside me if the wind allows. I think about all the pains from which I have been healed, all the trials and tribulations out of which I have been lifted, and I express my thanks, gratitude, and awe for the mercy the universe has shown to me. I usually make a promise at this time, an oath to the world that I will freely let whatever light is given me shine outward as brightly as possible. I renew my vow to the Divine that I will be an open channel through which the Goddess may do Her work.

When the morning comes, I'm fully ready for a fresh start, eager to get back into the swing of things. I make a list of all my goals for the next few months, taking an inventory of the "seeds" I want to plant at this time. What new projects do I hope to begin? What energies do I want to welcome in my life? What are some ways in which I can grow to become a better person? I place this list on my altar, and I energize and empower these goals with a pair of crystals that have been charged with a combination of piezoelectricity and magick. (You can try this process for yourself with the ritual included later in this section.)

To me, embracing the season of Imbolc means cleaning up the spiritual debris of winter and getting in gear for a great spring season ahead. It is both a head start and a fresh start, a time to let go and a time to get going, a time to unplug and then reconnect at full power.

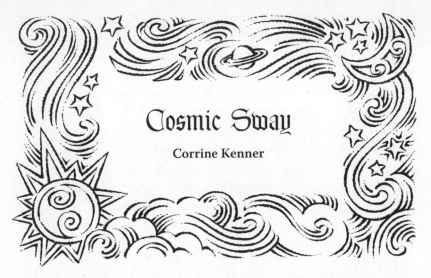

Cosmic Sway

Corrine Kenner

IMBOLC CELEBRATES THE COMING of spring. It falls at the midpoint between the winter and spring equinox, when the Sun is halfway through the sign of airy Aquarius—which is also the halfway point between the winter solstice and the spring equinox. It's a cross-quarter holiday that's also known as Brigid, Candlemas, or Brigid's Day.

In the Celtic calendar, Imbolc marked the start of the lambing season. The word itself means "in the belly," and it signifies pregnancy and the quickening of new life.

Mythic Astrology: Venus, the Goddess of Love

Almost everyone knows that Venus was the goddess of love, beauty, and desire—but what often goes unsaid is that her physical desirability inevitably led to pregnancy and childbirth, too.

Happily, she held boundless affection for men and children.

Venus—Aphrodite to the Greeks—was the daughter of the sea. She rose from the waves, gently shook her long, flowing hair, and the droplets of water that fell were transformed into glistening pearls.

All the gods wanted her as a wife, but Jupiter gave her to Vulcan, the celestial metalsmith, for the service he had rendered in forging thunderbolts. It was the height of irony: the most beautiful goddess was married to the ugliest god. He was the son of Juno, queen of the gods—but he was a squalling, red-faced child. Horrified at his appearance, Juno threw the child from Mount Olympus. When he landed, he broke his leg, and he was left permanently lame.

His marriage to Venus was doomed from the start. Not only was he miserable to look at, but Vulcan was also mean-spirited and cruel.

Plus Venus was too much for one man. She had a long string of torrid affairs with gods and men alike.

While she never had children with Vulcan, she did have several with Mars, including Cupid, the god of love, and Concordia, the goddess of harmony. They were also parents to twins Phobos and Deimos, the personifications of fear and terror, who accompanied their father into battle.

After a rendezvous with Bacchus, she gave birth to Priapus, a fertility god with an oversized phallus.

Mercury—also known as Hermes—fathered her child Hermaphroditus, the original hermaphrodite.

Venus took mortal lovers, too, including Prince Anchises. He fathered her son Aeneas, who founded the city of Rome. When Aeneas was wounded in battle, she raced to save him and was wounded herself.

She had a mythic love affair with Adonis, the most handsome man on earth. When Adonis was killed by a wild boar, Venus went mad with grief—until Pluto, the god of the Underworld, agreed to let him spend six months of every year with her, while he spent the other six months in the realm of the dead.

Venus was generous with her power, too. She owned a magic belt that she loaned out to lovesick women, because whoever wore it was imbued with Venusian grace and beauty, which made them irresistible to men.

Venus's placement in a horoscope chart, by sign and by house, describes your most heartfelt desires, romantic pursuits, dalliances, and desires.

Ancient astrologers referred to Venus as the lesser benefic; like Jupiter, Venus was generous and kind. In an astrological chart, Venus graces everything she touches with ease, comfort, affection, and enjoyment.

Venus rules two signs: Taurus, the earthy sign of creature comfort and spiritual values, and Libra, the airy sign of social grace and balance. She also rules two houses of the horoscope: the second house, where astrologers look for information about property and belongings, and the seventh house of marriage and partnership.

Reading the Signs

The Sun moved into airy Aquarius on January 19. It will move into Pisces on February 18.

On Imbolc, the Sun and Venus are conjunct in Aquarius, where their energy is focused on visionary causes. Venus moved into Aquarius on January 18. It will transition into watery Pisces on February 10, and fiery Aries on March 6.

At the moment, Venus is in an uncomfortable square with Jupiter in watery Scorpio. Their discomfort is minimized, however, by the fact that both are benefic planets; if anything, they're probably at odds about how to distribute favors and blessings. In Aquarius, Venus is focused on groups, while Jupiter in Scorpio wants to benefit private partnerships.

Jupiter will probably win this argument, and the benefits it bestows will be tangible. That's because Jupiter is in a powerful sextile with Pluto in earthy, businesslike Capricorn, where it's poised to reward hard work and commitment.

Saturn, the ringed planet of boundaries and limitations, is also in earthy Capricorn. In this case, Saturn's rings don't merely confine us: they can also define us.

Planetary Positions

- Sun in Aquarius
- Moon in Virgo
- Mercury in Aquarius
- Venus in Aquarius
- Mars in Sagittarius

- Jupiter in Scorpio
- Saturn in Capricorn
- Uranus in Aries
- Neptune in Pisces
- Pluto in Capricorn

There's a second power struggle underway in the Imbolc chart. Uranus, the planet of the unusual and the unexpected, has squared off in fiery Aries against Pluto, the planet of unavoidable endings.

Mercury is in Aquarius, in an easygoing sextile with Mars in fiery Sagittarius. The messenger planet will continue on into Pisces on February 18, and Aries on March 6. Mars will charge into Capricorn, where it's exalted, on March 17.

On Imbolc, the Moon is in earthy Virgo, in an opposition with Neptune in watery Pisces. It's a creative aspect that lends itself to art and dreamy self-expression. Write, draw, or paint—but don't try to conduct important business for most of the day. The Moon will be void of course from 2:07 am until it enters airy Libra at 4:47 pm When the Moon is void of course, it's suspended between signs, and if you try to force change, you'll only be spinning your wheels.

Phases of the Moon

On February 15, a New Moon in airy Aquarius invites you to get together with groups of like-minded friends and allies. New Moons occur when the Sun and Moon are conjunct in a sign. During a conjunction, we can't actually see the Moon because its dark side is facing the Earth. In a day or two we'll see a silvery crescent in the sky.

On February 15, a partial solar eclipse will be visible from the southern tip of South America. Historically, solar eclipses were said to impact emperors and kings—which means it could bring political news to light in the southern hemisphere.

On March 2, a Full Moon in earthy Virgo reflects the light of a Pisces Sun. It's a good time to meditate and seek emotional well-being for the sake of your physical health.

On March 17, a New Moon in watery Pisces could offer an escape from the harsh realities of your physical existence and invite you into the dreamlike world of cosmic mysteries.

Practical Astrology

All of the planets are constantly traveling through all twelve signs of the zodiac. Occasionally, one of those planets will find itself stuck in a sign that seems completely foreign to its own basic nature.

Venus, for example, loves being in Libra, the sign that she rules. But send her to Aries, 180 degrees from her usual home, and she feels like a stranger in a strange land. She's forced to work with elements, energies, and an environment that are completely different from her own—which means she's at a distinct disadvantage.

Astrologers use a system of essential dignities to clarify how the planets will feel—and function—in the various signs of the zodiac.

Planet	Dignity (Domicile)	Exaltation	Detriment	Fall
Sun	Leo	Aries	Aquarius	Libra
Moon	Cancer	Taurus	Capricorn	Scorpio
Mercury	Gemini/Virgo	Virgo	Sagittarius	Pisces
Venus	Taurus/Libra	Pisces	Aries	Virgo
Mars	Aries/Scorpio	Capricorn	Libra	Cancer
Jupiter	Sagittarius/Pisces	Cancer	Gemini	Capricorn
Saturn	Capricorn/Aquarius	Libra	Cancer	Aries

Dignity (Domicile): Planets feel at home in their domiciles, the signs they rule. The Sun is at home in Leo, for example, while the Moon is at home in Cancer. A planet in its own home is said to be in its highest form of dignity.

Detriment: Planets that find themselves 180 degrees from their usual placement are as far from home as they can go. They're forced to function in a land of opposites. They're weak; the placement is a detriment.

Exaltation: Each of the seven traditional planets has its exaltation in one zodiac sign, where their energy is compatible. Planets in exaltation are honored guests in another planet's home. According to some astrologers, the exaltations were the original domiciles of the planets, before Adam and Eve's fall from grace in the Garden of Eden.

Fall: On the other hand, planets in fall are in a sign 180 degrees from their exaltation. Rather than being honored guests, they're unwelcome visitors—humbled, dejected, and at their absolute weakest.

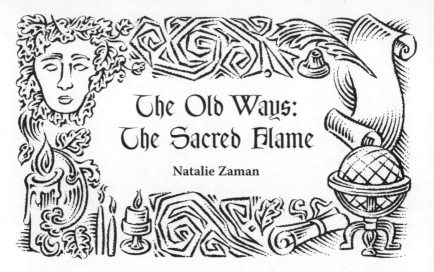

The Old Ways: The Sacred Flame

Natalie Zaman

IT'S DARK AND COLD—seasonal for a winter night in Rome. But despite the chill there's warmth in the air—from the press of bodies and the thousands of flickering candles as the procession winds its way through the streets. It's the feast of Juno Februata in her guise as "the Purifier," and this candle-lit ritual walk reminds all who participate that the long nights are on the wane.

The Latin root of February is *februa*, which means to purify or cleanse. In the ancient Roman world, the month of Februarius (February) would be dedicated to just that: a temporal and spiritual cleaning out to prepare for spring, only weeks away. Fire was and is a means of purification—burning away the old so the new can blossom forth. Its power is symbolized in the candle, an easily obtainable and portable means of illumination and devotion.

The veneration of Juno Februata with candles as well as February as a month for purification and preparation was absorbed by the Catholic Church in the fourth century and renamed Candlemas. Imbolc and Candlemas are often used interchangeably, but the Catholic celebration of Candlemas was not derived from the Celtic festival of Imbolc. Candlemas first came into being via Greco-Roman traditions, and when its rituals and celebrations were eventually brought to Ireland and the British Isles, Christian missionaries found yet another set of older traditions—with some uncannily similar threads to those existing on the continent—to assimilate. Names and rites would blur and change, but the reverence of the Divine Feminine and her power of inspiration and renewal would not be extinguished.

In the fourth century the Venerable Bede recorded that Candlemas was a celebration of the presentation of Jesus in the Temple, but it was to the Divine Feminine that the day remained dedicated. The early Februarius (February) feast of Juno the Purifier became the celebration of the Purification of the Virgin Mary. If December 25 is accepted as the birth of Christ, then the beginning of February would be the time when Mary, properly cleansed after the birth, could reenter life. (Jewish law dictated that a woman must be isolated for forty days after the birth of a son, eighty for the birth of a girl.) Alternatively, Pope Innocent XII related the co-opting of the tradition to the worship of Demeter and Persephone:

Why do we carry candles in this feast? Because the Gentiles dedicated the month of February to the infernal gods; and as at the beginning of it Pluto stole Proserpine [Persephone], and her mother Ceres searched for her in the night with lighted candles, so they, at the beginning of this month, walked about the city with lighted candles. Because the holy fathers could not wipe out this custom, they ordered that Christians should carry around candles in honor of the Blessed Virgin; and thus what was done before to the honor of Ceres is now done to the honor of the Virgin.

Be it Ceres and Persephone, or Juno, it wasn't difficult to connect the rites and rituals of the day to Mary. And what of Brigid? A powerful goddess in her own right, she was demoted to sainthood, a mere intercessor. However, she would not be replaced. Called "Mary of the Gaels," melding mythos sprang up around her: She was the midwife of Christ, or the foster mother of Christ (an important position in Celtic culture). A being of light, she was given her own candle tales: crowned with candles, she is credited with distracting Herod's men, allowing Mary, Joseph, and the baby Jesus to escape his wrath, then later using the same guise, she distracted elders so that Mary could enter the temple with the young Jesus for his presentation.

All were queens: Juno, Queen of the Gods; Ceres, Mother of Earth; Persephone, Queen of the Underworld; and Brigid, then Mary, Queen of Heaven—essentially, all aspects of the Divine Feminine, though in very different aspects.

And so at Candlemas, the flame-lit processions for the Greek and Roman goddesses came out of the streets and into the churches. During the ritual, the priest would bless the candles that would be used by the church during the course of the liturgical year. This preparation included a magical charm of sorts. Candles were given to the congregation, who would process around the church with them, imbibing a blessing, just as they had in the streets of Greece and Rome and the fields in Ireland where Brigid was invoked to purify and enliven the earth. Whatever was left after the ceremony was kept as protective amulets for the coming year:

> *This done, each man his candle lights,*
> *Where chiefest seemeth he,*
> *Whose taper greatest may be seen;*
> *And fortunate to be,*
> *Whose candle burneth clear and bright:*
> *A wondrous force and might*
> *Both in these candles lie, which if*
> *At any time they light,*
> *They sure believe that neither storm*
> *Nor tempest doth abide,*
> *Nor thunder in the skies be heard,*
> *Nor any devil's spide,*
> *Nor fearful sprites that walk by night,*
> *Nor hurts of frost or hail.*

Keep the fires of Candlemas alight; bless your candles, light one, then walk around your home or sacred space, invoking the love and protection of the Divine Feminine who purifies and loves always and in all ways.

Additional Reading

Chambers Book of Days: A Miscellany of Popular Antiquities In One Volume. Edinburgh: Chambers Harrap Publishers, 2004.

Dyer, T.F. Thistleton. *British Popular Customs Present and Past.* London: George Bell and Sons, 1900.

Illes, Judika, *The Encyclopedia of Mystics, Saints and Sages: A Guide to Asking for Protection, Wealth, Happiness and Everything Else.* Harper Collins: New York, 2011.

Mankey, Jason, "The Right and Wrong of Imbolc." Patheos Pagan, January 1, 2015. http://www.patheos.com/blogs/panmankey/ 2015/01/the-right-and-wrong-of-imbolc/.

Took, Thalia. "Juno Februtis." The Obscure Goddess Online Directory, 2004. http://www.thaliatook.com/OGOD/februtis.html.

Walsh, William Shepard. *Curiosities of Popular Customs and of rites, ceremonies, observances and miscellaneous antiquities.* Philadelphia: F.B. Lippincott and Company, 1898.

Feasts and Treats

Laurel Reufner

By this point in winter, our ancestors were relying pretty much on what stores they'd put back months earlier, all while looking for signs of the coming spring thaw. This menu tries to draw on that. It's time for some warm comfort food.

Cheesy Bacon and Potato Soup

It's a little embarrassing how easy this soup is, but it's so danged tasty that I had to share. The good news is that this dish is very easy to make vegetarian—just leave out the bacon. Or maybe substitute in some of the bacon bits you have left over from Yule.

Prep time: 25 minutes
Cook time: 45–60 minutes
Servings: 8

2 tablespoons butter
1 onion, sliced
3 tablespoons garlic
16 cups potatoes, cubed
3 carrots, shredded
64 ounces of vegetable broth
½ cup bacon, chopped or crumbled

2 cups baby bella mushrooms, chopped
2 cups low fat cheddar cheese, shredded
1 cup Greek yogurt
½ cup fresh chives, chopped

Get out your largest pot. Add the butter to the pot and heat to let it melt before adding in the onions and garlic. Stir them once or twice while they brown. While that's going on, wash the potatoes and chop them into cubes that are at least ½" big. After 4 or 5 minutes, start adding in the potatoes as you chop them up. Add the carrots and vegetable broth to the pot along with enough water to cover. Bring to a boil, reduce to a simmer, and allow to cook for half an hour or so, stirring every so often.

About 15 minutes before you want to serve, stir in the bacon, mushrooms, cheese, yogurt, and chives. Let the cheese melt. Top with the chives to serve.

Homemade Crackers

Yep, crackers are super easy to make at home. And you can top them with all kinds of fun stuff! I kept these simple so they wouldn't compete with the wonderful flavors of the soup.

Prep time: 30 minutes
Cook time: 30 minutes
Servings: 50 crackers

¾ cup flour
¾ cup whole wheat flour
1 teaspoon sugar
1 teaspoon salt
2 tablespoons light olive oil
½ cup water

Desired toppings: ½ tablespoon sesame seeds and a sprinkling of salt.

In a mixing bowl, whisk together the flours, sugar, and salt. Add the oil and water, stirring until you have a soft and sticky dough. If there's a lot of loose flour left unincorporated into the dough, add a little more water, a bit at a time, until you can get it all mixed together.

Now you want to break the dough into halves and set one off to the side. On a lightly floured surface, shape the other half of the dough into a square shape and then begin rolling it out. You'll need to be very patient with this part, as you need the dough to be about ⅛" thick. Keep checking every so often to make sure it's not sticking to your surface. Also, dusting your rolling pin with flour will help. Preheat oven to 450 degrees F.

Brush the dough's top surface with water and then sprinkle on half of your toppings. Using a sharp knife or a pizza cutter, cut your dough into crackers that are about 1"× 2".

Transfer them to a floured baking sheet with a metal spatula and bake for 12 to 15 minutes at 450 degrees F. You'll want to keep an eye on them and pull them out as the edges start to brown. Transfer to a wire cooling rack and repeat all over again with the remaining dough. Makes about 50 crackers.

Sweet Potato Tarts

The credit for this dish goes entirely to my eldest daughter, Rowan. This has got to be one of the most amazing, tastiest things you can do with sweet potatoes.

Prep time: 30 minutes
Cook time: 25 minutes
Servings: 2 dozen

2 tablespoons butter
3 cups sweet potatoes, cooked and mashed
½ cup brown sugar
2 teaspoons fresh ginger, finely chopped
½ teaspoon vanilla
¼ teaspoon cinnamon, ground
Pinch salt
Pie crusts for a double crust pie

Put the butter in a medium-sized saucepan and allow to melt on a medium heat. Add the sweet potatoes and the remaining ingredients. Stir well to combine it all. Continue to stir often while the ingredients heat up. This will take about 5 minutes if the sweet potatoes are already warm. If they aren't, wait until they warm up in the pan and then let it cook for another 5 minutes. Turn off the heat and set aside.

Meanwhile, carefully roll out your crusts on a lightly floured surface and cut out 3" circles. (I used a drinking glass that was about 3¼" across.) Tuck your circles down into the wells of a muffin tin. They won't come completely up the sides, but that's okay. Preheat oven to 375 degrees F.

Carefully fill the pie crusts with the sweet potato mixture. It will take about 2–2½ tablespoons if you use 3" circles of crust. Bake in a 375 degrees F oven for about 25 minutes or until the tarts are heated completely through and the crust edges are browned.

These tarts are pretty good as is, but I also think they're tasty served with some whipped cream on top and a sprinkle of nutmeg. Makes about 2 dozen.

Scrumptious Hot Chocolate

Finish off your warm and tasty meal with one of the above tarts—or two!—and a cup of this decadent hot chocolate.

Prep time: less than 5 minutes
Cook time: 10 minutes
Servings: 6

6 cups milk*
½ cup sugar
½ cup dark chocolate cocoa powder
1 teaspoon cinnamon
½ teaspoon nutmeg
Mini marshmallows or whipped cream—maybe what's left from serving the tarts?

In a heavy-bottomed saucepan, combine about 1 cup of the milk, sugar, cocoa powder, sugar, and spices and bring just to a boil over a medium heat. Stir in the rest of the milk and let it heat through, stirring constantly. You do not want it to come to a boil again or you may scald the milk.

Serve with marshmallows or whipped cream, maybe sprinkled with a little cinnamon or nutmeg on top—or maybe a sprinkle or two of chocolate. Makes about 6 servings.

*I use boring 1 percent or skim milk here at the house since I'm lactose intolerant. If you don't have to worry about such things, and you don't mind the extra calories, go for the whole milk for your cocoa.

Crafty Crafts

Linda Raedisch

HOLD ON TO YOUR pointy hats, my dears! To explain the inspiration behind the next craft, I'm going to take you on a brief detour into ancient Christian ritual. And why not? As the glacier of Christianity made its inexorable way across Europe, it picked up many of the Old Ways and incorporated them into the church's still uncertain new rituals. Then, as that glacier began to subside, those little bits of the native religions were exposed, picked out, and thrown aside like so much gravel. It's up to the Witches to sweep them up again and take them into their sacred keeping.

Conceived in Rome in the seventh century, the feast of Candlemas changed little over the course of the Middle Ages, except for the candles themselves. At those earliest Candelaria processions in Rome, each supplicant would have carried a candelarium, or mullein torch. With its tapering head of yellow flowers, a fresh stalk of mullein already looks like a candle. Once the stalk was dried and dipped repeatedly in hot fat, it actually became one.

Later, the wealthier townsfolk would carry sleek tapers of beeswax while the peasants trooping in from the outskirts brought tallow candles that smoked and spluttered, the drops of fat freezing instantly on the cobbles. The candles they carried were blessed by the priest at the altar and then used throughout the year for all sorts of magic, some of it sanctioned by the church, some not. The candles burned at the bedsides of the sick, the dying, and women in labor. They were used for love charms and to deflect lightning from the house. Red candles were supposed to keep Witches away—the malevolent kind, of course.

As they neared the churchyard, expectant mothers peered anxiously through the lichgate, for Candlemas Eve was also a night of augury. As long as enough snow fell to cover the graves, all would be well and spring would arrive by Easter. If only a little snow had fallen, then as many women would die in childbirth as there were bare patches of earth in the churchyard.

Paper Candle Collar

This craft will ensure both candlelight and a flurry of snowflakes for good luck in the coming spring. As the candle burns down, the cut paper snowflakes will become better illuminated. Note: Don't try this with a candle less than 2¾" in diameter. Even if the paper collar doesn't catch fire, you'll have hot wax gushing out through the holes.

Do I really need to remind you not to leave a candle burning unattended? Consider yourself reminded. Especially if you have cats.

Time frittered: Less time than it takes to read the instructions!

Cost: Less than $5.00, unless you buy a really, really fat candle

Supplies

White pillar candle (minimum 2¾" diameter)

Colored tissue paper* (I like pink for the glorious post-snowstorm sunsets we see at this time of year.)

White all-purpose glue*

For a 3" pillar candle with a 2¾" diameter, you will cut a strip of tissue paper 3" wide and 9¼" long. This will give you room for three repetitions of your snowflake pattern as well as about a ¼" overlap for gluing. If your candle is larger, you will need a wider, longer

strip. No, you don't have to measure; simply lay the candle on the tissue paper and it will be your guide.

Here comes a little origami lingo: A "valley fold" is a fold in which the crease becomes a valley. A "peak fold" is a fold in which the crease becomes a ridge. Valley folds and peak folds are really the same thing, but they convey which way the paper is moving in relation to the folder (that's you). So: valley fold the edge of the strip into a triangle. Now peak fold that triangle back behind the strip, and valley fold and peak fold until you have only that ¼" strip left. To make sure you've got it right, unfold it and check your crease pattern against the one in the illustration.

Now fold it back up again and snip out your snowflake pattern with a pair of sharp scissors. Unfold, wrap around your pillar candle, and glue in place.

Medieval Snowflake

By now, those frost-ferns you put in the window at Yule are probably looking a little tired. Take them down now and throw them away, or burn them if you prefer. You can have the fun of making them all over again next year. We will replace them with paper snowflakes—no, not the kind you made in first grade! The design of this one is adapted from a medieval Oxonian inlaid paving tile. Medieval English tiles are an example of those last little bits of Paganism I was telling you about. Though they were made principally to cover the floors of monasteries and cathedrals, if you look at them with a Witch's eye, you'll see plenty of Pagan symbolism: holly leaves, oak leaves (lots of oak leaves!), hares, stags, sun wheels, and happy little dragons. When Henry VIII broke away from the Catholic Church, he put an end to all that sacred embellishment and the art of inlaid tilemaking sadly fell by the wayside along with the carving of gargoyles and the casting of really, really fat beeswax candles.

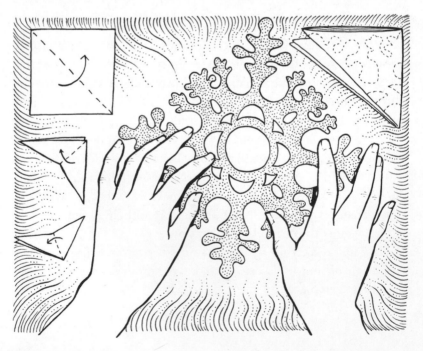

Did the craftsman who carved the wooden stamp for this particular tile intend it to look like a snowflake? Probably not, for the technology for looking at snowflakes close up had not yet been invented. More likely he saw a stylized city with cathedrals and watchtowers and tall fir trees—or are they oak leaves?

This snowflake can go in the window or in the center of the table. See how I left the center of the design empty? That's so you can place a pillar candle there.

Feel free to make your own adaptations to my design. Maybe you want to make those "oak leaves" look more like ghosts or the "cathedrals" more like Pagan temples. No two alike and all that!

Time frittered: Give yourself a good 20 minutes so you can cut and fold very carefully.

Cost: Mere pennies

Supplies

Lightweight white printer paper* (You're going to be cutting through several thicknesses of paper, so you don't want anything too heavy.)

Cut an 8½" square from an 8 ½" × 11" sheet of white paper. Fold this square into quarters then valley fold into a triangle. Cut out the design as shown, unfold, and let it snow!

Plants in Practice: Hellebore

Charlie Rainbow Wolf

IMBOLC IS THE TIME of year when, if you know where you're looking, you'll see the first signs of spring approaching. Around here, it's the hellebores that we watch. A member of the Ranunculaceae family, these hardy perennials take center stage, keeping their green foliage year round and blooming at the end of winter, even when there's still snow on the ground. There are several kinds of Helleborus orientals, and they come in many different colors, some with frilled petals. The different hybrids are often called Christmas roses or Lenten roses because of the wild rose shape of the blossoms and the time of year when they start to flower. Note that this is not the same plant as *Veratrum viride*, which is also sometimes called Indian hellebore or false hellebore.

Hellebores are an easy addition to the garden, particularly if you live in USDA zones 6–9. They seem to prefer partial shade (too much shade and the blooms won't be as prolific), but will do well in nearly full sun, too. They need a soil that is neutral and not too wet, and they shouldn't be planted too deeply into the earth, as this, too, will affect flower production. While this is a plant that will soldier on through deep snows and seasonal neglect, it will benefit from a bit of rotten manure or other composting materials in the fall and some late winter pruning. Don't put the discarded leaves into the compost heap, though; their leathery texture takes several months to rot down.

Division is the best method of propagation for hellebores. They will self-sow, but the plants that grow from this may appear where they're unwanted or not be true to the parent plant, so this should be discouraged. I've got my Lenten roses under a crabapple tree away from other plants, and for the most part I leave them alone—and they thrive, providing me with an early spring show of pale rose and lilac blossoms every year.

Hellebore isn't just for appearance, though. In folk medicine it was a powerful purgative and was used as a cure for insanity. Hellebore is highly toxic if ingested, and contemporary practitioners advise against its use because of this. All parts of the plant are very bitter to the taste, so the risk of a child or a pet accidentally poisoning themselves is very remote. Remember that toxins can be absorbed through the skin, though, so wear gloves if you're going to be handling it a lot, wash your hands immediately after working with the plant, and if you suspect that a child or a pet has indeed tasted it, seek medical advice immediately.

Even though hellebores are associated with Saturn and Mars, their element is water, making them an excellent plant to represent Imbolc and the watery snow that melts with the changing seasons. Their evergreen leaves remind us that winter only sleeps, while their blossoms promise us that spring is not far away. Imbolc is a time of new beginnings and of fire (Mars). It's a time for planning for the warmer weather, when gardeners start to conjure up ideas for their gardens. Others may turn their thoughts to romance, to fertility and new life. Wherever your focus lies, you can incorporate hellebore safely into the way you celebrate or honor this turn of the wheel.

An Imbolc Friendship Ritual

This will take thirty to sixty minutes, plus preparation time, depending on whether you're doing it alone or with a group. For this ritual, if you don't have hellebores, wild roses (*Rosa rugosa*) will be a suitable substitute—and if you've any hesitation about the toxins in hellebores, then go ahead and use rose. It's best to make a substitution than spend your festival worrying! You'll need a small fish bowl or circular goblet with water in it and some very simple food; beans and cornbread, pot stickers, seasonal stew, or something else that is filling, inexpensive, and local to your area. You'll also want ale or modest wine, or some kind of a fruit tea, and a flagon or wine glass.

On the day of your ceremony, prepare your simple food. If you're holding this as a group gathering, ask each attendee to bring an uncomplicated covered dish, something that was handed down through their family or reminds them of a loved one in some way. Place all the dishes apart from the main course on the table. If the main course is a soup or stew, put it in a tureen, or something else that's easily carried. If it is a simple meatloaf or meat pie, then put it on a platter.

At the time of the ritual, place the hellebore (or rose) flowers in the goblet that has the water in it, and put it in the center of your feast table or on your altar. The flowers that herald the spring are the focus for this ritual, for they're symbolic of the coming spring. It doesn't matter whether you do this solitary or in a group, the outcome is the same.

Next, put the main course in front of you. Say a prayer of gratitude—something like, "For the simple comforts in life: good food, a warm fire, and good friends, I (or we, if doing this with others) give thanks." Then take a bite of your food.

Now raise up your flagon of ale, your glass of wine, or your cup of tea, and make the toast "to absent friends." Pause for a moment and remember those who cannot be with you at this time, those who are far away, and those who are no longer walking on this earth. Drink to their memory and to the health of those still here. If you are doing this in a group, pass the drink around.

There's nothing left to do now but enjoy your feast. Dig heartily into the simple food that is already with you, and cast your thoughts forward to all that the coming season has to offer. Whether you're a gardener, a student, a parent, a young couple in love, or a new family, the rest of this year holds potential. The early flowers of the hellebore that appear even when the days are short and cold reminds you of what you hope to achieve, while the evergreen leaves bring a promise that you have the tenacity to move forward and make your plans manifest!

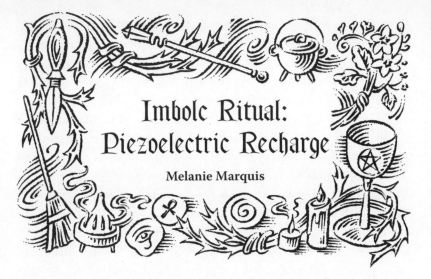

Imbolc Ritual: Piezoelectric Recharge

Melanie Marquis

THIS RITUAL MAKES USE of the piezoelectric properties of quartz crystal. Piezoelectricity describes the electrical charge produced by an application of mechanical energy on certain crystalline structures. Topaz, tourmaline, quartz, table sugar, your bones, your tissues, and even your DNA all have piezoelectric properties. When a piezoelectric substance is squeezed or subjected to friction, electrical charges are emitted. Hold a quartz crystal in your hand and squeeze it tightly, and both positive and negative electrical charges will build up on the opposite faces of the crystal. If you increase the mechanical stress even more by vigorously rubbing two crystals together, you will see sparks and glowing flashes of light. Your body's piezoelectric properties are similarly stimulated. Rubbing, pressing, or stretching your skin, for instance, activates your body's piezoelectricity which in turn increases circulation and kicks your innate healing mechanisms into high gear. This Imbolc ritual uses your body's piezoelectricity as well as the piezoelectricity of crystals to help give you a jump start toward a successful spring season ahead. It is best performed at night, any time after the sun has set.

To begin this ritual, you will need two large pieces of quartz crystal that you don't mind getting scratched up a bit. You will also need a piece of paper and something to write with. Wear something with short sleeves, or go nude. Go into a dark room. You'll need a candle or small lamp for light, just bright enough to read by. Place the crystals, paper, and writing utensil in front of you and sit comfortably on the floor, or in a chair if you prefer.

Sit quietly and take some slow deep breaths to help you feel calm and centered. If your mind is going crazy with thoughts, let the thoughts come until your head is clear, or at least as clear as you deem possible. Once your mind is settled, set it to thinking forward to springtime.

Pick up the paper and pen or pencil, and ask yourself what you would like to accomplish in the coming months. What are your career goals, family goals, relationship goals? Most importantly, what are your personal goals? Are there areas in your personal life that need attention? Are there any mental, emotional, or physical challenges that you would like to overcome? Are there any obstacles originating from outside of yourself that you would like to obliterate? Write these goals on the paper, phrasing each one in positive terms. You want to word each goal as an affirmation. For example, if quitting nicotine is a goal, write the goal as if you've already accomplished it: "I am a healthy nonsmoker" rather than "I want to stop smoking."

When you're finished making your list of goals, read it through slowly, one item at a time. After you read each item, repeat it over and over again in your mind as you rub your arms or massage them gently to stimulate your body's piezoelectric flow. Envision yourself successfully accomplishing each goal. Notice the details, and try to feel the emotions of the scene. Take your time with each goal, and continue to rub or softly massage your arms. If you like, you can stimulate the piezoelectric effect in other parts of your body besides your arms. Try stimulating your legs, hands, feet, chest, or other areas. Just remember to be gentle in your movements. As you think of each goal, think also of the electric charges now accumulating within your body.

When you've finished visualizing each goal on your list, rub the paper between your hands so that it can pick up your electric vibrations. Put the paper to the side, pick up the two crystals and extinguish the light. Hold a crystal tightly in each hand, pointed down and angled away from your body. Rub one of the crystals vigorously against the other, keeping the crystals at a safe angle and distance to protect your eyes and face in case any small rock fragments break off. Keep rubbing the crystals briskly until you witness the unmistakable piezoelectric effect. First you may see small sparks, then the crystal will begin to glow from within. The greater the friction, the brighter will be the glow. If it doesn't seem to be working properly, try applying friction to a different part of the crystal. If you're using a chunk of quartz that is asymmetrical or that contains other minerals, you might have to work with it a bit before you find that sweet spot. The better the crystals, the better the piezoelectric effect produced, but this will absolutely scratch up your crystals so you want to find that balance between good enough and too good to ruin.

Once your crystals start to glow, hold them just above the surface of the paper on which you've listed your goals. Visualize the electrical charges from the crystals falling onto and into the paper to further energize your intentions. When you've had enough fun making the crystals glow, gently touch the charged crystals to your body at the pulse points, as if you were applying perfume. Feel the energy going into your body. Then rub the crystals over your list of goals to complete the ritual. Place the list in a special place and leave the two crystals on top of it. Each day until you accomplish your goals, rub the crystals together briefly to generate some more piezoelectricity, then place them back on top of the paper.

If you enact this ritual at Imbolc and back up the magick with solid, sensible actions, success should be yours before the end of spring.

Notes

Notes

Ostara

The Amazons

Deborah Castellano

WHAT ISN'T EXCITING ABOUT an Amazon? She's depicted as wearing pants and carrying a shield in 470 BC artwork, already a modern woman! She can ride a horse and throw spears. She's great at archery. She's sexy. She's powerful. She has killed before and will kill again! She lives with her fellow Amazon sisters plotting military battles to acquire more land. She visits her male Gargarean neighbors once a year to get pregnant. She's fierce and everything about her threatens the patriarchy.

In folklore, Penthesilea was the daughter of Ares, the god of war and Otrera, her Amazon queen mother. Penthesilea became queen when her mother was killed in battle by Bellerophon. While out deer hunting with her sister, Hippolyta, Penthesilea accidentally killed her with a spear, causing herself so much pain and grief that she didn't want to live anymore.

As the Amazons were a warrior culture, the only honorable way for Penthesilea to die was in battle. She decided to fight with Troy in the Trojan War, bringing twelve of her Amazon companions with her so she can prove how badass Amazons are. She sets her sights high and decides that she will kill Achilles or die trying. If she kills him, she gets glory and bragging rights for the rest of her life. If she is killed, then mission accomplished for joining her sister and atoning for her sister's death.

She and her companions go into battle, and she is soon covered in the blood of her enemies from all the epic amounts of killing she does. Achilles is called into battle and she launches herself at him, but he immediately pierces her armor and stabs her directly in the heart and then kills her horse for good measure. Penthesilea falls to the ground. Achilles, being a class act, mocks her body because he killed her so fast in battle. It could be argued that Penthesilea had been busily slaying dudes all day and Achilles comes into battle hours later, fresh as a daisy and well rested, so it wasn't the fairest of fights to begin with. When he takes off her helmet, presumably to spit in her face or some other act of being a well-bred kind of guy, he sees that Penthesilea is not a man, but an incredibly beautiful and incredibly dead woman. He immediately feels terrible about being a jerk about killing her and falls in love with her because he has trouble figuring out how to do life in the right order. When Thersites sees his bro shedding man tears over Penthesilea's body, he gets right to mocking Achilles for having actual feelings, because his upbringing was apparently even worse than Achilles. Achilles has now had a rough day and is not in the mood for tomfoolery, so he kills Thersites because he doesn't want to hear Thersites' sass mouth. Then he buries Penthesilea with honors. I suppose the moral of the story is if you are going hunting with your sister, be aware who is standing where.

There's still a lot of argument about whether or not Amazons actually existed or whether they were folkloric tales. The current discussion revolves around the Scythians who lived north and east of the Mediterranean on the steppes of Eurasia. They were not a society comprised solely of women, but the women there hunted, fought, rode horses, and used bows like our mythical Amazons. They lived in small tribes so everyone needed to be able to defend themselves, and their tribes depended on horses. The romantic story currently popular is that the Amazons were kidnapped by the

Greeks from Turkey and put on a ship to go back to Greece. The Amazons bided their time and stealthily reclaimed their weapons and killed their captors. But, since the Amazons were horsewomen and not sailors, they didn't know how to steer a ship.

Eventually the Amazons landed in Crimea and started going about their business of plundering, looting, and considering new land conquests. The Scythians started hearing stories of these invaders and became concerned. The Scythians were settled, moneyed, and also used horses and bows. They didn't want their goods to be stolen from them. So the Scythians sent out a party to do some spying. When they were informed that these new neighbors were women who were also excellent archers and horsewomen, they were intrigued. Instead of sending off parties to stamp out this problem, they sent a party of handsome, eligible young bachelors to wine and dine the ladies. While the ladies had been enjoying themselves getting high around the campfire off of cannabis, tattooing each other, and being boisterous together, a bunch of cute guys were also of interest. While they didn't speak the same language, the men made advances to the women.

The women who were interested would hang their bows over their wagons (the equivalent to putting a sock on the door) and they would get down with whomever struck their fancy. There were no monogamous agreements made during this exciting time of cross-cultural shagging, but when they started to be able to understand each other, the men suggested that the women marry them and come live in town and be proper Scythian wives. The Amazon women looked at each other, possibly giggling to each other under their breath until one of them said "Pass." Listen, here's the deal. We like things the way they are. We think you are fun to be around, you're a good time in bed, you're decent with riding and archery, and these are all things that are relevant to our interests. We like to party and you're fun to party with. We're not super interested in marriage and being tied down to a house. We want to continue living the way we've been living. How about instead of us coming to live with you, you come and live with us? And we'll all be equal and it will be a good time. The guys thought about it and thought about how boring life was in town with their parents all up in their business and the women not being allowed to do anything awesome and decided that sounded like a very good proposal indeed.

Whether the Scythians were actually Amazons at one point, or whether they were folklore, the ancient Greeks were just as fascinated by them as our modern culture has had an on again off again love affair with the Amazon princess, Diana Prince, otherwise known as Wonder Woman. For the ancient Greeks, Amazons made plenty of appearances in artwork (even starting a kind of artwork known as Amazonomachy) and plays.

Amazons were exciting for both men and women in ancient Greek society (and even modern society!) because they didn't have to obey societal rules that were enforced primarily by men. They didn't have to act like a proper lady of that time period would behave, they could yell, kill, and be equal members of large scope battles like the Trojan War. They didn't need to sit at home worrying if their husbands were going to come home from war, they didn't have husbands, and they were already fighting in the wars. But in each of the known myths about Amazon queens, the queen always winds up killed by a man. Amazons are bad girls, they live outside the patriarchy. Bad girls have to be punished. They could be amazing warriors, they could be beautiful, they could be smart, but they couldn't ever fit in Greek society so they had to be killed at the end of each story and bested by a man to remind Greek women that this power was dangerous and would only get you a bad end. This is still prevalent in current media. Think: *Heathers, The Craft, Pretty Little Liars,* and *American Horror Story: Coven.*

And ... let's get real for a moment, my fellow Amazon sisters. When *Xena: Warrior Princess* came out in the mid-1990s, I was absolutely fascinated by its depiction of Amazons. I was a teenager and they seemed like the coolest thing ever. They had amazing battle cries! They were culturally diverse! Their songs and dances were breathtaking! They were gorgeous and fierce, somehow primal and perfectly coifed at the same time! And oh, those masks that they wore! Seeing this depiction laid down the groundwork for my interest in women's spirituality.

Cosmic Sway

Corrine Kenner

OSTARA MARKS THE FIRST day of spring and the long-awaited end of winter. For the next few months, the days will grow longer and warmer, but today, on the vernal equinox, there are just as many hours of daylight as night.

It's a time for fresh starts. When the Sun moves into fiery Aries at 12:15 pm eastern, the astrological year begins.

On the spring equinox, when day and night are balanced, we're reminded of the union of Pagan gods and goddesses, like Isis and Osiris, Freya and Odin, and Eostre and the Green Man. It's also reminiscent of the marriage of two ancient planetary gods—Uranus and Gaia, Father Sky and Mother Earth.

Mythic Astrology

In astrology, the first marriage between a god and a goddess was that of Uranus and Gaia—Father Sky and Mother Earth. Both were born from Chaos. Uranus represented the light and air of heaven, while Gaia was the sustainer of life.

Their firstborn child was Oceanus, the flowing ocean stream that encircled the Earth. Their other children included Aether, the highly rarified atmosphere that only immortals could breathe. Then came Air, which was separated from the Aether by cloudlike divinities called Nephelae. Uranus and Gaia also gave birth to the mountains and the sea.

Their union also led to the creation of two distinctly different races: the Giants and the twelve Titans. The Giants were brutally strong, but the Titans were both strong and smart.

The Titans included Saturn and Rhea, another married pair of deities who eventually would give birth to the gods of Mount Olympus.

Uranus both hated and feared his children. As soon as they were born, he confined them to Tartarus, the subterranean dungeon of the gods.

Gaia eventually rebelled against her husband and convinced the Titans to conspire against their father. Saturn agreed to her plan and castrated his father. When the old man was wounded, giants and nymphs sprang from drops of his blood, and Venus was born from the sea foam where he fell.

Saturn was the supreme power now—but as Uranus lay bleeding, the father god cursed his son and warned him that he, too, would fall victim to a similar fate.

In astrology, Uranus is the planet of rebellion, revolution, and reform. It rules radical ideas and people, as well as social groups that are dedicated to humanitarian ideals.

Its placement in a horoscope chart, by sign and by house, describes genius and individuality.

Because Uranus was discovered at the dawn of the Industrial Revolution, it's associated with new ideas, inventions, and discoveries. It's also linked to electrical energy and modern technology. Its glyph looks like a satellite: ♅

Uranus is an unconventional planet in our solar system, too. It literally spins sideways on its axis. It's horizontal, not vertical. It rotates on its side, so that its two poles face the Sun in turn. During its revolution, one hemisphere is bathed in light while the other lies in total darkness.

Uranus rules airy Aquarius, the sign of freedom and liberty. Uranus also rules the 11th house of the horoscope, where astrologers look for information about friends, social groups, and forward-looking causes.

Reading the Signs

At the moment, there are four planets in Aries: the Sun, Mercury, Venus, and Uranus. It's a fiery array that pumps a lot of energy into this season of new beginnings.

Venus is especially open to change because the planet of love and attraction is momentarily standing still, gathering strength and considering her options.

Venus moved into Aries on March 6. It will slide gracefully into Taurus, the sign that it rules, on March 31, and Gemini on April 24.

The Sun will stay in Aries until April 19, when it moves into Taurus.

Mars has been in earthy Capricorn, where it's exalted, since March 17. The warrior planet is more than comfortable with the hard-working energy of the sign, which rewards business success and single-minded determination for a cause.

Mars is squaring off at a 90-degree angle to the Sun and engaged in a sympathetic trine with rebellious Uranus. Those aspects are fueling the driving, aspirational energy of the moment.

Jupiter is moving backward through watery Scorpio, opposite the Moon and in sextile with Pluto. Until Jupiter moves forward into its own sign, Sagittarius, you may have to look inward for rewards. This is a good time to practice your positive self-talk and recognize your own worth and success.

Pluto is rubbing Mercury and Venus the wrong way, squaring the fast-moving planets of communication and love, but it's in an easygoing sextile with both Jupiter and Uranus. That has ramifications that could change your life for the better. Let it inspire you to release something that's holding your back: extra weight, surplus property, or a relationship that leaves you feeling burdened rather than energized.

Planetary Positions

- Sun in Aquarius
- Moon in Taurus
- Mercury in Aries
- Venus in Aries
- Mars in Capricorn
- Jupiter in Scorpio
- Saturn in Capricorn
- Uranus in Aries
- Neptune in Pisces
- Pluto in Capricorn

Phases of the Moon

On March 31, we'll be graced by a Blue Moon in Libra—the second Full Moon of the calendar month. The luminary, reflecting the full light of the Sun in fiery Aries, will emphasize the need for balance and equanimity in relationships.

On April 16, look for a New Moon in Aries. Each New Moon is a conjunction with the Sun. This one heralds a new cycle of individuality and personal growth. Set your sights on a new adventure or two: make definite plans, complete with a series of step-by-step goals and objectives that will help you measure your progress.

On April 30, a Full Moon in watery Scorpio will be charged by the light of the Sun in earthy Taurus. It's a powerful combination: in this case, the Sun's energy will channel emotional desires into physical energy. Don't be surprised if you find yourself seeking a physical outlet for pent-up emotions.

Practical Astrology

As they orbit the Sun, the planets pass through all twelve signs of the zodiac. While they're not comfortable in every sign, they do stay true to their essential nature.

The Sun, the central focus of cosmic energy and identity, highlights and personalizes everything it touches.

The Moon, the orb of reflection and intuition, adds emotional depth and compassion.

Mercury, the planet of speed and communication, adds a note of reason, logic, and intellectual understanding.

Venus, the planet of love, attraction, and beauty, graces everything she touches with affection and benefic gifts.

Mars, the warrior planet of aggression and assertion, powers its contact points with intensity, energy, and drive.

Jupiter, the largest planet in the solar system, brings expansion and good fortune to everything in its path.

Saturn, the ringed planet of limitations, boundaries, and restrictions, constricts everything it touches. While ancient astrologers thought of Saturn as a malefic planet, its influence isn't always a negative. Saturn also offers structure and discipline to those he meets along his path.

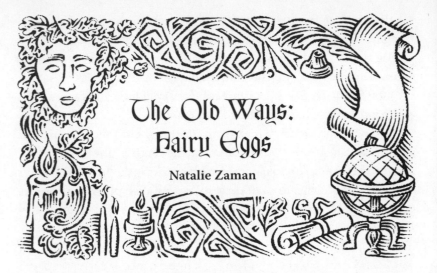

The Old Ways: Fairy Eggs

Natalie Zaman

THE EGG HAS BEEN a symbol of renewal and rebirth for thousands of years. Before Peter Carl Fabergé ever jeweled an egg, ancient Egyptians were decorating ostrich eggs as tomb treasure for the deceased to use in his next life. To nearly all cultures that embrace them as such, eggs have always been a positive emblem of life, rebirth, and promise. But eggs are also objects of mystery.

They pose questions: which came first, the chicken or the egg?

Medieval riddles puzzled their substance and form: "A white house filled with meat, but no door to go in and eat," or "A lady in a boat in a yellow petticoat."

Eggs could be used to predict the weather, death, and the marriage of partners. Eggs and their shells were the ingredients in magical cures as well as spells and curses; a cheating husband could be brought to heel by writing his and his lover's names on an egg and then smashing it—accompanied by the right prayers—against the eastern corner of your house.

Eggs are not so simple. Eggs are enigmas.

Thanks to their fragile packaging, eggs were and are something to be handled with care—not necessarily walking on eggshells, although that may be the origin of that turn of phrase—but it's possible that they're not so delicate. It was believed that egg shells had to be thoroughly crushed once an egg was broken. Witches or wicked spirits could use them as houses—being able to shrink themselves to fit, of course—or, as the riddle above suggests, boats in which they could take to the water and control the weather. It's important to note that these folk beliefs are about normal eggs.

Today encountering an abnormal egg usually means scoring a double-yolker in your dozen from the grocery store. Keep chickens (as was the case in many households in the past) and you'll inevitably encounter very different and even disturbing anomalies. Chickens can lay eggs without shells, the yolk and white encased by the thinnest of membranes, or eggs that are so small that they look like they've been passed by a wren. These tiny eggs are usually not whole and usually contain no yolks. They can occur early in a hen's laying cycle and will continue to form this way until her reproductive system regulates itself. Stress, infection, or even the presence of a foreign body in her oviducts (like the sand that forms a pearl in an oyster) can cause a chicken to lay an undersized egg. Before science provided explanations for this oddity (which are really natural functions of the chicken's body as it corrects itself), they were just considered bad luck, and sometimes, dangerous.

Our ancestors had colorful names for extra small chicken eggs: "Fart eggs," "dwarf eggs," and "runt eggs." In the Middle Ages, "witch eggs" or "cock's eggs" had fearful and fantastic lore attached to them. Cock eggs were the seeds of evil. It was believed that if they were allowed to incubate, a serpent would hatch from them, or worse, a serpent-chicken hybrid, better known as a cockatrice. (Or basilisk; the two were often used interchangeably—but both could kill with a look.)

Fortunately, the appearance of a monster was not guaranteed; the egg had to be laid by a rooster and warmed by a toad. Since it was never certain that someone would witness the entire process, it was best to be safe and handle such eggs with extreme caution. Bringing it into the house ensured bad fortune of the worst kind, and one couldn't simply destroy it. Eggs crushed under the wrong conditions could still result in trouble, like sickness or contamination. A cock egg could be neutralized only by tossing it over the family home without hitting the roof or by burning it.

In 1474 in Basel, Switzerland, a rooster was put on trial for laying an egg and was condemned to death. The rooster wasn't tried as an animal but as a sorcerer in disguise. A clever witch, whatever his or her guise, could use such an egg as a supernatural weapon to bring harm to others. It's uncertain as to whether the law in Basel believed that the egg in question would have hatched a cockatrice or if it was just a homegrown tool that would be used to lay a curse, but for the rooster, the results were fatal. The unfortunate bird was burned at the stake along with his purported progeny.

A few hundred years later in Victorian times, these tiny eggs took on a prettier, sweeter reputation as well as a more palatable name: fairy eggs. The fear of dangerous witchery was nearly dismissed, but a bit of magic still remained. (As late as 1892 it was still believed—at least in rural areas—that a chicken's health could be bewitched, though this was easily righted by adding a piece of iron to their drinking water.) Fairy eggs were used for wishing rather than cursing, though the ritual was the same: Make a wish, then toss the egg over the house. If it didn't make it, no harm done, but the wish might not be granted—fairies are, after all, perfectionists.

Should you ever have the (mis)fortune to find a fairy egg this spring as the chicks become hens and begin to lay, perhaps the best thing to do is to give it to the fairies. Write your desire on its tiny surface and place it under a toadstool. May the fae bless your spring celebrations and grant your fondest wishes!

Additional Reading

"Blog Post 139: Eggs." *New World Witchery: The Search for American Traditional Witchcraft*, October 10, 2011. https://newworld-witchery.com/2011/10/10/blog-post-139-%E2%80%93-eggs/.

Chambers Book of Days: A Miscellany of Popular Antiquities In One Volume. Edinburgh: Chambers Harrap Publishers, 2004.

Gielau, James. "The Case of the Cursed Eggs." *Mind Your Dirt*, April 17, 2016. https://mindyourdirt.com/tag/cock-egg/.

Murphy, Patrick J. *Unriddling the Exeter Book of Riddles*. University Park: The Pennsylvania State University Press, 2011.

Feasts and Treats

Laurel Reufner

THERE IS SOMETHING ABOUT spring that makes me start to change my eating habits for the year. We're starting to get more fresh things in and the warmer weather makes me want to eat lighter fare. The main dish for this menu features a couple of predominant symbols of the holiday—chicks and eggs!

Chicken Pot Pie à la Quiche

Quiche takes a little bit of time to put together, but it's really not difficult to make. And this one helps save on chopping time by making use of frozen vegetables. If you want to use fresh vegetables, just be sure to chop them to about ½" cubes. Also, this has an easy vegetarian workaround by simply omitting the chicken.

Prep time: 20 minutes
Bake time: 35 minutes plus 10 minutes to rest
Servings: 8

Pie crust
3 eggs, beaten
1½ cups milk
¼ cup pearl onions, frozen

1 cup cooked chicken, cubed
1 cup mixed veggies, frozen
Salt and pepper, to taste
1 tablespoon flour

You want a nice deep-dish pie pan for this quiche. Put the pie crust in the bottom of the pan and cover with a double layer of aluminum foil. Bake in a 450 degrees F oven for 5 minutes. Remove the foil and bake another 5 to 7 minutes. While the crust is baking, stir together the eggs, milk, onions, chicken, veggies, salt and pepper, and flour and mix well.

Once the pie crust is baked, turn the oven down to 325 degrees F and take the crust out to cool while you finish assembling the quiche. To do so, pour the egg mixture into your hot pie crust and bake at 325 degrees F for about 35 minutes. You'll know it's ready when a knife inserted into the middle comes out clean. If the crust starts to over brown, cover the edges in aluminum foil. Let stand for 10 minutes before serving. Cut into eighths to serve. (Just a hint, but you might want to make two while you're at it. I always need to.)

Spring Salad

This salad makes a nice accompaniment to the quiche. The spinach makes for a heartier salad than many other greens, while the straw-berry makes for a refreshing bit of sweetness.
   Prep time: 15 minutes
   Servings: 6

12–16 ounces of fresh spinach
1 cup pecans and walnuts, toasted
1 cup fresh strawberries, sliced
Strawberry vinaigrette dressing

Start by rinsing the spinach well and patting it dry with a towel. While it finishes drying, toast the pecans and walnuts by placing them on a baking pan in a 325 degrees F oven for 6–7 minutes. Watch them closely, tasting if necessary, as they can quickly burn.

Assemble the salad in a large bowl by roughly tearing the spinach leaves into smaller pieces. Toss in the strawberries and nuts and top with a strawberry vinaigrette just before serving.

Strawberry Vinaigrette

This vinaigrette helps really bring out the flavors of the spring salad. You could also use it for, well, any dish where you might want a nice splash of flavor.

Prep time: 5 minutes
Servings: at least 6

4 or 5 strawberries mashed into a puree
1 cup balsamic vinegar
1 tablespoon olive oil
Pinch of salt

Place all of the ingredients into a bottle, close the lid, and shake the heck out of it. Shake again before using. If you really want the ingredients well blended, pop it all into a blender and give it a whir for a few seconds until you're satisfied with it.

Will keep for about a week in the refrigerator.

Lemon-Rosemary Infused Water

If you are new to infused waters, then you're in for a taste treat. I'll be honest here—I don't like the taste of plain water. And sometimes it upsets my stomach. But add in some fresh flavor infusions and it's something totally different.

Prep time: 10 minutes
Chill time: 1 hour
Servings: 8

1 lemon
3 sprigs fresh rosemary, each 5–6 inches long
Ice cubes
1 gallon cold water

Cut the lemon into about ¼" slices. I usually discard the very ends. Place the slices into either a larger jar or a pitcher. Add the rosemary and top with the ice cubes. (They'll help keep everything from floating to the top.) Slowly pour in the water.

You'll want to let this sit for at least an hour before serving. If you want to make it look fancy, add a half-slice of lemon and a small sprig of rosemary to each glass.

Spiced Carrot Cake

My family's love affair with this cake recipe goes back nearly two decades, to when I was pregnant with our first child. All of a sudden I craved it strongly enough to decide on making one from scratch, complete with grating all those carrots by hand. Now its creation is made even easier with the acquisition of our food processor.

Prep time: 15 minutes
Bake time: 35 minutes plus 30 to cool
Servings: 12

2 cups flour
½ cup sugar
1 teaspoon baking soda
1 teaspoon baking powder
1 teaspoon cinnamon, ground
1 teaspoon nutmeg, ground
3 cups carrots, finely shredded
4 eggs
1 cup cooking oil

Combine the flour, sugar, baking soda and baking powder, and spices in a large mixing bowl. Add the carrots, eggs, and oil, then beat with a mixer until it's all combined.

Pour into a 13" × 9" greased and floured baking pan and bake at 350 degrees F for about 35 minutes. To test for doneness, insert a toothpick near the center of the cake. If it comes out clean, the cake is done. Cool for at least a half hour before serving.

If you want, you can finish your cake with the traditional cream cheese icing or perhaps a dollop of whipped cream to the side, but we're happy just sprinkling some powdered sugar on top and then gobbling it up.

Crafty Crafts

Linda Raedisch

"'EGGSES!'" AS GOLLUM HISSES in *The Hobbit*. "'Eggses it is!'" Well, what were you expecting? It's Ostara, after all.

In the past, I've pushed black and silver at Ostara, but black just isn't going to work for this project. The colors need to be translucent and one thing black is not is translucent. I'm partial to lavender and spring onion green. You can make single color eggs or have both colors on one egg by incorporating a broad stripe in the middle. Not quite Witchy enough? Though it will be painstaking, you can make narrow stripes of two alternating colors to achieve the look of a Swedish Easter Witch's stockings.

Yes, I know I've already written quite a bit about the Easter Witches, but I just can't get enough of these hags-in-disguise who clatter over the still snowy fields with their black cats and copper kettles. Of course they're hardly hags; they're the latest incarnation of the ancient bird goddesses who brought the springtime fertility and all good things to those who worshipped them.

Cosmic Glimmer Egg

Since it's only one color, this egg is the quickest. It only gets fussy when you're edging the inner cosmic egg in glitter. A tree full of these eggs in a variety of sizes and at least two colors will look very pleasing to passing Easter Witches.

Time frittered: Hours and hours. But the good news is you don't have to do this craft all in one sitting. In fact, you'll have to let your egg dry in between steps. You can always get started on a second or a third egg while the papier-mâché layer on the first one is drying.

Cost: About $13.00, assuming you buy the bag of foam eggs in assorted sizes; much less if you can buy just one.

Supplies
Newspaper torn into strips
White flour
Styrofoam egg
Small cups: an egg carton will work nicely
White all-purpose glue*
Plain white napkin or paper towel torn into bits

Cotton swabs
Egg cup
Colored tissue paper* torn into bits
Silver glitter glue*
Scrap of wax paper

The smaller your egg, the narrower your newspaper strips should be: you want them to wrap themselves around the egg smoothly. Discard the straight edges of the newspaper page: straight edges do not blend. When you've torn as many strips as you think you'll need, set them aside and make your papier-mâché paste.

In a tall jar or deep bowl, mix ½ cup flour with 1 cup water. This will probably be sufficient for more than one egg. Keep the spoon on hand because the flour tends to sink to the bottom and you'll want to stir it up again as you work.

Dip a strip of paper into the paste, wiping off the excess paste between two fingers as you draw the strip out. Paste the strip to your egg. Continue until the egg is covered, smoothing out any lumps or bumps with your fingers. This is the most difficult layer because things tend not to want to stick to Styrofoam. Let dry several hours until the egg is pale and no longer cool to the touch.

While the egg is drying, you can tear your papers. The white napkin bits can be half an inch to an inch square but the colored tissue should be no more than a quarter inch square. No, please don't measure! Pieces can and should be irregular. And remember: discard the straight edges of the papers. You can keep the torn bits in an egg carton until you're ready for them. Using a cotton swab, dab the torn edges of just a few tissue bits with silver glitter glue and leave on a scrap of wax paper to dry.

To apply the white napkin bits to the dry egg, dip a cotton swab in glue that has been slightly thinned with water. Lay the torn piece of napkin on the egg then dab it with the wet cotton swab. Cover the whole egg this way. You may have to let the egg rest in an egg cup for a spell: you don't want the gluey bits of napkin sticking to your hands. When the egg is all white, let it dry completely before proceeding to the tissue paper stage.

When the white egg is dry, sketch a small egg in the center of the egg with a light pencil.

We want the edges of this egg within an egg to glimmer. Glue on the glittered bits of tissue paper one by one around the sketched egg shape so that the glittered edges fall on the pencil line, defining the egg shape. Now you can go to town with the rest of the tissue paper until the rest of the egg is covered.

When this final tissue layer is dry, glue on a loop of thread and you're done. No, you are not going to decorate that plain white egg shape in the center. That's the cosmic egg, the calm at the center of the Ostara storm.

Stripedy Egg

To make a stripedy egg, you'll sketch lines on your dry, napkin-coated egg. If you just do one broad stripe in the middle, it won't take much longer than a single color egg. Just be careful to position your tissue bits so the colors stay separate and don't cross the lines. Narrow stripes will of course take longer and may require the tearing of smaller tissue bits, depending on the size of your egg.

Hang your egg or eggs from a birch or willow branch, set it in the window, and watch for approaching Easter Witches.

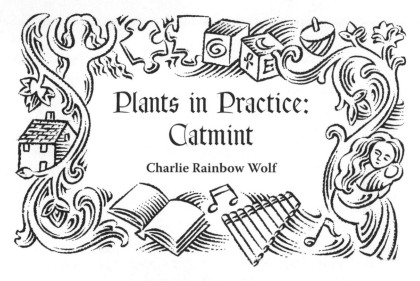

Plants in Practice: Catmint

Charlie Rainbow Wolf

CATMINT IS ALSO CALLED catnep, but it shouldn't be confused with catnip. While they're both a member of the mint family, catmint (*Nepeta mussinii*) is a much showier plant than catnip (*Nepeta cataria*), and has a much milder taste. There are well over two hundred species of Nepeta, and it's native to Europe, Africa, and Asia and has been naturalized in the Americas.

Catmint is easy to grow. It adapts to most soils but does seem to prefer something that is chalky and well-drained. The stalks are square and sturdy and can grow up to three feet high in some instances. The leaves are somewhat heart-shaped and covered in a slight fuzz, which gives them a pleasant downy appearance.

The flowers of the catmint are spiky and bloom from late summer until early autumn. They come in shades of pink, lavender, and mauve and attract valuable pollinators, such as bees, hummingbirds, and butterflies. Catmint is also useful at deterring aphids, squash beetles, and other garden pests, making it an appealing and beneficial addition to the herb garden—folklore even tells us that the roots will repel rats! Like all mints, though, it does have a tendency to spread, so make plans to contain it before deciding where it's going to grow.

While the blooms are very pleasing, it's the leaves that are the most important part of the plant when it comes to folklore and herbal use. You're probably aware of catnip's exhilarating influence on cats. This is due to the nepetalactone in the catmint stimulating the neurons in the cat's olfactory bulb. It doesn't have quite the same influence on humans, though, but don't rule it out just yet!

The leaves of the catmint are used in both cooking and herbal remedies. The best time for harvesting them is in the morning, after the dew has gone but before the sun gets too high in the sky. Choose the leaves from young stalks, as those on older ones tend to be a bit woody.

Catmint tea has a mild sedative influence, and when combined with lemon balm, it makes a very pleasant and pacifying bedtime beverage. It calms the nerves, soothes the stomach, and helps to relieve bloating and gas. It should be made as an infusion, though, because boiling water will decrease its healing properties. It's hard to overdose on catmint tea, but don't drink too much—it may act as a laxative!

Magically, catmint is associated with the planet Venus and the element of water. It's an ideal herb to use in springtime spells for love, beauty, and fertility. A sachet filled with catmint and rose petals is said to attract a lover or increase the bond between existing couples. If you're looking for love, catmint wrapped in a bit of pink or red cotton cloth and carried with you at all times is believed to draw a lover into your life.

An Ostara Ritual for Love

For this ritual, it's best if you've grown your own catmint, but purchasing it from an apothecary will do. You will also need a kettle in which to boil water, a teapot, teacups, green tea bags (available from most groceries or herbal stores), some honey, a teaspoon, two pink candles, and something with which to light them. You can do this solitary or with a group—the outcome will be the same—creating a place where love can grow.

At the appointed time, bring the kettle to the boil and pour the hot water onto the green tea bags in the teapot. Use one tea bag for every eight ounces of water that your pot holds. While this brews, put your two pink candles on your altar or ceremonial table. Let your tea steep for about five minutes, then add the catmint—a teaspoon if you're working on your own, or a good tablespoon if you're with others. Let the tea rest for another five minutes or so while you set out the teacup(s) in your sacred space.

Place the teapot and the honey (with the teaspoon) between the two ceremonial candles. As you light the first candle, think about what love you are projecting from your heart out into the world. Are you happy? Do people enjoy your company, are you pleasant and uplifting to others? What are your good points, what do you have to offer in terms of friendship and love? Focus on those, and envision them radiating from you. You might want to say something aloud (which can be recited in unison if you're with others—or each person can share their own thoughts). You can write your own or use this example:

Spring's light lengthens in the sky
Let my love from my heart shine
Friend and lover hold me near
May these words my goddess hear.

With the candles lit, pour the tea into the teacups. Add up to a teaspoon of honey per cup, depending on taste. Now focus on what is sweet about you. What do you share willingly, what do you hope to achieve this year? How can you start it now? Focus on those goals and envision them coming to you. You can state your intent out loud, or use something like this:

Sweet is the tea upon my lips
Sweet are my thoughts between my sips
Sweet is the love that shines from my soul
Sweet is the love that makes my life whole.

Quietly sip your tea, relaxing in its goodness, its warmth, its sweetness. If you're doing this with others, everyone can have their own cup, or you can share the one cup around as if it were a chalice. Spend some time with your thoughts, because you're setting yourself up for what you want to manifest.

After the tea has been consumed and the ritual is coming to an end, it is time to extinguish the candles. Either pinch them out or use an extinguisher (it's ill-advised to take a life force with a life force). As you do so, say a few words in closing. Again, this can be off the top of your head, something you've composed or something along these lines.

> *Tea and light have blessed me*
> *And now it's time to leave*
> *I thank you for the sweetness*
> *Of joys I will receive.*

Tidy away your items, keeping in mind what you have set in motion. If you garden, the tea (when it has cooled) can be tipped onto a flower bed or into your compost pile. All that remains now is to go forward and sow the seeds of kindness and light, and prepare to reap the harvest of joy and fulfillment. Catmint reminds you that when you relax and try to approach things from a calm and positive mindset, you can achieve a lot more than if you worry about them.

Thanking the Amazon Spirit

Deborah Castellano

IN MY CIRCLE, WE believe that while we may be cycling through the maiden (meaning: being free and in charge of yourself, not a virgin), mother (meaning: someone who has given birth to something be it a person, a business, an artwork and has been changed by it), and crone (meaning: someone who has acquired enough wisdom to guide others and is entering the final stage of her life, not just someone who doesn't menstruate anymore) and be in different stages of that cycle, the warrior Amazon spirit is our common thread because we are Amazons in all stages of our life. We need that fierceness to guide us through the most traumatic parts of life that we experience. We may not literally ride off to battle, but we fight battles big and small in our everyday life and we need to be able to draw from that strength to move us forward. A few years into attending circle, I started to do an annual Amazon rite so that we could draw strength from our sisters and from ourselves for our tribulations. The rite is always different: one year we made masks, one year we did Thorne Coyle's Iron Pentacle, one year we wrote letters to ourselves as if we were our own mothers and we wanted to give advice to ourselves as our own daughters, we've baked bread together, and we've done healing circles. Performing these rites on a yearly basis has helped me to dig down into myself to find the courage to face my own hardships and difficulties.

The feast aspect of this ritual is important. It's where you start to connect to each other (if you feast first like we do). I cook the feast myself because I offer it up as a fundraising dinner with a sliding scale. I pick a charity that I feel we could make an impact with and that will spend our money wisely. A potluck would also work because that gives you a chance to combine energy by eating each other's food. Pick a theme that's cohesive if you're cooking and try to be aware of your covenmates' dietary restrictions.

For example, my circle has some vegetarians and some garlic allergies. Last year my menu was:

Drinks: lemon rose spritzer (non-alcoholic)
Appetizer: fresh herb platter (sabzi khordan)
Salad: shepherd's salad
Dinner: pomegranate chicken (fesenjan) with orange scented rice
Dessert: rose madeleines with Fig Honey Sauce

The next important aspect to consider is who you want as your Amazon guest of honor. Possible choices for this ritual: Diana, Artemis, Kali, Durga, The Morrigan (especially Nemain), Mary Magdalene, Deborah and Jael, White Buffalo Calf Woman, Penthesilea, Otrera, Hippolyta, Antiope, or Melanippe.

Once you've settled on who the guest of honor is, if she is not someone you work with already, it's a good idea to spend some time, weeks or months, getting to know her through making offerings, doing research, and asking for omens from your guest of honor. When setting your altar space for this ritual, include things that she would like. Generally speaking, it's hard to go wrong with offerings of flowers, perfume, candles, and incense. Be sure to find out what (if anything) your guest of honor would be offended by and to avoid that.

Ostara is when spring is just starting to awaken, but it doesn't feel much like it when the weather is so gray and dismal. If you live in a place that has four seasons in the Northern Hemisphere, the ground is generally half frozen, but the snow is melted so now you can see wilted grass, cigarette butts, and various animal poop that was previously hidden. It's not actually warm yet and it's pretty depressing. It's not the best backdrop for most rituals. So you need to think deeper. You need to think that even though the trees and plants aren't really budding yet, their roots are starting to wake up under the earth, so that by Beltane, everything will start to flower again. If you garden, you need to start planting seeds now or there will be nothing to harvest. But it must be done with care and consideration because a late frost could kill all of your efforts. It's a rather delicate time. It's also a good time for you and your sisters to contemplate where the root of their power comes from.

The ritual I am going to suggest is from my circle. If you feel you need to change any of the elements, please do! What works for us may not work for you. You are captain of your own ship and you need to be able to do what works for you.

Set up your altar area. Some potential ideas: pictures of women who inspire you, beeswax candles, statues or pictures of your guest of honor, offerings to your guest of honor, balsam fir needles, bay leaves, High John the Conqueror root, orchids, books about strong women, your grandmother's teacup, a shawl that always makes you feel powerful.

Set up a private area using an indoor tent, a small closet, a bathroom that doesn't have windows, etc. Make sure there is a mirror and enough room to sit or stand comfortably in front of the mirror. Have low lighting and a basket full of small comforts, such as oil for one's skin, hand cream, a pot of lip moisturizer, facial spray, cuticle cream, and perhaps a roller ball tube of cosmetic glitter. Have a dark bowl full of water in case scrying is desired and perhaps a deck of tarot cards. Before the ritual, write or type words where one's power could be rooted. Use good paper, nice fonts, or lovely cursive. Cut the words apart and roll each word toward you in a tiny scroll. Close each scroll with thread, yarn, or ribbon. Put these scrolls on a plate that is sacred to you and put it next to your basket of comforts.

Run through the ritual with your sisters so they know what to expect. Include aspects of your group's etiquette, an explanation of Ostara, a bit about your guest of honor, and the ritual you will be performing together.

Start your ritual by washing all of the participants' hands. Use a nice bowl, some good towels, warm water, and some rose water. Float some dried herbs, flower petals, and tumbled stones into the bowl. When washing your sisters' hands, hold their hands in yours and then dry them. Welcome them to your ritual as your sisters.

Consecrate the area you will be working in. Some suggestions: a pink Himalayan salt circle, sigils drawn in hallowed water, smoke from sage, lavender, and rosemary, chanting "I cast this circle" while catching the hand of your sister standing next to you.

Lead your sisters in a simple meditation to center everyone. Have them grow roots through the foundations of your home and into the earth, and have them draw up energy from those roots through the trunks of their bodies, and have them shoot it out through the branches growing from their heads up to the stars. Have them draw the energy from the stars down through the trunks of their bodies and down into their roots. Cycle this energy three times.

If you invoke the elements, here is a good place to do that. If you don't, do whatever you do to raise energy to work with: sing, chant, drum, dance, whatever you do together.

Here is where you will invoke the spirit of your fellow Amazon sisters. Think of women who are your ancestors, historical figures, friends, family members, and fictional characters that embody the Amazon spirit through their bravery, strength, and fierceness. Say their names out loud. Let the names overlap as they spill from your sisters mouths' together. When you feel that everyone has called in their Amazon sisters, welcome them to your ritual.

Now that you are surrounded by your sisters and the spirits of these Amazons, invoke your guest of honor. Use words that come from your heart. Speak as simply or profusely as you feel called to do, but let it come from your spirit and not a piece of paper. Let your guest know what offerings you are giving to her.

Start a chant or a song and let each sister journey into the private area to find her word of power.

After each sister has found her word and has rejoined the group, give them the opportunity to talk about their experience if they want to or to pass if they don't. Have each sister hold the scrolled word to her heart chakra and seal it into her heart.

If cakes and ale or libations are shared, here is a good place to do that. Thank your sisters, your fellow Amazon spirits, and your guest of honor for joining you for your ritual. If elemental spirits were invoked, thank them too. Release the energy you have generated by smudging the salt circle, opening the circle, or doing whatever you usually do.

Notes

Beltane

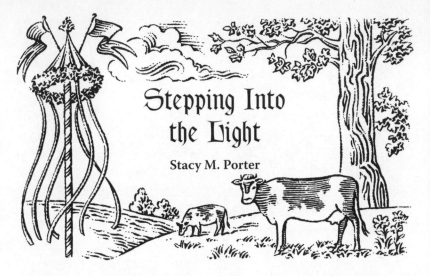

Stepping Into the Light

Stacy M. Porter

THE ONE THING ABOUT life that never changes is that everything changes. It is a funny thought to wrap your mind around. At first it might seem overwhelming. It means that no matter how tightly you hold on to something, it will always slip away. But it also means that something better will be waiting for you just around the corner. It means that there is always an opportunity to grow as a person and to experience something new and exciting.

Spring is the season of change. The sun's strength is building, breaking through the dreary gray of winter. April showers are soaking into the earth, making the fertile soil we need so flowers can bloom brightly this May. This is the time of the year when we cut away the past, clear the garden of the previous year's work, and open the path before us for new and glorious things.

Beltane, also commonly referred to as May Day in the northern hemisphere, is the last of spring's fertility rituals and is literally translated as bright fire. The ground might be muddy from all the springtime rainstorms, but most people recognize May to be the real shift between the seasons. In some Wiccan traditions, the focus of Beltane is the battle between the May Queen and the Winter Queen. The May Queen, who comes from the fairies, has been depicted throughout history as Maid Marian in Robin Hood tales and Guinevere in the Arthurian legends. She is the goddess of flowers and is associated with new life, youthfulness, and innocence. With her come fertility, love, and light. The Winter Queen is the dark mother and the crone. She is weighed down by experiences, maybe even turned hard or cold from what she has witnessed in her life. With her comes death, grief, and darkness.

The Wheel of the Year tells their story. Since Samhain, the Winter Queen has ruled, but now it is time for life to be returned and brightness to take the throne. It is a fight to the death and the Winter Queen will eventually lay resting while the light takes over the earth for the coming months, until we reach Samhain and it is her turn once again to walk the earth. The Wheel of the Year is always turning, always bringing change to the earth and to our lives. It is not only about the seasons, but about the obstacles we all face and the lessons we all must learn.

In many ways we are all the May Queen, with her innocence and hope, and also the Winter Queen, with her pain and life experience. We were born the May Queen and become the Winter Queen as we age. We also play their different roles during different times of the year, encompassing their spirits during the spring and summer when hope springs eternal and during the fall and winter when we are surrounded by death and darkness. I also believe we have a choice, throughout the year, as to whether we want to live a life full of hope and color or a life that is negative and bleak.

At this time of year, after we have spent months in the dark, we too are raging an inner battle as the light is trying to overturn the hold the shadows have over us and the world. While we can literally see the fight taking place between the May Queen and the Winter Queen by looking out the window and watching the earth change, we are also fighting as we struggle to release the stagnant energies of winter and the past that want to cling to our hearts and affect us as we try and live our lives.

It is a lifelong struggle to find a perfect balance between the light of our soul and the shadow that lives within us all. It can be a battle or it can be a dance. We can constantly fight against the darkness or we can welcome it, knowing that we all have lessons to learn from the shadows of the world. We can struggle against the light, thinking we are unworthy or not ready for all it has to offer, or we can bravely step into it, knowing that life only sends us things we can handle.

For months we have dwelled in the darkness. The winter months are a time for rest, but spring is the time for action. For the next few months, we will dance in the light. Some of us have craved the feeling of the sun on our skin. Others have found comfort in the cool darkness and might be afraid to leave that space. While it is healthy to grieve, mourn, and take care of yourself, we must be willing to change as the earth does, to follow the natural course of life. Beltane is the perfect time for us to release that struggle, to give our problems and worries to the universe. Let them burn in the fires. Let your pain burn away and be purified, allowing new opportunity to be born from the ashes and hope to bloom in the garden.

I remember being a little girl and spending a whole day in the car with my mom as we drove up the coast to meet our coven in beautiful Upstate New York. I remember making hair wreaths with brightly colored ribbons and flowers, and the whole house would be vibrating with drums and chants. Outside, we would dance around the maypole while the fire grew strong in its pit. Then we would jump the fire so that our wishes would be taken by the flames and lifted up into the heavens by the smoke so that the universe would hear them and make them come true within the year. Even years later I can remember feeling the presence of fairies on those magical days.

I think that is what most people think of when they think of Beltane: bonfires and fairies. It is a hot, fierce, and passionate time when magic can be so thick you can actually taste it. This is primarily because Beltane, like Samhain, is when the veils between worlds are at their thinnest. It is when fairies come out to play. It is when you are literally watching life spring up all around you as the earth wakes up from winter's slumber and the world is surging with colors.

One year, I was so excited that the sun was finally out that I ran outside, set up my lawn chair, and sat in the warmth reading a book for hours. It was absolutely glorious until I went back inside later that day and realized that nearly every inch of my body was sunburnt.

There are not-so-nice aspects about everything, even the light. Though that is not something people really like to think about. The light is supposed to be pure love and joy. It is supposed to be heavenly and inviting. It is not supposed to hurt. The reality, though, is that sometimes the light is too bright and powerful, especially when we are not prepared or already feeling vulnerable.

All of that fiery energy can actually be overwhelming for people. We are leaving behind the more solitary, darker months of the year. We have just spent so much time with our focus turned inward on the internal aspects of life and spirituality. Since Samhain, which is Beltane's true opposite on the Wheel of the Year, our focus has been on death and closure. We have been journaling, meditating, and giving ourselves permission to think of the past so that we may learn from what we have already experienced. We have been holed up inside, wrapped up in blankets or hiding under coats and scarves to protect our bodies from the harshness of winter's bite.

The brighter half of the year is more external, more outgoing and loud. Now is the time for us to take everything we have learned over the past few months and express it.

Sometimes the brightness of Beltane, of spring, can seem very sudden. You are literally stepping outside for the first time in months, so it is natural to feel a little blinded.

Time goes on and now, even though Beltane holds such beautiful memories for me, I have come to celebrate the day very differently. As a child, it was pure magic and pure love. Now that innocence has faded and sometimes it is hard to turn off my adult mind and once again see the world filled with light. I think that is a transition we all face, as we ourselves say goodbye to the innocence of the

May Queen and start becoming the Winter Queen as we grow older and experience more parts of this life on earth. Maybe it is because whenever you turn on the television or open the paper, it is so easy to get bogged down by the problems of the world that it seems selfish to go frolic with the fairies. Maybe you have experienced a loss or trauma and the darkness is still too real and fresh for you to even want to be consumed by the intense bright light of this time of year.

But no matter our age or where we are on our personal path, the light continues to shine for us. The light will always be there to welcome us home. Just as the May Queen fights off the Winter Queen, so that the earth may be fertile and abundant, we too must stand tall against our fears and have the courage to release the hold the shadows have on us. We must be brave and step into the light, to feel the warmth of the sun, and to give the world a chance to see and hear the message our soul is here to share. We must be willing to feel the burn so that we can shine, to heal our hearts and the hearts of others, and to truly make a difference. Beltane is not just trivial fun and games, it is a time of passion that is rich with meaning and purpose. This is the time when we can share our dreams with the world, with the universe and the Lord and Lady, and know that they will come true.

Rituals come in all shapes and sizes. Sometimes, especially as we are beginning our journey back into the light, we want to take things slowly. Enjoy your morning cup of tea or coffee in a place where you can watch the sun rise, take a walk in the sunshine, tend to your garden, or spend a day at the beach. Make a list of all the things you are grateful for to invite more of those vibes into your life. You can always wait until the night of Beltane, when the night is dark and cool, and light a candle. This is physically symbolizing your return to the light, showing the power of a small light in the midst of shadow.

Never doubt that light will always return. The Wheel of the Year is always turning. There is a time for everything, whether it is mourning and internal growth or joy and dance parties. Be patient and follow what your body, your mind, and your spiritual path desire. You know what you need.

No matter how you decide to celebrate this fire festival, remember that Beltane is the perfect time to open your arms to possibilities, adopt the innocent worldview of a child, and embrace the hope of a better, brighter future. Nothing is ever perfect, but that is what makes life beautiful. So, no matter where you are in your life, you should always have hope, for you never know what lies ahead on your path.

Cosmic Sway

Corrine Kenner

Beltane, commonly known as May Day, marks the halfway point between the spring equinox and the summer solstice, when the Sun is midway through the sign of earthy Taurus. It also marks the beginning of the planting season.

Farmers want their seed to take root and grow to fruition, so Beltane is a fertility celebration. It's closely linked to the procreative power of Mars, the ancient god of war, and—surprisingly—agriculture.

Mythic Astrology: Mars

Mars was the god of war—passionate, hot-blooded, and hot-tempered. He was the protector of his people, as well as their leader and guide on the field of battle.

Mars was the son of Jupiter and Juno. He had five attendants in his bodyguard: Eris, or Discord; Phobos, Alarm; Metis, Fear; Demios, Dread; and Pallor, Terror.

The early Greeks regarded Mars as the god of spring. He vanquished the brutal cold of winter and nurtured the agricultural arts.

The Romans gradually stripped him of his peaceful nature and established him as the god of war. He marched into battle before them and served as their invisible protector, and his priests danced in full armor.

Mars ruled the weapons of war and conquest, along with any warrior who carried weapons into battle to stem the red tide of death: soldiers, surgeons, and metalsmiths. Mars was the master of tools that can sever and pierce flesh, excise dead and unhealthy tissue, and make necessary sacrifices for the greater good.

Mars was still the god of agriculture, who could turn swords into plowshares. He encouraged farmers to plant and tend their crops, because he knew that an army marches on its stomach.

Mars and Venus—the Empress—had a long and storied romance. Unfortunately, Venus was a married woman, and her husband Vulcan arranged for both of them to be caught in a web of their own deception, and exposed them, naked and *in flagrante delicto*, to the entire pantheon of gods.

In astrology, Mars is the red planet of blood, sweat, and tears. It symbolizes sexuality, stamina, and strength. It's the planet of passion and pain. It's closely linked to confidence, courage, and conflict, as well as action, assertion, and bold aggression.

Mars rules Aries, the first sign of spring. It also rules the first house of the horoscope, where astrologers look for information about physical appearance and first impressions.

Not surprisingly, Mars also represents the machinery of war, sheer physical strength, and brute force. At times, the unrestrained warrior is also responsible for accidents, crashes, and careless cuts.

Mars also rules sports and competitions—war games that take the place of battle during peacetime. It represents athleticism, training, and preparation for combat.

The glyph for Mars looks like a shield and spear: ♂

Reading the Signs

The Sun moved into earthy Taurus on April 19. It moves into airy Gemini on May 21.

At the moment, the Sun and Saturn are in an easy trine, where the Sun's radiant energy can supercharge Saturn's Capricorn dedication.

The Moon has slipped into fiery Sagittarius.

Mercury is in fiery Aries, squaring off against the boundaries and limitations of Saturn. Mercury moves into earthy Taurus on May 13, and Gemini on May 29.

Venus moved into airy Gemini on April 24. It will move into Cancer on May 19.

Mars is in earthy Capricorn, square Uranus and conjunct Pluto. You might feel edgy: use the energy of the moment to make important decisions in business and career. You can focus on friends and social groups when Mars moves into Aquarius on May 16.

Jupiter is in watery Scorpio. It's moving backward in a dreamy trine with Neptune and a soft sextile with Pluto. Big decisions will seem easy, and they'll lead to marked improvements in your life.

Uranus is slowly transitioning from Aries to Taurus. As it changes signs, it seems to take two steps forward, then one step back. The outer planet will move into earthy Taurus in mid-May, but then it will backtrack into fiery Aries on November 6, where it will linger until March 2019.

Neptune is in watery Pisces, in a gentle sextile with the Sun.

Planetary Positions

- Sun in Taurus
- Moon in Sagittarius
- Mercury in Aries
- Venus in Gemini
- Mars in Capricorn
- Jupiter ℞ in Scorpio
- Saturn ℞ in Capricorn
- Uranus in Aries
- Neptune in Pisces
- Pluto ℞ in Capricorn

Phases of the Moon

On May 15, a New Moon in earthy Taurus signals an ideal start to the growing season. This is a great time to plant seedlings or prepare a garden, either literally or metaphorically.

On May 29, a Full Moon in fiery Sagittarius will be completely illuminated by the Sun, which is on the other side of the zodiac in Gemini. As you gaze upward at the night sky, you'll feel like sharing your philosophical views—and you'll talk with anyone, whether you're spending time with your sister or a stranger from across the world.

On June 13, a New Moon with the Sun and Moon conjunct in Gemini promises closer connections with friends and neighbors. This can be a practical Moon: use Gemini's energy to run errands, make phone calls, and catch up on family news.

Practical Astrology

As you bask in the beauty of spring, take a look at your own birth chart. Most of us know our own Sun sign, but we don't usually stop to consider the fact that all of the planets and signs follow suit. Each of us is a living, breathing constellation of signs and symbols.

On major holidays—which are, after all, markers of annual calendar events—it's fun to compare and contrast the position of key planets in the sky to their placement on your chart. In this case, find Taurus on your chart and look for the 15-degree point. That's the halfway mark between the spring equinox and the summer solstice, when we celebrate Beltane. Do you have any planets there? If so, that planetary energy will be triggered when the Sun passes over in real life, and you can expect to see changes and developments in that sphere of influence.

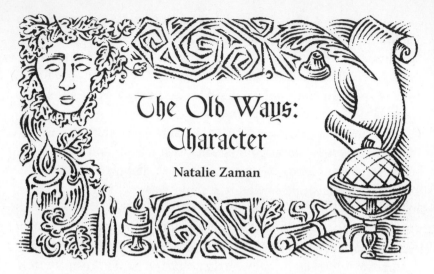

The Old Ways: Character

Natalie Zaman

FLOWERS, FIRES, AND MAYPOLE dances are the essential elements of a Beltane celebration, but this sacred day also has a whimsical side, one that's all about pageantry, parades, and personality. A unique cast of characters has been welcoming in May Day for centuries with song, dance, and some carefully constructed costumes.

A custom of the British Isles, Morris Dance can refer to a May Day pageant or parade, or specifically to the dance and the group performing it. Uniformed dancers (costumes vary from region to region, and troupe to troupe) maneuver—in formation—through a series of steps and jumps, tapping sticks, clashing swords, or waving handkerchiefs. Folks who dance today will tell you that both steps and props have a purpose. Dancers wear shin pads lined with jingle bells, their steps keeping time to the tunes. Steps and sticks imitate things going on in the fields: "The dance called 'The Balance of the Straw' ... actually follows two taps of the fork vertically before passing the hay up to the dray cart." Music to accompany the dance was played on pipe and tabor, and later, concertina and fiddle. Folk songs about rural life on the farm and in the village (sometimes with bawdy lyrics) were sung as well.

The origin of Morris Dancing is uncertain. There are suggestions that it came from Italy where it was called morisca. It's also possible that John of Gaunt brought it back from Spain when he did a tour of duty there in the fourteenth century. The spiritual dances of the Sufi have been compared to Morris Dancing, "Morris" evolving from "Moorish." There are regional dance groups in Britain that blacken their faces for the dance, but rather than it being an attempt for the dancers to become "Moorish," it's possible that it dates back to the sixteenth century as a disguise that allowed seasonal workers to beg during fallow times and hide their identities.

Shakespeare linked Morris Dancing specifically to May Day festivities in *All's Well That Ends Well*, although the dances were incorporated into church and agrarian festivals throughout the year. Whenever and wherever it's performed, Morris Dancing honors the coming together of nature and spirituality and the sacred and secular life that continues to this day. (Visit *http://themorrisring.org /find-side-near-you* for a partial listing of Morris Dancing troupes other related resources.)

In the early 1700s, a maypole was a permanent fixture in London's Strand, but once it was removed by the Puritan government, it nearly wiped out May Day festivities in the city. Thanks to the milkmaids they continued—and evolved. On this day, the maids called on their clients balancing flower pots on their heads to collect some extra cash. Not to be outdone (and with time on their hands, being seasonally employed), the chimney sweeps concocted something far grander. Their creation came to be known as Jack in the Green, a conical cage covered in foliage and crowned with flowers with Jack peeking out from inside. Perhaps as a nod to (or in mockery of) the milkmaids, Black Sal—a man dressed in women's clothing—and a host of other sweep characters, such as Dusty Bob and May Day Moll, danced alongside Jack and performed songs like this one, sung by the sweeps of Cambridge in the eighteenth century:

> *The first of May is garland day,*
> *And chimney sweeper's dancing day.*
> *Curl your locks as I do mine*
> *One before and one behind!*

Jack also made appearances in rural areas, sometimes parading with a bevy of attendants who harangued the watching crowd for money, whacking them with bladders on sticks to encourage them to pay up. It's no surprise that in addition to the Green Man, that Pagan spirit of nature and the wild wood, that Jack also became associated with Robin Hood (though it's likely that the sweeps kept any money they collected for themselves).

Jack's May Day celebrations live on in revivals staged in London and a handful of smaller towns and villages throughout the United Kingdom. Today's Jack is accompanied by boogies or bogeymen, not the nightmare sort, but Puckish green-man spirits. (Visit *https:// thecompanyofthegreenman.wordpress.com/jack-in-the-green/* for a listing of current celebrations that feature Jack in the Green.)

A curious creature rounds out our May Day mummers, one that is exquisitely portrayed in the 1973 version of *The Wicker Man*. The film's hobby horse is true to historical descriptions: a large patch-work cape-skirt to form the body, and a snapping head. The character is thought to be based on an actual horse, an Irish breed popular in the twelfth century, now extinct.

In putting on a horse's "hide," the player embodied the essence of the animal, in this case unbridled virility and fertility—the spirit of the day. The horse had a handler called a teaser or fool, who egged him on by whacking him with a bladder on a stick—that May Day ritual tool no reveler could do without—as they paraded through the streets to the sound of rhythmic drumbeats, the pulse of life in the earth that awakens at Beltane. Unlike Jack who collected money and put on a show, the hobby horse moved through the streets flick-ing water at people in the crowds or capturing women under his skirts, a fertility rite as it guaranteed pregnancy in the coming year.

One of the oldest Beltane celebrations that features a hobby horse—or *'obby 'oss* if you go by the local accent—takes place every year in Padstow, Cornwall, where three 'osses are featured: a children's 'oss, the blue peace 'oss, and finally the old 'oss, in use before WWI.

Merriment and fun have always been a part of May Day. May your Beltane celebrations be blessed with song, dance, and character!

Additional Reading

Grimassi, Raven. *Beltane: Springtime Rituals, Lore & Celebrations.* St. Paul: Llewellyn Publications, 2001.

Martin, Gary. *Hobby Horse. The Phrase Finder.* www.phrases.org.uk /meanings/hobby-horse.html.

"Morocco: The Home of Morris Dancing." *The View From Fez,* July 21, 2010. http://riadzany.blogspot.com/2010/07/morocco -home-of-morris-dancing.html

Walsh, William Shepard. *Curiosities of Popular Customs and of rites, ceremonies, observances and miscellaneous antiquities.* Philadelphia: F.B. Lippincott and Company, 1898.

"The Traditional Jack-in-the-Green." *Company of the Green Man.* https://thecompanyofthegreenman.wordpress.com/jack-in -the-green/.

Whitcombe, Chris. "Earth Mysteries: Morris Dancing." *Brittania: America's Gateway to the British Isles Since 1996.* 3 January, 2015. http://www.britannia.com/wonder/modance.html.

Feasts and Treats

Laurel Reufner

AH, BELTANE AND THE merry month of May! Spring is definitely here and all of nature seems like it's conspiring to pair everyone and everything up. This holiday's menu focuses on light foods that will fill you up without weighing you down like the comfort foods of the past few months. All the better to head out for some frolicking in the beautiful spring weather.

Spring Greens Salad

It's almost embarrassing how easy this salad is, and yet it's one of my favorite things in the spring. What follows are only loose guidelines based on what I can find here locally. Feel free to switch up whatever greens you use based on what's available in your area. The amounts given are for one salad, as I think this particular one is best assembled individually.

Prep time: 5–10 minutes plus harvest time
Servings: 1 (or 2 small)

½ cup small dandelion flowers
¼ cup wild violet flowers
1½ cups mixed wild violet and dandelion greens*
Raspberry vinaigrette dressing

Harvest your flowers fresh, then rinse them well and pat dry with either a kitchen towel or some paper towels. Set for a few minutes to finish drying.

Combine everything in a small bowl and top with the vinaigrette just before serving.

I've included an easy dressing recipe below, but you could also use a good bottled one.

*When harvesting your dandelion leaves, go for the small, tender new ones. The big ones tend to become bitter. I also prefer to pick the violet leaves before they get very big as well, simple because they're more tender tasting.

Raspberry Vinaigrette

I like the tartness of a good balsamic vinegar as opposed to the oiliness and added calories of oil in my salad. Feel free to adjust the following ratios.

Prep time: 5 minutes
Servings: 4–5

¼ cup balsamic vinegar
3 tablespoons olive oil
1 tablespoon seedless raspberry preserves, or fresh raspberries, pureed
½ teaspoon onion powder
¼ teaspoon salt
⅛ teaspoon pepper

Place all of the ingredients into a glass jar, put the lid on, and shake until well combined.

Fabulous Beer-Battered Fish

Any fish recipe that makes me willingly dig in is a keeper. The same goes for my younger daughter. So, how fabulous is this fish? The day after I made it the first time, she asked if there was any left. The next time I made it, I had to triple the recipe so everyone could get enough.

I'm including it here not just because it's good, but because fish is such a wonderfully light dish for a holiday that fully embraces the fertility of spring. This does require a little bit of refrigeration time, which gives you time to assemble the salads.

Prep time: 20 minutes

Cook time: 30 minutes

Servings: 4

¾ cup flour

½ cup flat beer (quality doesn't matter)

2 tablespoons. plus approx. 1 cup vegetable oil (for cooking)

1 egg, separated

1 pound white-fleshed fish fillets, cut into 6" long pieces

In a small bowl, combine the flour, beer, and two teaspoons of oil. Cover and refrigerate for about 15 minutes to an hour. Also, the bowl will need to be big enough to dip the fish in when you go to fry it.

When the refrigeration time is up, stir the egg yolk into the flour mixture and then beat the egg white in a medium bowl until soft peaks form. Gently fold the egg white into the other mixture.

Pour a couple of inches of oil into a heavy-bottomed pan or a cast iron skillet, and heat the oil to 365 degrees F. Once oil is at temp, you're ready to begin. Moving quickly, dust the fish with flour, dip it in the batter, and shake off the excess against your bowl, then gently lower it into the hot pan.

The fish should only take about 6 minutes to cook and should be turned only once. Be careful not to crowd it in the pan with too many other pieces of fish.

When it is cooked through, drain on a paper towel–covered plate.

May Wine

I tend not to use alcoholic beverages, since I want to keep any drinks more accessible to a larger audience. However, May wine is such a classic Beltane beverage that I decided to include my take on it. Unfortunately, this may not be a good last minute drink unless you already have some sweet woodruff growing in among your herbs. It proved harder to find than I suspected. Lucky for me, I live near Companion Plants[1] and was able to drive out and buy a couple of plants. If you have to, go online and order the dried version.

Prep time: 5 minutes
Steep time: 8 hours, minimum
Servings: 5–6

1 bottle of sparking white wine
5 sprigs of sweet woodruff, about 3 tablespoons dried
3–4 thin orange slices

This is so easy to do—simply put it all in a big enough glass container and let sit overnight. Strain the next day. Serve cold.

Rose Petal Scones

I think these scones will go well with the rest of the menu. The certainly make a nice, light finish to the meal.

Prep time: 15 minutes
Cook time: 12 minutes
Servings: 8–12

2¼ cups flour
2 teaspoons sugar
2 teaspoons baking powder
½ teaspoon baking soda
¼ teaspoon salt
¼ to ½ teaspoon ground cinnamon

---

1   Companionplants.com is one of the best herbal resources in the world. If you've read Scott Cunningham's books, you may have come across a reference to it. Lucky for me, I live about a 15-minute drive away, but they also ship plants to you.

4 tablespoons unsalted butter, cold
1 cup cream
1 teaspoon rose water
¼ cup dried rose petals that are food safe

Combine all of the dry ingredients in a large mixing bowl and whisk well to mix. Using a pair of knives, a pastry blender, or some combination thereof, cut the butter into the mix until you have a coarse crumbly mixture. (That part always seems to take the most patience.) Preheat the oven to 425 degrees F.

Next you want to stir the cream and rose water together. Either cut or chop the rose petals into small pieces and add to the cream. Finally, stir the cream mixture into the flour mixture and stir until you have a soft dough.

You can either form the dough into a flattened circle and then cut into wedges before baking, or drop it by heaping tablespoonfuls onto an ungreased baking sheet. Bake in the oven for 10 to 12 minutes or until the scones have turned a lovely golden brown.

Serve as is or dust with confectioner's sugar before serving.

Crafty Crafts

Linda Raedisch

In my article, "All One Family: Secrets for Beltane" in *Llewellyn's 2016 Sabbats Almanac*, I waxed mystical about the number nine. I also expressed a burning desire to play Nine Men's Morris (the game, not a folkdance) with giant kokeshi dolls—you know, the painted wooden dolls shaped like clothespins whose heads squeak when you turn them? This year, I'm striking a compromise: Nine Dolls' Morris played with tiny kokeshi dolls made mostly out of paper.

In Japan, dolls play an important role in springtime fertility rituals. They are often made out of paper painted with stylized apricot blossoms, and they are often sacrificed to running streams.

You think that playing Nine Men's Morris with kokeshi dolls sounds a little far-fetched? It isn't really. We know the Vikings played the game, but the design of three concentric squares with four lines radiating out from the innermost square was drawn in ancient Egypt and in Sri Lanka where it served as a sort of good luck charm.

The best time to play this game is during the nine nights preceding Beltane (or Walpurgis Night, as I prefer to call it), since that is when the magic is thickest in the air.

Nine Dolls' Morris

Time frittered: So many dolls and so little time! This one takes several hours.

Cost: About $20.00 if you use top-of-the-line washi or chiyogami paper, much less if you use the thinner, photo-printed kind.

Supplies

Eighteen old fashioned unfinished wooden clothespins, "legs" sawn
    off, or eighteen ½" unfinished wooden beads

Printer paper* or other paper (it won't show)

Origami paper in two contrasting patterns (This is all about spring-
    time, so go for cherry blossoms, fluffy clouds, or something
    green and leafy. The dolls will be playing on opposing teams, so
    make sure the two patterns are easy to tell apart.)

One 8" or larger square of cardboard or stiff paper

Metallic marker*

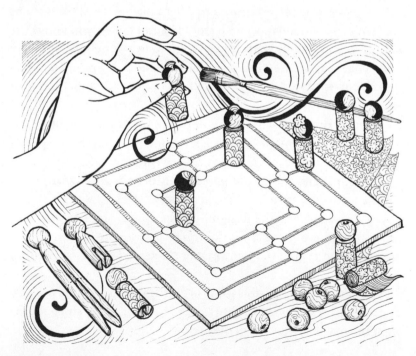

White all-purpose glue*
Black acrylic paint

If you are using a clothespin, roll all but the head in a strip cut from the origami paper, nine of one pattern, nine of the other. Glue in place. If you are using wooden beads, you will first have to make the body. Roll a 1" × 11" strip of paper into a tight roll and glue at end. No, rolling paper isn't as easy as you'd think but rolling it around a pencil or drinking straw makes it easier. Cover the roll with origami paper as for the clothespin, then glue the wooden bead on top to make a head.

Paint all dolls' heads black, leaving a space for the face, of course. Don't paint facial features! Let each doll decide what her own personality is going to be.

Find some small flower or leaf shapes among your scraps of origami paper and cut them out. Glue one on top of each doll's head. For the wooden bead dolls, this is to cover up the hole in the bead. For clothespin dolls, it's purely cosmetic.

Now to make the board. You'll need a square of cardboard or stiff paper no less than 8½". Draw on the lines as shown with a small circle at the corner of each square and at each point where two lines meet. That makes 24 circles: 24 points on which you can place a doll.

You and your opponent each get a "team" of matching dolls. Place your dolls, one per turn, on the circles on the board. At this point, you've got an eye out to placing three in a row, but it's not likely to happen, since your opponent will be out to thwart you at every turn, just as in tic-tac-toe.

Once all the dolls have been placed on the board, you and your opponent take turns moving them, one per turn, to empty adjacent circles on the board. There is no jumping and no ousting an opposing doll from her circle. When you've managed to shuffle three of your dolls into a row, you're allowed to "capture" one of your opponent's dolls. Dolls in rows are inviolate; they cannot be captured, unless there are no more free-ranging dolls of that team on the board, in which case they become fair game.

When one player has only two dolls left, the other player has won.

To be honest, I'm not how this game spread all the way from ancient Egypt to the Orkney Islands and the Indian Ocean. But my family seems to enjoy it, and I like making the dolls.

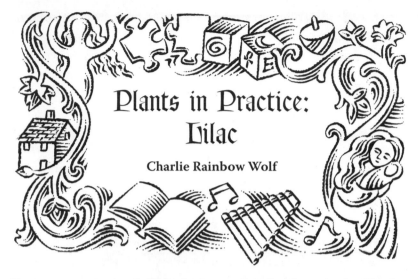

Plants in Practice: Lilac

Charlie Rainbow Wolf

THE HEADY SCENT OF lilacs is a sure sign for those in the Northern Hemisphere that spring is well and truly here. While there are many kinds of lilacs, it's the old-fashioned lilac, *Syringa vulgaris*, that dominates the hedgerows and flower gardens. Sometimes referred to as the common lilac, it's said to attract the attention of the ancestors.

Lilacs are hardy and easy to grow. They're usually seen as a shrub, but they can be trimmed into a tree. If you're going to let it grow as a bush, plan on giving it space, for they can grow up to ten feet tall and seven feet wide. Lilacs also need a moderate to full amount of sunlight—at least six hours a day, and they're fairly drought resistant. The leaves of these age-old beauties don't change their colors in the autumn, and they are somewhat prone to powdery mildew.

While lilacs flower every year, the flowers do seem to be more prolific every other year. To encourage flower production, make sure that the dead blooms are removed. Hard pruning of larger shrubs will also encourage better growth, but lilacs will continue to flourish even when neglected—they're hardy like that.

Lilacs are best propagated by taking suckers from the parent plant in spring. I've found it best to separate the roots below soil level and wait a few weeks before moving the cuttings. This gives the new shoot a better chance to establish its independence before being transplanted to its new home. Sowing seeds from the flower heads is not recommended.

Lilacs aren't just beautiful bringers of the spring sunshine, though. The essential oils are valuable in aromatherapy when it comes to lifting the mood and treating depression. Lilac also strengthens the spirit and increases sensuality. While the flowers may be eaten, they should be done so sparingly, for they are astringent and can have an adverse effect on saliva.

Massage oils made from the flowers are beneficial for rheumatism and neuralgic pains—not to mention very relaxing because of the sweet floral scent. These oils can also be helpful for skin issues, from minor cuts and bruises to rashes and simple burns—in fact, lilac is actually recommended for those with sensitive skin. The bark has also been used to reduce fevers, soothe the digestive system, and lessen pain.

Lilac is just as soothing to the spirits as it is to the body. In magical work, lilac is helpful when persuading unwanted spirits to leave, to protect you and your home, and to add positive energy to your practices and your environment. Lilac is also known to have a strong connection with the ancestors, and this makes it an exceptional addition when doing past life work, in ceremonies that involve birth or death, or procreation, or when exploring your spiritual heritage.

To make a very simple protection spray, put some lilac flowers into a pestle and mortar and gently bruise them. Place these in a heatproof glass or pottery dish (not plastic or metal), and cover them with boiling water. Leave to cool for at least two hours. Strain off the liquid and remove the flowers. Repeat this until you have a couple of cups of the lilac "tea," and then simmer this down until you have about four ounces. Put it into a spray bottle and keep it somewhere cool. When doing your protection work, simply use this to mist yourself and the area in which your working.

A Beltane Ritual to Call the Ancestors

At first it may seem odd to have an ancestral ritual at a time of fertility—surely this belongs at Samhain, and not Beltane? To those who responded in that manner, I have one question: where did you come from? Wasn't it the fertility of your ancestors that allowed you to be conceived, and take life? Puts a bit of a different perspective on things very quickly, doesn't it?

Beltane is traditionally a fire ceremony, so it's appropriate if you can light a bonfire of some sort. Should you want to dress your table or altar, then a light purple or mauve cloth is the ideal color. Think of the colors in banded amethyst (because amethyst is a very spiritual stone), and go for the more pastel shades. Put lilac flowers in a vase, or lilac oil in a diffuser. Wear lilac colors. Burn lilac scented candles and light lilac incense. Spray the lilac mist. Do any or all of these so that the sweet perfume of the lilac permeates everything, everywhere, and everyone. You'll also need seven white tealight candles and a heatproof surface on which to place them, a goblet, some red wine or red grape juice, matches or a lighter for the candles, and a candle snuffer if you have one.

At the appointed time, arrange four of your candles in a diamond shape, with a candle at each compass point. Place another candle above the north position, and one below the south. Leave a space in the center for the last candle. You can now cast the sacred circle, if you use one with your magic.

Light your candles beginning with the center one. As you light it, lift it skyward, and say:

I am the blood of my ancestors. Your life force flows through my veins. I am the summary of your existence, and for this, I give thanks and welcome you.

Now, use this candle and light the one in the east, placing the first candle in the center of the candles. As you light the flame, say:

I am the blood of my ancestors. Your life force flows through my veins. As the sun rises in the east and new life begins, so my life began because of you, and for this, I give thanks and welcome you.

Use the candle that was in the east to light the candle in the south. As you do, say:

I am the blood of my ancestors. Your life force flows through my veins. As the Sun shines down through the day, promoting life and growth, so I live and grow because of you, and for this, I give thanks and welcome you.

Replace the east candle in its position and use the south candle to light the one in the west, saying:

I am the blood of my ancestors. Your life force flows through my veins. As the Sun sets in the wast, bringing closure and fulfillment to the day, so my life is fulfilled because of you, and for this, I give thanks and welcome you.

Replace the south candle in its place, and use the west candle to light the north candle, saying:

I am the blood of my ancestors. Your life force flows through my veins. As the night falls bringing dreams and visions, so my life is full of dreams and visions because of you, and for this, I give thanks and welcome you.

Replace the west candle back to its position, and pick up the candle from the center again. Use it to light the candle above the north and below the south, saying:

I am the blood of my ancestors. Your life force flows through my veins. I know not what lies ahead of me, but I trust you to guide me. I trust you to continue to show me what I have brought forward with me through your life, so that above me and below me, all around me and within me, I honor you. For this life I give thanks, and I welcome you.

Now, pause and listen with your heart. If you do automatic writing, crystal gazing, or other scrying, divination, or shamanic journeying, this is an ideal time for those activities. You have summoned the ancestors and they have heard you. All that remains is for you to listen to them with your spirit ears and watch for them with your spirit eyes.

The best way to close the ritual is to let the candles burn themselves out. If that's not possible, then use a snuffer or pinch out the flame. It's a good idea to bid the ancestors farewell in some way, though. If you pinch out the flames, you can thank them for attending with the usual "Stay if you will, go if you must" parting. I usually do something more along the lines of:

I am watched by generations, and I thank you; for your life, for my life, and for the gift of your company. I carry you in my heart, even though my ceremony has ended.

Lilac teaches you that there's a season for everything—even you. You're connected to your ancestors by your DNA, and you will leave your life's essence behind you, long after you've taken your last breath. Even if you have no children of your own, you'll live on in your deeds and the recollections of others, so make sure that your footprints on their hearts are worth remembering.

Beltane Ritual for Healing

Stacy M. Porter

BELTANE IS OFTEN REFERRED to as May Day, as it occurs on the first day of May in the northern hemisphere. It is a fire festival where we celebrate and honor the sun as it grows stronger in the sky, bringing heat, passion, and flowers to us and the earth. It is a beautiful day, often filled with dancing, vibrant colors, and floral decorations that are associated with joy and love. However, sometimes we are not always ready for those happy emotions.

Spring is by far one of the most healing times of the year. Almost everyone has heard of spring cleaning—when we clear out the things we no longer need or vibe with to make room for new beautiful things that support us creatively and ignite a new light in our heart and soul. Beltane is the last fire festival of the year and is a day of pure passion, intense love, and a whole lot of unbridled energy that I intend to channel into a healing spell, which many of us need after the long dreary months of winter and mud. This May Day, we will be harnessing that marvelous Beltane energy and using it to honor and celebrate ourselves: our spirits, our bodies, and everything we have endured so far during this human experience.

With this ritual, we will step bravely into the light. We will have the courage to leave behind the shadows. We will have the strength to heal ourselves from the inside out so we will be ready, prepared, and excited for the bright months of summer. It can be a very emotional ritual, but the intention is to cleanse yourself of the pain of the past, so you are left feeling more awake and alive.

Preparing the Ritual

Most children see this time of year as being freeing, as they leave behind the school and welcome the happy days of summer vacation. As adults, we too can free ourselves of the prison walls' old energy and wounds that have etched into our skin and minds from this past year.

With Beltane comes the healing powers of the light, as we can see as the sun and rain bring life back into the earth. We too can harness that energy and draw on the pure love that Beltane embodies as we bravely step into the light.

This ritual will give us the strength we need to call on the Green Man and the fairies to bless the earth and our physical bodies. This time of year, as the wind carries away the clumps of leaves and other remnants of the cold and gray months, we too need to cleanse and prepare for the rich summertime ahead.

I designed the ritual for the solitary practitioner, because healing rituals are often very personal and can be extremely emotional, but it can easily be modified for a group.

Notes: It is best to do this ritual outside at dawn, at the first light of a new day or when the sun has reached its peak and is the most powerful. That waning energy is telling its own story, as the sun travels through its daily course, much like how the Wheel of the Year turns. That energy will help your ritual flow naturally and will give your magic a kick.

Wear pastel colors or white to honor the sun, spring, and the fairies. And you can never go wrong with a hair wreath or simply putting some flowers in your hair! Remember that the energy of Beltane is passion and fun. So have fun with your clothes and how you decorate your circle.

I recommend reading through the entire ritual before starting. That will help the ritual to go smoothly.

Items Needed

Dirt: This can mean that you're sitting outside in grass or that you have a potted plant. You need to be able to feel the earth with your hands.

Take a deep breath and know, right now before we even get started, that you are perfect just as you are. If you ever feel overwhelmed during the ritual, you can always take a moment to take another deep breath. Ground yourself into the earth and know that you are supported by the May Queen, the Lady, and the Green Man.

Now, prepare your sacred space and sit somewhere where you are comfortable and will not be disturbed. Be sure that you will be able to sit up straight, with a tall spine and an open chest. This posture alone will show that universe that you are present and that you are willing to have an open heart.

The Green Man Blessing

Draw your circle, creating a protective ring around wherever you will be performing your meditation and ritual. Simply walk in a clockwise circle three times around your workspace, starting at the north. Visualize a wall of light forming around you, starting at your feet on the first rotation, then watching it rise to your shoulders on the second time around, and finally so it goes over your head, forming a cone of power that reaches up into the heavens, allowing your mind and spirit to connect with the greater powers that be.

Once your circle is drawn, standing again at the north, stomp your foot on the ground and say, "In perfect love and perfect trust, this circle is sealed."

Find a comfortable seated position, whether it is in a chair or on the ground. Be sure that you can somehow touch the earth with your hands, whether your hands are weaving through blades of grass and your fingertips are sinking into the soil or you are holding a plant in your lap. Take a moment here to recognize that you are part of something so much bigger than just yourself. You are never alone and your path is so much wider, longer, and richer than you can see from where you are sitting now.

Take a deep breath, inhaling through your nose and exhaling heavily through your mouth. Do that two more times, sighing or even yelling when you exhale so that your body can truly feel a relief in the tension you have been carrying. When you are ready, say this chant:

> *I am a child of the light, filled with love and full of might*
> *I am ready now to fight, I am ready to release the night*

Close your eyes and take another deep breath. Make sure your spine is tall and straight and then turn your palms so they are facing up in your lap. Visualize the sky opening up above you, sending the gentlest of rays down to touch the crown of your head and your open palms. Feel the warmth of the sun and welcome the joy of the light. Then say:

> *I call on the forever young, the fairies who love to play*
> *I call on the Green Man, the spirit who chases away the gray*
> *And I call on the powerful sun, the bringer of the day*
> *Come forth into my circle, with your beauty and your might*
> *Please take away my darkness, please make the world so very bright*
> *With this prayer, I ask of you, to bless me with light*

Turn your palms down and dig your fingertips into the soil. Connect with the earth as the light shines down on you so you are both heavenly and earthly.

Stay there for a moment, meditating on the light and dark, feeling the battle happening inside you and watching as the sun cleanses away the darkness. Visualize the light consuming you, flushing the darkness out of you and into the earth, so that the energy can be transformed into something good for all.

This meditation can be short or long, depending on how you feel. Stay in this space for as long as you need.

When you are ready, slowly get to your feet and walk in a single circle, counterclockwise around your sacred space, drawing the energy of the circle into your arm or sacred tool. Once you are standing back at north, clap your hands together, scattering the energy from your circle into the air and earth around you, and say, "This circle is open, but never broken."

Then, step away from your sacred space and find some sunlight to stand in. Open your arms to it and close your eyes, greeting the sun with your heart and a clear mind.

As you go back to your regular day, remember that you are a force for good, worthy of the greatest joys that this life has to offer. Welcome those good things and shine brightly—directly from your soul with a smile—for the rest of the world to see and appreciate.

Blessed Beltane!

Notes

Notes

Litha

Welcoming Summer

Susan Pesznecker

LITHA (PRONOUNCED LEE-THUH), OCCURRING around June 21 at the moment of the summer solstice, means many things to different people. To the lay public, it follows the completion of the school year and heralds the onset of barbecues, camping trips, and summer vacations. To those of us magickal folks, it also means those things—but also much more.

The summer solstice is the proverbial longest day and shortest night of the year. In truth, several of the days before and after Litha are the same in length, and Litha isn't the only longest day—it's one of them. But there is a precise moment of the summer solstice that's measured astronomically. To an astronomer, this measurement is based on the Earth's axial tilt—the way it leans along its axis in relation to the sun. In simplest terms, visible to us, solstice is the time at which the sun reaches its highest annual point in the midday sky, leading to the phenomenon of the year's longest day and longest period of daylight. When the sun reaches that apex, it seems to pause there for a time and almost appears still. The word "solstice" in fact comes from the Latin *solstitium*, meaning "sun stopped" or "sun still."

The winter solstice in December stands opposite Litha on the calendar, occurring between Dec. 21 or 23. Known also as Yule, the winter solstice marks the year's shortest day and longest night. At the precise moment of the winter solstice, the sun creeps to its lowest position of the year, yielding a short day and scarce daylight. As with Litha, the winter sun also appears to pause briefly before setting in the western sky.

Together, the two solstices mark the sun's progression through the heavens and show the natural balance between the forces of light and dark. Summer days are long, warm, and vividly bright. The sun is high overhead and able to warm the earth directly, and even summer evenings remain mild, for the ground has little chance to cool during the short nights. In contrast, winter days are short, cold, and dim. The sun is low in the sky and exerts little warming effect, and the nights are long, encouraging a deep, persistent chill. Plants and animals thrive in the summer only to die or become inactive or dormant during the winter months. It's a tangible model of balance—the interplay of cyclic natural forces that keep the earth alive and vital.

Note that the schema discussed above applies to the Northern Hemisphere. In the Southern Hemisphere, the seasons—and the solstices—are reversed, with summer arriving in December and winter in June. But the effects and the idea of balance are the same.

Different cultures and traditions around the world have long marked the solstices with celebration and ritual—particularly with purifying bonfires and rituals aimed at helping young women find future mates. June and the time around midsummer is a popular time for weddings in many cultures, a trend possibly harking back to those ancient searches for a spouse but also honoring Juno, patroness of marriage, who gave her name to the month of June.

People have also long marked the summer solstice with archaeoastronomical monuments, i.e., workings of stone that track the alignments of the Sun, Moon, and stars. One of the most famous of these is Stonehenge, built by Neolithic people about 3,000 years ago. At the moment of the summer solstice, the sun rises over a special heel stone and shines into the stone circle. Another famous monument is the El Castillo pyramid at Chichen Itza, Mexico; the solstice sunrise illuminates the pyramid and creates the effect of a gigantic snake cascading down its steps. There are many other such monuments across the world, and their study is fascinating.

For magical folks, Litha—sometimes called Midsummer, although some reserve that title for Lughnasadh on August 1—is likewise celebrated in many ways but primarily as a veneration of the sun and its power. Many use this as a time for dedications and initiations or for charging magical belongings. Oaths and bonds are powerfully taken up at Midsummer, and it remains a potent time for weddings and handfastings as well as for the establishment of contracts of any sort. Rituals may focus on fire—the ability of light to penetrate and overwhelm the darkness—or on the sun itself, as in vigils involving the solstice sunrise or sunset. Many folks will appeal to solar deities at this time, perhaps addressing or offering to Apollo, Lugh, Hestia, Horus, or Juno, to name a few. Others gather for feasting and celebration. A Druid friend of mine caps her Grove's feast with an "Oath, Toast, and Boast" ritual, featuring brimming mugs of ale and mead.

Cosmic Sway

Corrine Kenner

WHETHER YOU THINK OF Midsummer as the first day of summer, the longest day of the year, or the summer solstice, it's both an astronomical and an astrological event.

Like most celestial phenomena, the summer solstice can be keyed to a specific moment in time. In this case, that's on June 21 at 6:07 am eastern, when the Sun enters watery Cancer.

That's also when the Sun reaches its northernmost position in the sky, directly over the Tropic of Cancer. In fact, the word solstice comes from the Latin words for "sun" and "stop." The Sun stops moving north on that day. At that point, the North Pole is tilted toward the Sun so its rays will shed light on the earth for the longest day of the year.

This is a day to celebrate both the Sun and the midsummer Moon—and to keep the party going through two eclipses in the next few weeks.

Mythic Astrology

The Moon has many faces. From dark to light, she shines in heaven and walks on earth, an archetypal figure of womanhood in all her guises.

To the ancients, she was Luna or Selene in heaven, Artemis or Diana when she roamed the forests, and in her darkened aspect, she was Persephone, queen of the Underworld.

At night, she rose from the mysterious depths of Oceanus and drove her silver chariot across the sky while her twin brother, Apollo, was fast asleep. She wore a crescent Moon on her forehead, along with a veil of stars, and she illuminated the earth with a glowing torch in her hand.

As the virgin goddess of the hunt, she was intimately connected to life and death. The crescent Moon was her bow, and she could take life to preserve it. She delivered her own twin brother, Apollo, and from that time on women would call to her during labor, pleading to be released from their pain or delivered from their suffering by death.

As Hecate, the goddess of the crossroads, her reputation was darker yet. In myth and legend, she had the power to summon demons and phantoms from the bowels of the Earth. She taught sorcery and witchcraft. She could be found wherever two roads crossed, on tombs, and near the blood of murdered persons. She herself traveled with the souls of the dead, and her approach was announced by the whining and howling of dogs.

The Moon moves through all twelve signs of the zodiac in a month. In the process, it waxes from a shimmering crescent to a luminous orb—but the Moon always has a dark side that remains hidden from the world.

The phases of the Moon parallel the phases of human life and experience, including the cycles of life: maiden, mother, and crone.

In astrology, the Moon is the guardian of dreams, the keeper of secrets, and the silvery orb of reflection and intuition. It symbolizes the rocky emotional landscape of memories and dreams, and embodies our most our primal needs and desires.

The Moon rules watery Cancer, the sign of motherhood, home, and family life. It also rules the fourth house of the horoscope, where astrologers look for information about early nurturing and one's childhood environment. It's also a symbol of public perception and popular opinion, because it represents how our gifts will be accepted and received by the public, when we leave home as adults.

Cancer's signature creature is the hard-shelled crab, with claws that pinch and a shell that's hard to crack. The crab's defenses are hard to crack, but they conceal a tender, gentle sensitivity. The glyph for watery Cancer looks like the claws of a crab or a pair of female breasts: ♋

Reading the Signs

When the Sun enters Cancer at 6:07 am eastern, five planets are either stationed or retrograde. It's almost as though the universe is taking a deep breath to rest and reflect before time marches forward.

The Sun is in a wide opposition to Saturn, which is across the zodiac in Capricorn. Saturn is the ringed planet of boundaries and limitations, and its opposition to the Sun reminds us to reinforce boundaries at work and at home. Saturn is also moving retrograde, which means you might also need to be a little stricter with yourself when it comes to deadlines and personal commitments.

The Moon is in airy Libra, square Mercury in watery Cancer. It's a fast-moving aspect, but for a day or two, you might want to be especially careful about how you talk to your loved ones. Give other people the benefit of the doubt when they talk, too, because even simple observations and statements of fact are bound to rub people the wrong way.

The Moon is also square Saturn, which is retrograde in Capricorn. Normally the Libra Moon would be glowing with social grace—but tonight, it's fumbling and bumping into walls.

That awkward energy is compounded by the fact that Mars is in more of a fighting mood than usual. It's in the relatively cold and unfeeling sign of Aquarius, and it's standing still, generating energy that could easily be interpreted as hostile.

If that weren't enough, both Mars and Venus are in an uncomfortable square with Jupiter, the planet of generosity and good fortune. At the moment, Jupiter is retrograde in watery, secretive Scorpio.

Mercury is also opposite Pluto, which is moving backward through Capricorn, so people are especially susceptible to their darkest fears.

Both Jupiter and Mercury are in an open trine with Neptune—but Neptune is stationary in watery Pisces, which only confuses and obscures our true feelings and intentions. Be as transparent as possible. The more you broadcast messages of love and acceptance, the better you'll be received.

The Moon is also in an easy sextile with Venus, the planet of love and affection.

Venus is across the zodiac from Mars, so their line of communication is wide open.

The Moon also has an open channel to Mars's sense of reason through an airy, intellectual trine.

Venus is in fiery Leo. The planet of love and beauty will glide into Virgo on July 10. When it does, Leo's long nights of passion could lead to a long-term commitment.

Planetary Positions

- Sun in Cancer
- Moon in Libra
- Mercury in Cancer
- Venus in Leo
- Mars in Aquarius

- Jupiter in Scorpio
- Saturn ℞ in Capricorn
- Uranus in Taurus
- Neptune in Pisces
- Pluto ℞ in Capricorn

Phases of the Moon

On June 28, a Full Moon in earthy Capricorn sheds light on issues of business, career, and social status—all subjects that are completely opposite the Sun's position in watery Cancer, the sign of home and family life.

On July 13, there's a New Moon in Cancer—its own sign. The luminary's entrance ushers in a brief period of domestic tranquility. It's a good time to enjoy life in your own domicile, or to invest in home repairs and home improvements.

There's also a partial solar eclipse on July 13, followed by a total lunar eclipse on July 27. Eclipses almost always bring new information to light.

On July 27, a Full Moon in airy Aquarius will bask in the light of the fiery Leo Sun.

Practical Astrology

Make the most of lunar astrology by actually looking for the Moon each night. Pay special attention to every Full Moon, which rises at sunset and sets just as the Sun rises. Full Moons represent culmination and completion, and you can time your most important projects to peak when the Moon is at its brightest.

It's also interesting to note that a New Moon occurs when the Moon and the Sun are conjunct—which means they occupy the same sign and degree of the zodiac. When the Moon is New, it's a great time to initiate projects, because your head and your heart will be on the same page.

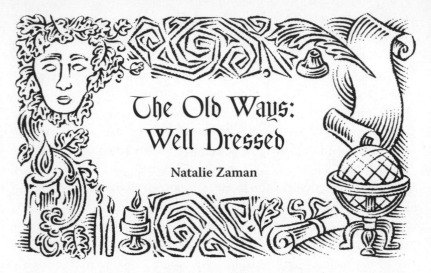

The Old Ways: Well Dressed

Natalie Zaman

WALK ABOUT TIDESWELL IN England's Peak District about the time of the summer solstice and you'll come upon a curious and beautiful sight. On Fountain Square one of the village's four long unused water sources is hidden from view behind a colorful mosaic screen. The central image is an ancient cathedral surrounded by a border filled with visions of the English countryside—wrolling, green patchwork hills dotted here and there with snowy sheep. The words "For the beauty of the earth, For the beauty of the sky" crown the picture. Come a bit closer and you'll see that this is an impermanent display. Not made of tiles or stones, the image is rendered completely in flowers, seeds, even a bit of fruit here and there—still fresh, for it's only a day old. What you're looking at is a well dressing, a Tideswell tradition (with some lapses) for over 750 years.

Wells, springs, and the like have been sacred Pagan sites for millennia. Then as now, water was essential to life, and springs and wells had deities attached to them—often though not always female—to whom offerings would be made to ensure a fresh and abundant supply. Because the source of the water is underground, these sites were associated with the womb and birth. Springs, like Aquae Sulis dedicated to Minerva in Bath, England, and various wells all over Ireland dedicated to Brigid were sacred to local folk, but became places of pilgrimage. It was commonplace for people to leave offerings of thanks, or petitions as was discovered during excavations at Bath where jewels and curse tablets were retrieved from the drain.

The earliest well dressings were more like offerings, and they were very simple. Flowers and other natural materials were arranged around the water source when they were available. Over time the offerings took on a Christian hue though they still had an underlying Pagan nature. Anna Franklin says that foxgloves (a flower associated with fairies) were used in England to dress wells dedicated to Nechtan, the husband of the Celtic river goddess Boann. In the Middle Ages Nechtan became St. Nectan whose hermitage was under a waterfall in Cornwall—essentially the same deity, though in a different guise.

Eventually the church banned well dressings, dismissing them as being too Pagan, but after the Black Death swept through in the fourteenth century, the practice was revived and survived in rural and isolated Derbyshire. Simple well offerings can be seen the world over, but the Peak District is the only place where this tribute, both Pagan and Christian in practice, lives on, on a large scale.

June 24 is designated as Well Dressing Day, but villages create dressings from May through September. Most go up in the summer, particularly in June and July when the materials to make them—flowers, fruit, and seeds—are abundant. Once the dressing is complete, the well is blessed, kicking off a week of celebrations, or "wakes." Today, Wakes Week (which lasts a little longer than the dressing, which is fresh for only a handful of days) culminates in a carnival or fair as it has for hundreds of years. (Check out *http://welldressing.com/calendar.php* for a schedule of well dressing dates and locations throughout the district.)

When well dressings became formal, community affairs is uncertain, but we have the Victorians to thank for the elaborate large-scale dressings seen today. When piped water became available, taps and pumps were dressed as well, thus many of the villages of the Peak District have several water sources to decorate. Because of this, entire communities can be involved in their creation and the festivities that follow.

The process is much the same as it's been for centuries. First, wooden trays are built in different lengths and widths, but with a depth of only one to two inches. These trays are soaked, usually in a natural water source such as a pond or stream after which they are filled with a mixture of clay that's been "puddled" (mixed thoroughly until it's completely smooth) with salt water. The shallow depth of the tray and the saturated wood helps to maintain the moisture necessary to keep the dressing fresh for as long as possible.

When the trays are prepared, a cartoon of the chosen design that has been drawn on paper first is pricked into the clay before the picture is "petaled." Whole flowers, petals, leaves, moss, and other fodder from forest and field are used to fill in the images, some of which are as intricate as a Renaissance painting. Modern dressings have included tributes to the Olympics held in London in 2012, and the 150th anniversary of *Alice in Wonderland* in 2015, but as of old, a combination of biblical, historical, and nature and folkloric themes will always be found in well dressing art.

At the solstice, find a water source that is sacred to you. Whom do you perceive as its patron god or goddess? Leave a floral tribute, no matter how simple, and a word of thanks. Water is life.

Additional Reading

Barrow, Mandy. "Well Dressing." *British Life and Culture: Calendar of Special Events and Celebrations*, 2010. http://resources .woodlands.kent.sch.uk/customs/questions/welldressing/index. html

Castelow, Ellen. "Well Dressing." *Historic UK The History and Heritage Accommodation Guide.* http://www.historic-uk.com/ CultureUK/Well-Dressing/

Franklin, Anna. *Midsummer: Magical Celebrations of the Summer Solstice.* St. Paul, MN: Llewellyn Publications, 2003.

Schama, Simon. *A History of Britain: At the Edge of the World?* New York: Hyperion, 2000.

"Well Dressings." *Peak District Information.* http://www.peakdistrictinformation.com/features/welldress.php

Williams, Glyn. "More About Well Dressings." Welldressings.com, 2011. http://welldressing.com/extra.php

Feasts and Treats

Laurel Reufner

This entire menu was made with grilling and eating outside in mind. We held our Midsummer ritual in the pool and then gathered around the grill after for the feast.

Marinated Veggie Kabobs

This recipe is easy to make either with or without meat. I've written the recipe to use tofu, but if you want to make it for your more carnivorous friends, simply switch out the tofu for chicken. Or you can please everyone and offer both!

Prep time: 1–2 hours
Cook time: 10–15 minutes
Servings: 4–6

1 block of extra firm tofu
1 batch balsamic rosemary marinade (see page 210)
8 ounces baby bella mushrooms
1–2 green bell peppers
1 sweet yellow onion
2 small zucchini
8 ounces cherry tomatoes

Press the tofu to remove the excess water. I've found the easiest way to do this without a tofu press is to use two plates, a clean kitchen towel, and a few bags of dried beans. Carefully wrap the tofu in the towel and place it between the two plates. Then just pile on the bags of beans until you've got 3 or 4 pounds pushing down on the tofu. This method works well because the bags can more easily conform to the curve of the plates. Let it press for at least half an hour before continuing.

Cut the tofu in half lengthwise, then cut each of those sections into fourths, finally cut those fourths so that they're half as thick. This should give you 16 pieces. Place in a plastic ziplock bag along with the marinade and refrigerate for 30 to 45 minutes. (Do not over-marinate.)

If using chicken, cut into roughly 2 inch pieces and marinate for 1 to 2 hours.

Clean the mushrooms, cutting into halves or fourths if they are really large. I'd suggest maybe making an extra batch of the marinade and letting the mushrooms soak alongside the tofu.

While your protein of choice is marinating, chop up your vegetables into roughly 1½ to 2 inch pieces and place in separate bowls. Cut the onion into small chunks, unless you know that everyone likes a really good mouthful of the stuff. Also, if you're using wooden skewers, start them soaking in water so they aren't flammable on the grill.

I like to let everyone assemble their own kabob. To do so, set everything out in bowls and place the skewers nearby. The trick to this is to remember which kabob belongs to which diner, but hopefully they can remember what they put on their skewer.

Grill on a medium heat for 5–10 minutes or until everything is heated evenly. Chicken will probably need longer to cook, perhaps up to 15 minutes. Make sure it is cooked through before serving.

Balsamic Rosemary Marinade

With a good, flavorful marinade, you can take any dish to new levels, especially those containing tofu. It's great for absorbing whatever you want to flavor it with. This particular recipe is a nice change from all of the Asian-inspired ones out there, which makes for a great summertime flavor boost.

Prep time: 5 minutes

2 tablespoons olive oil
1 tablespoon garlic, chopped
1 tablespoon fresh rosemary
½ tablespoon brown sugar
½ cup red balsamic vinegar
Pinch of salt and pepper

Place together in a small bowl and whisk to combine.

Rosemary-Onion Potato Packets

Start these cooking while the kabobs are being assembled. Serves 6.

Prep time: 20 minutes
Cook time: 10–20 minutes
Servings: 6

6–8 potatoes
3 carrots
1 medium onion, chopped small
5 tablespoons olive oil
1½ tablespoons dried rosemary
1 teaspoon dried thyme
Salt and pepper to taste

Clean your potatoes and cut them into ¾ inch pieces. Clean, peel, and slice the carrots into ¼–½ inch pieces. Boil for about 10 minutes or until crisp-tender—a fork goes in, but not without some pressure. Drain and give a quick rinse under cold water.

Mix the rest of the ingredients in a large bowl and add the potatoes. Toss to evenly coat, then portion out evenly onto 6 pieces of aluminum foil. Wrap up tightly.

Cook on a medium heat for about 10 minutes or until the potatoes are easily pierced with a fork.

Swedish Pickles

These pickles are a traditional Swedish Midsummer dish. Everyone who has tried them has loved them.

Prep time: 40 minutes
Chill time: 2–24 hours
Servings: 8

1 cup white vinegar
½ cup sugar
½ cup water
1 teaspoon caraway seeds, either crushed or coarsely ground
2 English cucumbers
2 tablespoons sea salt

Bring the vinegar, sugar, water, and caraway to a boil in a medium saucepan until the sugar dissolves. Set it aside to cool to room temperature.

While the brine is cooling, wash the cucumbers and slice them thinly. Leave the cucumbers unpeeled. Place them in a large bowl and toss with the salt. You want to set them aside for 10 to 15 minutes, allowing the salt to start extracting some of the moisture out of the cucumbers.

You will now need a second bowl, because you're going to pick up small handfuls of the cucumber slices and squeeze out the extra liquid. You can continue on at this point, although I like to let them sit for another 15 minutes or so and repeat the whole squeezing process.

Once the brine has cooled to room temperature, pour it over the cucumbers and stir well. Transfer to a sealable container and chill for a minimum of 2 hours before serving.

Lemon-Berry Trifle

Out of all the desserts I made for the *Almanac*, this might just be my favorite. It's light and fluffy, sweet without being cloying, and a perfect accompaniment for any warm weather meal.

Prep time: 30 minutes
Bake time: 35 minutes
Servings: 12

1 yellow cake
1 pound strawberries
Lemon whipped cream (recipe follows)

I'm going to be perfectly honest here—I used a boxed butter cake mix found at the Dollar Tree. It has an amazing flavor that was far better than any of the yellow cake recipes I tried. Whatever you decide on, make your cake and set it aside to cool. While it's cooling, wash and slice your strawberries.

Once it has cooled, cut it into 1 inch pieces. To assemble the trifles individually, place a few pieces of cake in the bottom of your dish, add on a layer of the strawberries, and top with a dollop of whipped cream. To make one large trifle, place a layer of cake in the bottom of your dish, top with a strawberry layer, followed by a layer of whipped cream and then repeat the layers all over again.

Store it in the refrigerator until serving.

Lemon Whipped Cream

This truly whips up quickly if you start with everything cold, including the bowl. Try putting it in the freezer for a few minutes.

Prep time: 10 minutes
Servings: 12

1 cup heavy whipping cream
2 tablespoons sugar
½ tablespoon fresh lemon juice
½ teaspoon vanilla

When you're ready to go, combine everything in the chilled bowl and beat with an electric mixer, at medium speed, until soft peaks form.

Keep refrigerated until needed. Makes about 2 cups.

Crafty Crafts

Linda Raedisch

IT'S AT MIDSUMMER THAT I pine most heartily for a garden house. Garden houses are the best kinds of houses. When designing one, you don't have to worry about plumbing or kitchen fixtures or closet space. A garden house just has to look pretty and offer a view of the roses outside. There ought to be room inside for the owner and a few guests to sit down and drink tea and eat cakes, but that's all. A garden house is to an ordinary house as a fairy tale is to a novel.

Throughout Europe, but especially in the north, there was a craze among wealthy eighteenth-century landowners for building "pagodas" in their gardens. These were usually based on sketches made by someone who had been to France and seen some other sketches made by someone who may or may not have actually been to China or India or Japan. This third-hand art evolved into an endearingly whimsical and distinctly European decorative style known as chinoiserie.

China in those days was also known to Europeans as "Cathay." Cathay, as depicted in the wallpapers, ceramics, and garden houses of Europe, resembled Fairyland far more than any real place on earth. So what if it never really existed? Those little Cathayan fairies still need a place to go to drink their tea, eat their cakes, burn their incense, and enjoy the long summer nights.

You might be wondering to what religion do those fairies subscribe? I can tell you with all confidence that they are devotees of the goddess Ki Mao Sao. Wearing a golden three-petalled crown, jewels and either a purple or yellow robe, Ki Mao Sao was a popular subject of chinoiseries. But was she ever a genuine Eastern goddess? As far as I can tell, all depictions of Ki Mao Sao derived from the French painter Watteau's work "Decoration for the Chateau de la Muette: Ki Mao Sao in the Kingdom of Mang in the Country of Laos." Had Watteau ever been to Laos? I doubt it.

Chinoiserie Fairy Garden House

Make just one or make a whole village. You might want to use a heavier paper, but any white printer or drawing paper will do. While you should encourage your fairies to burn incense inside their garden house, tea lights are strictly verboten—I know, I tried. Here's another tip: fold your sheet of paper into quarters, both bookwise and lengthwise, and the only measuring you'll have to do is for the peaks of the roof.

Time frittered: About half an hour, more if you draw a lot of details on your house.

Cost: About $12.00. This includes a Morning Star brand box of two hundred incense sticks with small holder. And, of course, once you have the supplies, you can make as many houses as you want.

Supplies

One 8½" × 11" sheet of white paper, not too thin*
Fine blue markers
Metallic marker*
Craft knife*
Clear tape*
White all-purpose glue*
Stick incense (broken in half)
Small incense holder

First, draw and color the walls and roof of your garden house on your sheet of paper as shown. Use your imagination. I used light and dark blue pens for a "Blue Willow" look, with gold blossoms on the trees, but you can use as many colors as you like. Use a sharp craft knife to cut out the doorway of your house—otherwise, how are the fairies going to get in and out?

Since the garden house takes up only half the page, you can draw your four roof edges on the other half. Remember to make them longer than the roofline itself so that the perky tips stick out on assembly.

Cut out your house all in one piece, i.e., do not cut the walls apart. Sharpen the creases between the walls and the house will practically assemble itself. All you have to do is tape the one wall and roof seam on the inside. Lastly, glue on the roof edges. Pinch the tips together at the corners so they stick out exotically.

To dedicate the house to Ki Mao Sao, light a half stick of sandalwood, patchouli, or jasmine incense. Place the stick in a small incense holder, place the house carefully over it, and watch the fragrant smoke wafting up through the hole in the roof.

Plants in Practice: Chamomile

Charlie Rainbow Wolf

I DON'T KNOW ABOUT you, but for me the idea of chamomile tea conjures up warm June afternoons and sleepy star-filled evenings. Chamomile smells sweet, earthy, sensuous. It's a favorite among herb gardeners and one of the first plants I explored when starting my journey into plant totems and helpers. Looking similar to a small daisy, its presence is welcome in the garden for many reasons.

The most popular chamomiles are *Matricaria chamomilla*, or German chamomile. Some people refer to this as the true or wild chamomile. *Chamaemeium nobile* is also popular, and it goes by many names, including English, Russian, Roman, or common chamomile. They both have the very similar growing habits and uses.

The main differences between the two chamomiles is that the German chamomile is taller, sometimes reaching two feet in height, while the English chamomile is a low-growing creeper and more of a ground cover. They're both hardy in USDA growing zones 3–9, and neither need a lot of watering once they're established. Partial shade is preferred, but they'll tolerate full sun, too. It's easily propagated by splitting the parent plant.

This little miniature daisy has many assets in the garden. Folklore says that if healthy chamomile is planted next to another weaker plant, the sickly one will start to revive. It's pleasant to look at, smells nice when bruised, and is a wonderful companion plant to a garden, for it helps to keep bothersome pests away from the vegetables. It's particularly advantageous for onions and members of the cabbage family.

In herbal medicine, chamomile has a variety of benefits, internally and externally. Chamomile tea is a tried and tested sedative, known to relax and soothe the nerves as well as quiet a grumpy tummy. It's used to reduce fevers, and it is even said to prevent bad dreams.

A poultice made from chamomile flowers helps to lessen bruising and discourage swelling. Cold chamomile infusions can be used on hair as a conditioner and on facial skin to tone it after cleansing. The dried flower heads can be added to herbal sachets that, when put into a pillowcase, will help to promote a good night's sleep.

Magically, chamomile is an excellent herb for dreamwork and divination. Chamomile oils can be used to anoint crystals and mirrors used for scrying. Added to mojo bags and charms, chamomile is said to attract love. It encourages a feeling of general happiness and peace of mind, as well as helping to act as protection against negative energy. It's sometimes used as a money-draw herb, too.

A Chamomile Dream Ritual

Litha is the time of year when the days are at their longest and the energy of the Sun is at its peak. What better time to do a ritual to assist you in dreaming big dreams, and then work hard to make them manifest? After all, the nights are going to start drawing in after the solstice, where you'll have more time to focus on dreaming. Set your intent, and then start to make it happen!

You're going to need some chamomile tea. Loose flower heads are okay, or you can get chamomile tea bags and tip out the herbs. You'll need additional herbs for this one, too; hops, catmint or catnip, lilac, lemon balm (also called melissa), and rose petals. You'll require a cotton muslin bag, a needle and thread, and a pen and paper, too. If you're doing this in a group, make sure that everyone has their own bag, pen, and paper, and that there are enough herbs and threaded needles for everyone to share.

At the appointed time, write out what you want the coming six months to bring to you. What do you dream will happen? Be as detailed as you can—but not so lost in minutiae that the universe doesn't have some wriggle room! For example, you might want a new love; focus on that person being kind, respectful, fun to be with, and loyal—rather than him having blond hair, blue eyes, and driving a green car. If you want a new house, choose the neighborhood, rather than a red house with blue shutters and two lampposts in the yard.

When you have written down your dream, fold the paper to fit into the muslin bag. As you fold it up, envision those words being locked into a reality. You're setting your intent. You're about to make real magic happen.

Place the paper in your bag, and then start to fill the bag with the herbs. Put just a pinch of each. Say an affirmation with each one. Something like this would work:

Chamomile: Don't be lazy, my little daisy!

Hops: Hop to it and make my dream come true!

Catmint: We won't let the cat out of the bag yet!

Lilac: We'll gather lilacs in my dreams!

Lemon balm: There's nothing sour about this intent!

Rose petals: Oh, rose, I knows you knows!

Have fun with it. Make up rhymes, and don't be afraid to giggle. The more laughter and merriment you put into this little sachet of intent, the more joy you'll have working toward its fulfillment. Yes, it may seem simple. Yes, it may seem frivolous. Just trust me on this one—it works.

When you've filled your bag, it's now time to sew it shut. Focus on what you wrote with every stitch so that you blend your active energies with your dreams. Once this is shut, so that the herbs cannot escape, the sachet can be put into something more decorative, such as a lace bag. I often knit my dream pillow holders, echoing my intent with each stitch. If you're crafty, you could crochet or sew one. It doesn't matter how you make it. It doesn't even matter if it's store-bought. What matters is how much oomph you put into this and how much you're going to focus on making it happen.

Now get on with your solstice merrymaking, celebrating however you choose. Before you go to sleep, put the pouch you've made in your pillow. You might want to keep a journal next to your bed so that it's easy to record your dreams upon waking in the next weeks. Your unconscious mind will speak to you through visions and images as you sleep. Watch for repetitive patterns and for things that really stand out. Above all, though, don't think that the ritual is finished just because you've made your pouch and placed it in your pillow. Chamomile teaches you that you really can make your dreams a reality. They're waiting for you to step into them, but wishing isn't enough. Thoughts without deeds are lost opportunities. You still have to do the work in the real world to match the dreamtime work for anything tangible to manifest.

A Summer Welcoming Ritual

Susan Pesznecker

THE FOLLOWING DAY-LONG ritual is designed for one person but could be adapted to include more people as well. It focuses on the balance and interplay of cycles related to the summer solstice. The ritual immerses a participant in cyclical activities of light and dark and focuses on the balance between the two.

This ritual begins in the morning and finishes at bedtime. It's designed to fill a typical day while also setting that day "apart" as a magical space. The first half of the day is an homage to the sun and the energies of the longest day, while the second half is a connection with the coming darkness—both light and dark being part of the summer solstice. A midday ritual links the two halves and echoes the idea of balance.

You can adapt this to a shorter time as suits your purposes. Begin by reading through carefully.

Time	*What to do*	*What You'll Need*
7:00 am	Lie in bed. Stretch gently, aware of your body and its vigor. Offer thanks for the coming day.[1]	A prayer, poem, or other words of gratitude
7:10 am	Rise and stand near a window. Stretch again, taking deep breaths. Feel your body responding to the new day and its light.	
7:20 am	Shower. Dip your head in and out of the shower stream, repeating at first dip: My cares are washed away, at second—"I am cloaked in light", at third, "I am protected by the sun." Dry with a fresh towel. Anoint your heart chakra with rosemary essential oil, envisioning the heat of the sun and the heat of your beating heart. Dress in clean clothes.	Clean, fresh towel Rosemary essential oil Clean clothes. Choose light fabrics, natural fibers, and bright, sunny colors.
7:45 am	Prepare and eat a simple breakfast that references the sun. Wash your hands before eating as an act of purification. Offer a blessing, prayer, poem, or other words over the food.[2]	Think round and golden, yellow, or orange foods: eggs (sunny side up!), fresh-squeezed citrus juices, peaches, round biscuits, toast cut with a round cutter and topped with apricot jam.

[1] You might substitute a yoga sun salutation here.
[2] The meal reminds us that the sun gives all life here on earth.

Time	What to do	What You'll Need
8:30 am	Put away your dishes and tidy the kitchen. Tidy up the bathroom, too, and make and fluff your bed.[3]	Housekeeping tools
8:50 am	Check your e-messages and emails and reply to anything urgent. Once that is done, please power down your electronics and digital devices and put them away until the ritual is finished.[4]	Phone, tablet, and laptop, and a secure hideaway for them during the ritual.
9:00 am	Move about your house, opening your window coverings and windows. Be aware of the light that fills your living space and the way the energy changes.	A sense of intention, mixed with "presence in the moment."
9:10 am	Make changes in your home's adornments to recognize summer. You might put on a seasonal tablecloth, hang a dried flower wreath, bring in a floral arrangement, and so forth. Be aware of how this changes the surroundings and their energy.	Summer adornments

[3] Your surroundings today are ritual space, and should be in order to maintain the peace and balance of the event.

[4] Electronics have their own powerful effects and are not part of this ritual. By minimizing distractions, you'll be ready to participate and reflect throughout the day.

Time	What to do	What You'll Need
9:30 am	Sit for a few minutes and journal about your day so far. Reflect on how you feel on this longest day of the year. Note what you're thankful for. Write about or draw the summer sun in all its glory.	Paper (or a journal or notebook), pen, or pencil. Optional: sketching art tools.[5]
9:45 am	Take a walk outside, dressing for the weather. Be aware of the morning light and the sun's position in the sky. Feel the ways the sun warms and brings light to the earth.	Comfortable walking shoes and outerwear.
10:15 am	Make a cup of herbal tea.	Teapot, cup, spoon, fresh or dried herbs. Chamomile, lavender, and mint are summer associated and tasty.
10:30 am	Spend time journaling about your morning walk and sipping tea. Add a small treat if desired.	Treats!
10:45 am	Activity time! Work on an activity aimed at personal or magical growth. You might study, create a tool or altar piece, write a story, sew an item of garb, embroider, etc. Consider your act of creation and the energy you put into the work—much the same as the way the sun energizes us.	Activity materials

[5] Drawing, sketching, etc., are acceptable ways to journal if you prefer that to writing.

Time	What to do	What You'll Need
11:45 am	Prepare and eat a simple lunch that references earth, air, water, and fire. Wash your hands before eating as an act of purification. Offer a blessing, prayer, poem, or other words over the food. Clean up carefully after the meal.	**Earth**: bread, root veggies **Air**: fruit or vegetables from trees or vines **Fire**: spices, seasoning **Water**: a favorite beverage, prayer, poem, or words of gratitude.[6]
12:30 pm	Pause for journaling again. Consider what you wish to accomplish in the upcoming ritual. You'll account for your growth over the past season (light), and you'll prepare for your personal "harvest" and the quiet months to come (dark).	Journaling materials
12:45 pm	Work with your favorite divination tool, using it as a tool to help you focus on the upcoming ritual. Journal about your discoveries.	Favorite divination tool
1:30 pm	Prepare the space and set up for the upcoming ritual.[7] Preparation could be via smudging, sweeping, ringing bells, etc. For set up, arrange the materials and make sure everything is at hand.	Purification materials Ritual materials

[6] Referencing the elements invokes the idea of balance in all things.

[7] Select a room or space that can be both light and dark.

Time	What to do	What You'll Need
2:00 pm	Prepare for the ritual. Don robes, jewelry, or other garb. Wash hands and face. Meditate briefly, pray, or otherwise prepare.	Garb, jewelry, etc.
2:30 pm[8]	Carry out a ritual that honors the gift of light (the longest day) and welcomes the coming darkness. Begin by acknowledging the longest day: raise energy, sing, dance, do spell work, take oaths, etc. Recognize the coming darkness: bring the energy down, pledge to a plan or course, ground and center, etc.	Include whatever usual ritual trappings or components you like to work with: calling quarters, appealing to deity, making offerings, etc. Ritual materials
3:15 pm	Use your favorite divination tool to assess the ritual results. Journal about the results of your divination and ritual.	Favorite divination tool
3:45 pm	Put away your ritual materials and tidy the area.	A sense of reflective accomplishment.
4:00 pm	Prepare and eat a small, nourishing snack aimed at restoring energy.	Chocolate is good for this.
4:15 pm	Reading time. Pick a magical text or just relax with a favorite book!	A cup of tea, if desired.

[8] Assuming you rise at 7:00 am and go to bed at 10:00 pm, 2:30 pm is the midway point, i.e., the day's balance.

Time	What to do	What You'll Need
5:15 pm	Prepare and eat a hearty supper: the kind we'd eat as the nights grow long and cool. Wash your hands before eating as an act of purification. Offer a blessing, prayer, poem, or other words over the food. Clean up carefully after the meal.	Sample items might include soups, stews, curries, etc. (foods that warm and nurture us through the dark months. Prayer, poem, or other words of gratitude.[9]
6:15 pm	Take a second walk outside, dressing for the weather. Be aware of the sun's changing position. Envision the darker nights that soon will arrive.	Comfortable clothing
6:45 pm	Spend a few moments journaling about your walk.	Journaling materials
7:00 pm	Activity time, focusing on the introspection that comes with longer nights. What do you wish to accomplish in the quiet darker times as the days shorten toward winter? Make a plan for a project, a significant activity, or a course of study, and set a date to begin.	Your choice of journaling materials or a separate notebook (or other tool) for planning.

[9] In the morning, the meal focused on the sun and light. Lunch balanced us by considering the four elements. Now we're looking ahead to the approach of winter—hence heartier foods.

[10] Your project can begin immediately or could be delayed until a future time.

Time	What to do	What You'll Need
8:00 pm	Close the windows and blinds, and turn off the lights. Sit quietly for a few minutes and imagine the coming darkness. Light a candle, and consider the gift of light.	Candles and a sense of quiet contemplation
8:15 pm	Once again, work with your favorite divination tool, using it to assess the work you've done today and asking questions about your path in the months to come.	Favorite divination tool
8:40 pm	Journal about the evening. Reflect on how you feel this moment, on this shortest night of the year. Write about the coming darkness.	Journaling materials
9:00 pm	Slip outdoors and study the evening sky. Greet the darkness—acknowledge it as a balance to the light and as a positive force.	A flashlight, if needed
9:15 pm	You've worked hard all day: now it's time for pampering. Draw a deep, hot bath with your favorite salts, bubbles, or other props. Settle in. Enjoy.	Bathing materials
9:50 pm	Dry off and don nightclothes. Prepare for bed. Offer a prayer, poem, or spoken gratitude for the gifts of light, dark, and balance in the multiverse.	Clean towel and night-clothes

Ritual can be a powerful tool for connecting us to the mundane and magical worlds around us. I hope you have enjoyed this homage to the sun and the energies of the longest day while connecting with the coming darkness.

Notes

Notes

Lammas

Feast of the Loaf

Suzanne Ress

THE NAME LAMMAS IS an English corruption of the old Saxon Hlaf-mass, or Feast of the Loaf, the first harvest festival of the year.

Lammas is often used interchangeably with the name Lughnasa, an ancient Celtic harvest celebration centered on the twenty-four hours from sundown on July 31st to sundown on August 1st, and the two weeks preceding and anteceding that date. Lughnasa honored the sun god Lugh, with Olympic-like games and sports contests, and celebrated the first fruits of a successful harvest season.

When the medieval Christian church tried to suppress paganism and its traditional festivals, Lughnasa was renamed Lammas. Loaves of bread made from the newly harvested wheat were blessed by priests and either buried at the top of a hill or broken into four parts, which were placed in the four corners of the barn to protect the grain and ensure a bountiful autumn harvest. Bread, the staff of life, has symbolically represented the human body for a long time. Bread was regarded as sacred, essential to human life. Grain cultivation is responsible for the human transformation from living day-to-day as hunter-gatherers to being able to settle down into stable societies, where the arts, science, philosophy, and more could flourish. We owe a great deal of humanity's development to cultivated grain, and to bread.

The Christian Church was not very successful in suppressing the Pagan origins of this agricultural festival, and Lammas was widely thought of as being one of the four major Witch Sabbats, which also included Halloween (Samhain), May Day (Beltane), and Ladies' Day (Imbolc).

The beginning of the harvest is considered an auspicious time for hand fasting, the initiation of a new romantic relationship, and marriage. *Lughnasa* means, "An Assembly for Lugh". This was when the sun god wed the earth mother, and the consummation of their relationship was celebrated.

Nowadays many of us have little or no awareness of the importance of a successful harvest to an agriculturally based society. We may try to buy local, buy organic, perhaps even grow our own herbs or veggies, but if heavy rains destroy a crop or drought prevents proper growth, or if pesticides from a cornfield kill all the pollinators, there is a supermarket always mysteriously full of fresh produce, flour, bread, and all the food anyone could dream of and beyond, just down the road.

In olden times, when the last year's grain ran low or finished, the newly harvested grain was cause for riotous and happy celebration. Having successfully harvested the grain, survival through another winter was secure.

Last November I decided to plant two ¾-acre fields with wheat. These two fields, strangely situated in the middle of a woods, had caused me endless frustration ever since I'd bought them five or six years earlier. They'd been over run with black locust saplings and mugwort when I'd purchased them, hardly recognizable as the hay fields the deed said they were. We cleaned, cleared, and ploughed. The following year I planted both fields with borage and set up several beehives at the end of one. Unfortunately, the borage did not grow quickly enough to compete with the returning mugwort, and it was soon over run.

I resorted to applying the oft ill-spoken of Glyphosate to kill the mugwort, and attempted the borage planting again the following year, but once again the mugwort won out.

The next year, in the Spring, we ploughed the emerging mugwort underneath as a green manure, and I planted buckwheat, hoping my bees would make buckwheat honey. By late June the fields were beautiful, full of white buckwheat blossoms, but the bees, for reasons only they knew, wouldn't go near them. Once the buckwheat died down the mugwort came back with a vengeance.

This past fall's weather was unseasonably warm. In a stroke of what I believed was genius I decided to plant winter wheat, which, because of its long over wintering growing season, and head start in the Spring, would surely kill off the mugwort.

I placed my order with an organic seed company for 300 pounds of antique variety Verna wheat seed. A couple days later it was delivered in large burlap sacks on a pallet.

The fields had been ploughed and tilled, and my husband and I borrowed a seeding machine on November 14th to plant the wheat in long even rows.

"If the weather stays warm another ten days, you'll see the seedlings emerge," my farmer friend told us. "But it's risky to plant this late in the season—most people do it in October—the weather could turn cold any day."

We hoped for the best.

Ten days later, and no sign yet of frost, I rode my horse to the wheat fields, and, from a distance, saw the first rows of green emergence! I telephoned my farmer friend to tell him.

"Great!" he said. "You've been lucky. Now all should go well, unless—"

"Unless?" My heart sank a bit.

"Unless there is too much hard rain in the spring. That can ruin wheat."

Within a few days the weather turned cold and we had our first frost.

I wondered, because it seemed wonderful, how a plant could start to grow, then become dormant for the winter, and resume its growth in the spring when earth and air warm up. This process is called vernalization—the plant requires a one to two month period of air temperatures around freezing in order to flower in the spring, something like daffodil, crocus, or hyacinth bulbs, which must be planted in the fall for spring blooms.

Over the winter we had a couple of snows. The little wheat plants were covered completely.

By late February the snow had melted and the woods paths were muddy. I rode my horse to the wheat fields one morning, and saw, with much irritation, the deep tracks of a large off road vehicle that had entered and turned a wide circle over the tender plants.

My husband and I spent the weekend erecting a post and wire fence.

Within a few weeks the wheat began to grow again, slowly at first, and then, as the days grew longer and the sun warmed the earth, more quickly. All seemed to be going well, until, in early April, I noticed something else growing in the spaces between the rows of wheat—mugwort! It was shorter than the wheat, but I knew it would not stay that way for long.

Although I had wanted the wheat to remain organic, I wanted even more to eradicate the mugwort, knowing well that if I did not it might smother the wheat, and, at the very least, would make harvesting difficult.

Once again I succumbed to the tempting ease of a selective broad leaf herbicide, using it only on the affected field.

By Beltane I was pleased to see that the mugwort was turning yellow and had quit growing, while the wheat grew taller and more beautiful, like rows of spiky coarse grass.

The mugwort was dead by the end of May, but then the heavy rains began. The rains turned my horses' paddocks into gigantic mud puddles and tore the black locust blossoms off the trees, smashing hope for a good first honey harvest.

When I could, I rode to the wheat fields, and saw, with dismay, that the rains had pushed large swaths of the tall green plants, which had just begun to flower, to prone position on the ground.

Wheat (*Triticum*) is a domesticated grass, probably created by humans, intentionally or not, more than 10,000 years ago by crossing three different grass species and selecting for big seeds. Around 8,000 years ago humans were grinding wheat grains with stones to make flour, and 3,000 years later the Egyptians were using yeast to make leavened bread baked in wood fired ovens. By the year 1180 there were windmills to grind wheat throughout Europe and England, and in the Middle Ages, every village had its water or wind powered mill close to the wheat fields.

Wheat and bread have been with us a very long time indeed. Combined with legumes, wheat forms a perfect protein source. It is also higher in fiber, B vitamins, iron, magnesium, and potassium than either corn or rice.

In recent years wheat has gotten a bad rap as more and more people seem to become sensitive to gluten. A 2013 study showed that this is likely due to the greatly increased number of gluten based additives in processed foods rather than any change in the amount of gluten in modern wheat varieties versus antique varieties, as some people hypothesized.

By mid June the weather stabilized and grew hot. The chestnut trees came into bloom for the second local honey flow. Every few days I passed by the wheat fields and plucked off a spike, picking out and chewing the berries to test for ripeness.

After a month the green plants had dried to beige under the hot sun, and the wheat berries were hard and dry. It was time to harvest!

There was only one problem: the woods paths leading to the fields were only 8 feet 10 inches wide, highly banked on both sides, and modern harvesting machines measure 9 feet 10 inches from wheel to wheel.

"Try asking Daniel," said my farmer friend. "He has an older, smaller harvesting machine."

Daniel, a tractor mechanic with an agriculture hobby, was the man I'd bought the buckwheat seeds from a couple years earlier.

"No, no," said Daniel. "I can't do that work for anyone but myself. No insurance on the machine, you see."

My farmer friend had estimated we should harvest about three thousand pounds of wheat from those fields. I began to fear that my husband and I would have to harvest by hand, the way it was done for thousands of years. Reaping by hand, using a scythe, it takes about an hour to harvest 6 pounds of grain. I quickly did the math—my husband and I would be in the fields cutting grain for about three weeks if we worked twelve-hour days. The thought of this was dreadful.

Then I remembered an acquaintance mentioning a couple from the mountains who had a small, hand-pushed motorized wheat harvesting machine. I inquired, and was relieved when they said they would come July 18th and, for a fee, do the work.

July 18th was sunny and blistery hot. The mountain couple arrived about 10:30 am, and we started harvesting by 11. Claude pushed the machine, which cut and separated all the plants it could reach, leaving the stems on the ground and spewing the grain into a fifty-pound sack attached to its chute. The rest of us used scythes or sickles to hand cut all the spikes at the edges of the fields, and the ones that lay prone, putting them into the machine when it passed. Whenever the sack was full it had to be removed, and a new one attached.

At one point, cutting through the border wheat with my scythe, I visualized myself as the Grim Reaper. This representation of Death, which has been with us since about the year 1400, carries a scythe because he comes to harvest human beings' souls at the end of their season on earth.

During the course of the afternoon, several neighbors stopped by and joined in to help as their time allowed.

We emptied the full sacks into the trailer attached to our tractor and took turns sifting out the bigger pieces of grass and stems that were left in it. The trailer filled slowly. I began to doubt my farmer friend's estimate of 3,000 pounds. As the afternoon wore on it became apparent that our harvest would be much smaller than expected. The machine left much of the grain behind. Antique variety wheat's yield is naturally lower than modern varieties.

After seven hours without a break, all of us hot, sweaty, hungry, and thirsty, the harvest was concluded. I paid the mountain couple and gave them a few sacks of grain, then bid them goodbye. My husband drove the tractor with its trailer of grain through the woods and home, where we refreshed ourselves and then collapsed.

At seven the next morning I spread two old white cotton bedspreads on the south-facing uncovered patio, and we dumped and spread the grain there to thoroughly dry for 12 hours. During the day I turned it several times with a shovel, noticing lizards scampering across the warm grain. Later I realized that the lizards had provided a valuable service by eating the stinkbugs and shield bugs that had followed the grain home from the fields.

As the sun set my husband and I shoveled the perfectly dried grain into fifty pound sacks, a little dismayed to discover there was even less than we'd thought—only 900 pounds, including the two hundred we'd given to the mountain couple. We left the open sacks on the covered front porch to cool overnight, and the next morning tied them up tight and carried them to the dehumidified cellar for storage.

In the meantime I had called around to several nearby mills to find out about grinding the grain into flour. Two of these ground only corn. The third would grind wheat but only quantities over 2,000 pounds. I looked for alternatives.

I found an old man with a portable mill. He said he'd sell it to me, as he no longer used it. But when we tried it the motor quit. I took the motor to be repaired, but when I brought it back in working order two days later the old man had decided not to sell the mill.

"I'll grind your wheat here for you," he said. "You can pay me with honey."

In a couple of hours we ground enough grain to make 7 pounds of flour and 4 pounds bran, but I knew I would not return, as economically the exchange made no sense for me. I'd find another way. At any rate I had a big paper bag full of lovely whole-wheat flour. I also had a paper bag full of bran, which is the outer shell of the wheat grain. This made a nutritious treat for our hens and horses.

The next day, July 31st, I baked bread, carefully following the "Basic Whole Wheat Bread" recipe from *The Laurel's Kitchen Bread Book*[2]. While it was rising I telephoned our helpful neighbors, inviting them for dinner.

From start to finish, it took 6 hours to make 2 one pound loaves of bread.

July 31st at sundown, Armando, Herman, and Alice arrived. It was the start of Lammas, and we sat down altogether to a dinner of homegrown vegetables, omelets made of freshly laid eggs from our hens, and, to my immense joy and satisfaction, the most delicious bread any of us had ever tasted! Home baked bread made from freshly ground grain really is something to celebrate!

Notes

1. Kasarda, D.D. "Can an Increase In Celiac Disease Be Attributed to an Increase in Gluten Content of Wheat as a Consequence of Wheat Breeding?" *Journal of Agricultural and Food Chemistry.* Vol. 61, No. 6 (2013): 1155–1159.

2. Robertson, Laurel. *The Laurel's Kitchen Bread Book: A Guide to Wholegrain Bread Baking.* New York. Random House 1984.

Cosmic Sway

Corrine Kenner

THE CROSS-QUARTER HOLIDAY of Lammas falls during the hottest month of the year as the Sun makes its way through fiery Leo. The Sun rules Leo, which means that as temperatures rise, energy and emotions are heightened, too.

Among ancient Pagans, the first harvest of Lammas was a hopeful time—but the flip side of the coin was fear. If the crops failed and the harvest wasn't fruitful, a long, dark winter of hunger and deprivation was in store.

On a symbolic level, the holiday of Lammas celebrates the fact that we do hope to be rewarded for hard work. We know we'll be held accountable for our actions. If we worry that our shortcomings will be revealed, or that we'll be punished for our failures and misdeeds, we can raise our standards and live up to our own better natures.

Mythic Astrology: Saturn

Saturn may seem like a formidable foe. In fact, ancient astrologers referred to him as the Great Malefic, and he stands in stern contrast to the benefic nature of his son Jupiter.

He's a fearsome figure by any definition. Saturn is the god of time, and ate his children—just as the years eventually destroy all of the world's creations.

We're used to seeing Saturn depicted as an ancient Father Time, garbed in a hooded robe and carrying an hour glass or sickle. In more modern depictions, Saturn resembles the Grim Reaper. He's a skeletal figure who cuts short the lives of the young and harvests the souls of the old.

In Roman mythology, however, Saturn was the god of agriculture. He taught the ancients how to trim the vine and the olive, and his civilizing influence helped establish societal order and control.

Once a year, during the festival of Saturnalia, that social order was upended. Slaves were treated like royalty, and their masters dressed in rags to wait on them. Children received presents, and everybody feasted.

Saturn had three sons: Pluto, Neptune, and Jupiter, and three daughters: Vesta, Ceres, and Juno. Saturn had castrated his own father, Uranus, and he feared that his children would someday rebel against him, too, as his father had predicted.

Saturn managed to preserve his rule for years by eating his own children. Every time his wife gave birth, he snatched up the child and ate it. Eventually his wife grew tired of losing all her offspring. When Jupiter was born, she hid the infant in a safe place and wrapped a boulder in a baby's blanket. Saturn swallowed the stone without a second thought, and Jupiter was saved.

When Jupiter was grown, he drugged his father, forcing him to throw up all his other children. They'd been sitting in Saturn's stomach all along.

Saturn never forgave his wife or children—and even now, he works overtime to enforce boundaries and limitations.

In astrology, the ringed planet symbolizes discipline and clear-cut definitions.

Most people, of course, rebel at boundaries. They like to feel free and unencumbered. Saturn brings us down to earth and teaches us the practical realities of material existence. Saturn proves the old adage: what doesn't kill us makes us stronger.

Saturn reminds us that reasonable people recognize their limits and make wise choices to make the most of the time and space they're allotted. Time is the best teacher, and most people are willing to trade youth and innocence for the wisdom and experience of age.

Even though Saturn's rings imply a certain number of limitations and restrictions, they also delineate boundaries that can help us define our position and relate to other people without losing our own individuality. Boundaries keep outside forces out and contain what belongs inside. In other words, Saturn's boundaries don't merely confine us: they define us.

Ancient astrologers called Saturn the Great Malefic and associated him with misfortune. Today, astrologers are less fatalistic, and they'll usually point out that Saturn also clears the way for new beginnings.

Its placement in a horoscope chart, by sign and by house, describes authority figures as well as how we manage our own authority with lesser beings and subordinates.

Saturn rules earthy Capricorn, the sign of the goat. Saturn also rules the tenth house of the horoscope, where astrologers look for information about career and public image.

Reading the Signs

On the Solstice, five planets were either standing still or moving backward through this signs. If you thought that would change, you're right: now six planets are either stationed or retrograde.

Despite the slowdown in those planets, you'll have energy to burn. The Sun in fiery Leo is trine the Moon in fiery Aries.

The Sun is also beaming energy straight at Mars, which is across the zodiac in the opposite sign of Aquarius. Mars is also tapping into lunar energy from a sextile with the Moon in fiery Aries. That means Mars is soaking up the light of the Sun, building up its reserves of strength. It might discharge that energy in unexpected ways: the Moon is in an uncomfortable square with Saturn, the ringed planet of limitations and restrictions. Mars and Uranus are also in an uncomfortable square, and Uranus is the planet of rebellion and revolution.

Jupiter's expansive nature is hampered a bit by its square to the Sun, as well as its trine with Neptune, the sign of mysticism and illusion. The giant planet is in Scorpio, where it takes on a brooding quality. You can use the aspect to your advantage by immersing yourself in mystery. Now is the time to seek answers to the philosophical questions—like what, and who, you value most.

Uranus, which is stationed in Taurus, is square the Sun and trine Saturn. This is a good time to take inventory of your belongings and get rid of anything that isn't beautiful, useful, or loved. You might be surprised at how easy it is to liberate yourself from people and property that are actually weighing you down.

Two planets will be coming into their own soon, which could jump-start your love life. Venus, the planet of beauty and attraction, is in self-possessed Virgo right now, but she moves into her own sign of Libra on August 6.

Mars, the virile planet of action and assertion, moves into his traditional home of Capricorn on August 13.

Planetary Positions

- Sun in Leo
- Moon in Aries
- Mercury in Leo
- Venus in Virgo
- Mars in Aquarius
- Jupiter in Scorpio
- Saturn ℞ in Capricorn
- Uranus in Taurus
- Neptune in Pisces
- Pluto in Capricorn

Phases of the Moon

On August 11, a New Moon in fiery Leo will reinforce the Sun's emphasis on accomplishments and awards.

At the same time, a partial solar eclipse will fascinate Northern and Eastern Europe, and North and West Asia.

On August 26, a Full Moon in watery Pisces will fill the sky, illuminated by the Sun in earthy Virgo. The Full Moon in Pisces is actually featured on the Moon card in most tarot decks. A watery Pisces Moon promises psychic dreams and intuitive flashes of insight.

On September 9, a New Moon in earthy Virgo will move the harvest season even further ahead.

Practical Astrology

Retrograde planets are one of the most fascinating phenomena in astrology.

Every now and then, from our viewpoint on Earth, the planets seem to move backward through the zodiac. It's an optical illusion that occurs when Earth passes other planets in our orbit around the Sun. Just as a car you pass on the highway seems to go backward as you pull ahead of it, planets look like they're moving in reverse when we pass them in space.

People seem especially attuned to Mercury retrogrades. As Earth passes Mercury in its orbit around the Sun, the small messenger planet seems to travel backward through the stars. Other planets go retrograde, too, but none seem to have the same upsetting effect on our daily lives. That's because Mercury rules the stuff of everyday life—messages, errands, appointments, neighborhood jaunts, and family connections.

When Mercury is retrograde, double-check details, cross your T's and dot your I's, because the trickster energy can wreak havoc with communications. Check and recheck your work, and back up important files.

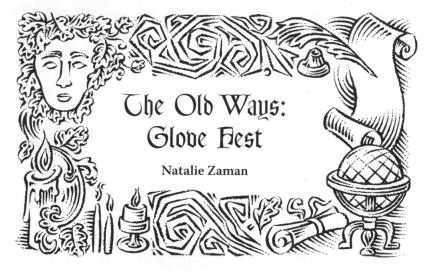

The Old Ways: Glove Fest

Natalie Zaman

AUGUST USHERS IN THE first of the year's harvest festivals. Lughna-sadh, also called Lammas (the names are used interchangeably), were, and still are, marked by festivals where games and competitions, as well as livestock dealing and other commerce take place. The fairness and trust required for these activities was symbolized by a little acknowledged article of clothing that one doesn't usually associate with August and late summer. The must-have accessory for the first harvest was a pair of gloves.

For many rural villages, fairs—which revolved around the cycles of nature and, subsequently, the church holidays that were new expressions of older traditions—were rare opportunities to buy and sell. Sometimes whole livelihoods could depend on doing well at these fairs, particularly those held at the harvest. Fair dealing and justice were especially important. The presence of a glove guaranteed smooth and honest operations.

Chambers Book of Days describes the opening of a Lammas fair in Exeter beginning with the mayor reading a proclamation (dating to the 1300s) followed by the raising of the "white glove," a large white leather glove stuffed to resemble a hand open in greeting. In Barnstable, the glove was bedecked with dahlias and suspended from a pole on the top of the "Quay Hall"—the oldest building in the town. At the end of the day the glove was taken down, and each day before it was put up again, it was exhibited in front of the town hall. Displayed this way, the glove not only welcomed revelers to the fair, but also ensured the protection of the king. An open hand is an age-old gesture of welcome, but also a sign of fair dealings and generosity—or justice and retribution when warranted.

Because they cover the hands, the most expressive part of the human body aside from the face, gloves conveyed messages. Like a magical tool, they became an extension of the person; what the hands did, so the glove expressed. To this day, a handshake conveys agreement and trust. To "throw down the gauntlet" means to pose a challenge. Gloves were worn when handling objects too precious to be touched by mere mortal flesh, and so express reverence. In the Middle Ages, knights wearing ladies' gloves as a favor was a sign of love and devotion.

Being a harvest festival, Lammas was a time for expressing thanks. It was traditional to present servants with the gift of a pair of gloves for good services rendered over the previous year and in anticipation of the cold winter to come. These were tokens of gratitude or, depending on the servant, an acknowledgment of the authority and responsibility given to him or her. If gloves weren't given outright, money earmarked for the specific purchase, called "glove silver," was given. Considering the price (household accounts from the fourteenth century show two shillings paid for gloves for over a dozen servants) the gloves for servants were probably the practical, protective kind, rather than something bejeweled and costly.

Lughnasadh may be named for Lugh, but the festival itself originated (at his command) as a tribute to his stepmother the goddess Tailtiu, who died of exhaustion after making the fields of Ireland subtable for planting, thus ensuring the survival of its people. Teltown (named for her) is considered the site of the first Lughnasadh celebrations—and of what would be called "Teltown marriages." The forerunner of betrothals, "troth-plights," and our modern engagements, these unions were temporary with an eye to becoming permanent. Unions could last for the duration of the festival or, more commonly, the entire year until the next festival, after which the couple could go their separate ways (even if they cohabited) or cement the union permanently with a proper handfasting. Gloves were often exchanged as tokens of these semipermanent commitments.

In his nineteenth century treatise "Gloves: their annals and associations," scholar William S. Beck suggests that the exchange of gloves for marriage (a pledge of trust) was an ancient custom, quoting, among others, the seventeenth century poet Robert Herrick who wrote:

> *What posies for our wedding rings,*
> *What gloves we'll give and Ribanings [ribbons][1]*

Even though white didn't become a fashionable wedding color until the nineteenth century, it was, perhaps because of its association with purity and new beginnings, the color of choice for marriage gloves, although pale yellow was also worn by wooing couples:

> *Next march the Glovers, who with nicest care*
> *Provide white kid for the new-married pair.*
> *Or nicely stitch the lemon-colour'd glove*
> *For hand of beau, to go and see his love.[2]*

And what about Lugh, the Celtic god for which Lughnasadh is named? It's possible that he had a hand in the making of these traditions. Pagan blogger Trina Roller offers an interesting theory that perhaps the glove is a nod to him: "The name Lugh-Lamhfhada means 'Lugh of the Long Hand,' and Llew-Law Gyffes, another name for the same God (Welsh), means 'The Lion with the Steady Hand.' It seems to us that the glove might simply be a symbol

---

1   Robert Herrick, "Hesperides."

2   A poetical description of glovers from an eighteenth century trade procession as recorded in *Gloves, Their Annals and Associations,* by William S. Beck.

for Lugh, with whom the festival has often been associated (as in Lughnasadh)." Could the hand of justice be his?

Revive the Lammas-tide custom of glove giving. Select or make a pair and bless them, then give them as gifts of trust, gratitude, and love—all celebrated at the first harvest!

Additional Reading

Beck, William S. *Gloves, Their Annals and Associations*. London: Hamilton and Adams, 1883. (Reprint from the collection of the University of California Libraries.

Dickens, Charles (conductor). *All the Year Round, A Weekly Journal*. Vol. XXIII. London: Chapman and Hall, 1879.

Fergusson, Rosalind. *Chambers Book of Days*. Edinburgh: Chambers Harrap Publishers, 2004.

Marquis, Melanie. Traditional Lughnasad with a Modern Twist. Llewellyn Journal, 2013. http://www.llewellyn.com/journal/article/2514

Roller, Trina. "Lammas, Traditions and Celebration." *Pagan Is Us*, August 1, 2013. http://paganisus.blogspot.com/2013/08/lammas-traditions-and-celebration.html.

Feasts and Treats

Laurel Reufner

By THE TIME LAMMAS rolls around, it's very hot here in Ohio. The last thing I want to do is stand over a hot stove while cooking. Besides, there are lots of wonderful veggies coming in the garden by now, and this holiday's menu tries to make use of them.

Simple Pasta with Sautéed Summer Squashes

Please do not discount the amazing, light flavor of this quick and easy summer dish.

Prep time: 15 minutes
Bake time: 20 minutes
Servings: 4

1 pound spaghetti
1 smallish zucchini (8–10 inches long)
1 smallish summer squash (8–10 inches long)
4 oz cherry tomatoes, approximately, or 1 large tomato
1 tablespoon olive oil, plus some for browning
1 tablespoon garlic, minced

Start the water boiling for the pasta, tossing in some salt for added flavor. While that is working, begin slicing your vegetables. The zucchini and summer squash should be cut into slices about ¼ inch thick and you may want to cut the larger diameter slices in half. Either halve the cherry tomatoes or chop a larger tomato into slices about ½ inch thick.

In a large skillet, heat enough oil to cover the bottom and toss in the garlic to let it lightly brown. Add zucchini and squash and sauté until tender. Toss in the tomatoes and gently stir until heated through. Remove from heat.

Once the pasta water is boiling, add about 1 tablespoon of olive oil. Break spaghetti sticks in half and add to water. Cook al dente, about 8 minutes, then drain.

To serve, dish out a helping of spaghetti noodles on a plate, add a nice serving of sautéed veggies on top. Finish with a little butter and a little salt and pepper. (You could also use a splash of olive oil in place of the butter, but I really love the way the butter and a little salt and pepper bring out the flavor of everything else.)

Garlic Bread Sticks

I really, really wanted to give you folks a home-baked, yeast bread option for Lammas, but it's become apparent that my bread-making skills need more work. However, not every sabbat's dish has to be made from scratch. These breadsticks are a nice, quick option if your bread-making skills also need some work.

Prep time: 10 minutes
Bake time: 8–10 minutes
Servings: 8

2 packages refrigerated crescent rolls
1½ tablespoons butter, melted
1 teaspoon garlic, minced

A quick tip before we get started—keep the crescent rolls refrigerated until you are ready to open the package and work with the dough. Otherwise they'll become a gooey mess.

Mix the melted butter with about a teaspoon of chopped garlic, adjusting to suit your tastes.

Remove one package of dough from the refrigerator and open it. Working on a lightly floured surface, you'll want to separate the dough into quarters. Using a pastry brush, a small spatula, or even the back of a spoon, spread some of the garlic butter mixture evenly across the exposed dough. Then roll the dough up lengthwise and place on a baking sheet. Repeat with the other package of dough.

Bake according to package directions or until they are lightly browned on top. Best when served warm.

Lemony Blueberry Zucchini Bread

My zucchini bread is considered amazing by pretty much everyone who's ever tasted it. And I always put some kind of addition in it. However, I've never used fresh fruit... until now. My daughters have declared this their favorite zucchini bread combination ever. You can make it without the lemon, but that little bit of zest really does amp up the flavor. Don't want to heat the house up during the day? Simply bake it an evening or two before you'll need it.

Prep time: 20 minutes

Bake time: 1 hour plus 10 minutes to cool

Servings: 16

¾ cup sugar

1 cup zucchini, unpeeled and shredded

¼ cup cooking oil

1 egg

1 lemon peel, zested

¾ cups all-purpose flour

¾ cups whole wheat flour

1 tablespoon flax seed, ground

½ teaspoon baking soda

¼ teaspoon salt

¼ baking powder

¼ teaspoon nutmeg, ground

1 cup fresh blueberries

I like to start this dessert with the wet ingredients first. Pick a big bowl, because it's the one that everything will wind up getting combined in. Place the sugar, zucchini, oil, egg, and lemon zest in the bowl and let it sit while you mix the dry ingredients. This will give it time for the sugar to start pulling moisture out of the zucchini and leave you with a nice soupy mix.

In another bowl, whisk together your flours, flax seed, baking soda, salt, baking powder, and nutmeg. Give the wet ingredients another good stir and then start adding in your dry ingredients, about a cupful at a time, stirring between each addition. Once it's all combined, gently stir in the blueberries.

Pour the batter into a greased loaf pan and bake at 350 degrees F for about an hour, checking toward the end of baking for a knife or toothpick inserted in the middle to come out clean. Let cool for at least 10 minutes before cutting.

Blueberry-Peach Shrub

Our ancestors used to make a very refreshing summer drink using vinegar, called shrub or switzel. I'm offering up a fruit-flavored variation to drink with your Lammas feast. This will need a minimum of 2 days prep time, but most of that is spent in refrigeration. Give it a try.

Prep time: 10–15 minutes
Chill time: 2 days
Servings: 8

6 ounces fresh ripe blueberries
10 ounces fresh ripe peaches
½ cup sugar
¾ cup white wine vinegar
Seltzer water, chilled

Wash the fruit well. In the case of the peaches, you'll want to pit them, as well as cut out any bad spots, but don't remove the peels; they'll only add to the peachy flavor. Put the fruit in a glass bowl and mash it up some so the juices are released. Stir in the sugar, cover in plastic wrap, and then chill it in the refrigerator for a good 24 hours.

Pull the fruit out of the refrigerator and stir it well, making sure the sugar is fully dissolved in the juice and then strain. Add the juice to a glass jar and pour in the vinegar. Put back in the refrigerator and allow to sit at least another 24 hours before using.

To use, mix 1 to 2 ounces of fruited vinegar to 6 ounces or so of the seltzer water. (Adjust to suit your taste.) Sit back and enjoy.

If you want to make it fancy when serving, try freezing some ice cubes that each contain either a lemon balm or mint leaf and add them to your drink.

Crafty Crafts

Linda Raedisch

IT'S A WAVE! IT'S a scroll! It's a shell! It's...rococo! The rococo decorative style prevailed in Europe for the first half of the eighteenth century, about the same time those Cathayan fairies from the previous project came into being. The name "rococo" comes from the French word *rocaille*, meaning "rockwork." What is rockwork? I'm not sure, but it's the shell, not the rock, that is the hallmark of the rococo. I adapted this one from a far more intricate design on a sandstone chimneypiece in an old Swedish manor house. The house, Sandemar, was actually built during the baroque (from Portuguese *barroco* "rough, uneven"), but like most old Swedish manor houses, Sandemar subsequently underwent the rococo before it was relieved by the altogether cleaner lines of the Gustavian.

August is the month when everyone seems to be making a last dash to the beach. It's an especially poignant place at this time of year, when the sun is beginning to set just that little bit earlier and the crickets are increasing the tempo of their tunes. You can glue the following pattern to the lid of the box in which you keep all those shells and bits of shore glass you collected over the summer, or use the pattern to make invitations to a late summer gathering at your manor house overlooking the Baltic Sea.

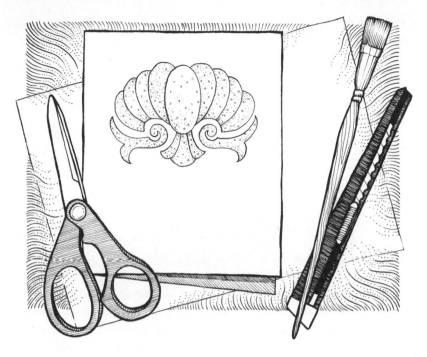

Rococo Cut-Paper Shell

Cut paper is one of my favorite media. Here we achieve the look of tarnished, brushed-on gold by cutting out pieces of scantily painted paper and gluing them to a background of the same paper. The design as it appears here was drawn to fit on the front of a small card. You can reduce or enlarge it on a photocopier to meet your needs, but don't reduce it too much or the scrolls will be too tricky to cut out.

Time frittered: About an hour per card, so if you're using them as invitations, you might want to trim the guest list.

Cost: If you haven't bought any of the starred supplies yet, this craft will run you about $25.00. But surely you've bought some of them already?

Supplies

Tracing paper*
Gold acrylic paint*
Craft knife* (optional)
Broad paint brush*
White all-purpose glue*
Smooth charcoal paper or light cardstock in either pale gray, pale
    blue, or pale pink.*

You will cut the shell from the same paper that you use for the background, so you only need one color. A sturdy white drawing paper will also do.

Fold and cut a portion of your paper to make a card. Set aside.

Lightly brush another portion of your paper (large enough to accommodate the shell) with the gold paint. Use a fairly dry brush and don't worry about unevenness. You don't want a solid coat of paint; you want the color of the paper to shine through. Set aside to dry.

Use a soft lead pencil to trace the shell design onto tracing paper. When the gold paper is completely dry, turn it gold-side down and transfer the design onto the blank side by tracing over the traced design again, pressing firmly with the pencil so the lines are transferred. Make sure the tracing paper is face down before you start!

Cut carefully along the pencil lines. Scissors are best, but you may want to use a craft knife for those pesky scrolls. Start with the central oval of the shell. Glue it onto your background (gold-side up, of course!) before cutting out the next piece. If you glue each piece on as soon as you've cut it out, you won't have to worry about losing any little pieces—a real danger if you have cats.

When gluing the pieces down, don't use so much glue that the paper gets soggy but do use enough that you can slide the piece around a little to get it into its proper position. Refer to the drawing to assure correct positioning. They should fit together quite easily, but do take care not to leave gaps and not to overlap.

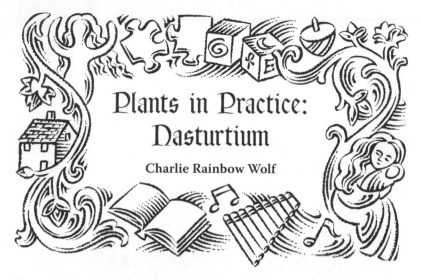

Plants in Practice: Nasturtium

Charlie Rainbow Wolf

THE LOVELY GOLDEN COLORS of the highly attractive nasturtium are still blooming, even though the season for summer flowers is coming to an end. The hues mirror the longer evenings and the warmer glows of the coming autumn. There are about eighty different types of nasturtiums—*Tropaeolum*—and they're native to South and Central America. Not only are they pretty and easy to grow, but they're excellent garden companions for all kinds of other growing things—and all parts of nasturtiums themselves are edible.

While a few nasturtiums are perennials in some areas, most of these festive additions are easily grown from seeds as annuals—and colorful they are! They commonly come in shades of orange and gold, but variegated, striped, yellow, purple, red, pink, and even blue are available! Depending on where you live, you have the choice to start them indoors or plant them directly into the earth. They like full sun; they will grow in partial shade, but may not be quite so hardy, producing more foliage than flowers. They don't need a lot of fuss, either, preferring poorer soil quality and no extra plant food.

Nasturtiums are fabulous in the vegetable garden. They attract pollinators and other beneficial insects. They repel unwanted pests that might jeopardize crops. They'll really earn their keep in with the cabbages and other members of the brassica family, for these brilliantly colored blooms will keep fungal infestations away, deter aphids, and trap squash bugs, cucumber beetles, and cabbage worms. Potato bugs don't like them and pumpkin beetles will stay away. In fact, there doesn't seem to be anywhere that these blossoming soldiers aren't welcome!

If you've never tasted nasturtiums, you're in for a treat. They have a nutty, slightly peppery flavor that compliments most dips and spreads. Go beyond the garnish and experiment with some herb pâtés and dips. Blend half a cup of silken tofu with some sunflower oil until it's the consistency of mayonnaise, then add half a cup of nasturtium petals—or just add the petals to mayonnaise. This makes a great spread for harvest breads or crackers.

Magically, nasturtiums are just as friendly and helpful as they are in the garden. They're seen as a symbol for abundance and loyalty, for good spirits and a community that works well together. Nasturtiums are a positive addition to spells and rituals that are aimed toward mending friendships, creativity, protection, and teamwork.

A Lammas Ritual for Abundance

Lammas is traditionally the time for harvest, the first grain. If you're doing this alone, make sure you've got some of your favorite foods on hand to indulge in once the ceremony is over. If you're working with others, let them know that this is a potluck feast, and have them bring their favorite harvest dish.

For this feast you're going to need a special loaf of bread—and if you use a home-baked one, even better (we're rather fond of tiger bread, because the colors seem autumnal somehow, but any bread will do). You'll also need a knife to slice the bread and a cutting board or plate on which to slice it, ale (again, home brew is best, but an artisan ale or a non-alcoholic beer work), a tankard for the drink, and a plate and serving knife for the bread, a large, smooth stone (a tumbled river rock is ideal), some peppermint oil (available at most health food stores or apothecaries), and some sunflowers—real, artificial, or even a picture or other representation. You should also have a few packets of nasturtium seeds. They're not expensive, and they're available from garden centers and farm shops.

At the appointed time for your rite, gather all items together. If you want a cloth on your altar or table, choose golds and oranges and other harvest colors. Place the tankard of ale and the loaf of bread onto the table, along with the stone, the peppermint oil, and the nasturtium seeds. Cast your magical circle now, if you wish. As you slice the bread, say out loud all the things for which you are thankful. Should you be gathered with others, take turns with this, and let everyone slice the loaf while doing so. Make it fun, rather than solemn; this is a time of harvest and celebration!

When the gratitudes have been spoken and the bread sliced, put a drop of the peppermint oil on the stone. As you do, offer up a prayer of thankfulness for all that you have and all that you're about to harvest in the upcoming months. You can write your own or you can use this one:

> *Lord and lady of the grain*
> *We're here to thank you once again*
> *For bread and ale and company*
> *And joys to come, so mote it be.*

Pass around the platter of bread and let everyone take a bite, followed by the ale, and let everyone take a sip. Next let everyone hold the stone. The idea is that the community shares everything, whether it is the first bread of the harvest or only a stone and some hope. Finally, pass around the nasturtium seeds for everyone to share and take home with them as a symbol of community, of looking after each other, working together, and being both useful and beautiful. Even if you're doing this solitary, you can hold the stone and know that you're not alone, for you have those in your life who strengthen you, and you always have the encouragement and support of the ancestors.

There's nothing left to do now but enjoy the feast. Dig into the bread, make merry with the ale, and keep the stone as a reminder to be thankful for the little things in life. Nasturtium teaches you that everything is easier when you share it. Teamwork halves the troubles and doubles the joys, and makes the work seem less of a chore. This often overlooked cottage garden favorite is a constant reminder that it is the simple pleasures that make the best memories and are the most rewarding in the long run.

Goodbye to the Sun God

Suzanne Ress

AT LAMMAS WE GATHER to celebrate the first harvest, especially that of grain. On a deeper level, we are also celebrating the symbolic sacrifice of the sun god, which enables his descent to the Otherworld, that dark hidden place of the spirit.

The ceremony must take place outdoors, and should start at sundown on July 31st, but in case of inclement weather, it can be postponed a day or two.

If possible, set up your altar in a newly cut wheat field, but if this is not a possibility, any open space outdoors will suffice.

Ritual Preparations

Collect some dry straw from a newly cut wheat field or otherwise procure a small amount. Weave this dry straw into a small braid, big enough to fit in the palm of your hand, and tie each end securely with yellow or gold thread.

Bake or purchase a fresh whole loaf of grainy bread.

Prepare a small vial of massage oil, using a few drops of sandalwood essential oil in jojoba or another carrier oil.

Items Needed

An orange candle and a windproof lantern or hurricane lamp to protect it

A carafe or bottle of red wine and a chalice

An athame

A wide, heatproof dish containing salt, sand, or fine gravel

If the ritual is to be performed in a cut wheat field or other unusual location, you will need a fireproof surface to serve as your altar. This can be improvised using several firebricks, a slate paving stone, or a heatproof board or small table.

At sundown, all participants shall gather at the selected location and the altar shall be set up. At the center of the altar, place the orange candle in its lantern with a lighter or matches. To the east of the candle, place the vial of scented massage oil, and below it, the dish of salt, sand, or gravel. To the west of the candle, place the carafe of wine and the chalice, and below it the braided straw. The loaf of bread and a knife for slicing shall be placed above the candle. The athame shall be laid below the candle.

Participants should form a circle as the selected leader lights the orange candle. Using the athame, she shall slowly trace the form of a pentagram in the air above the altar, starting at the top point and moving diagonally toward the lower right side point, and saying:

I invoke the elemental lord of fire, representing the sun god, to present himself for sacrifice, by joining us in our celebratory circle

All present shall cheer, "Huzzah! Welcome!"

Moving the athame slowly from the lower right point of the pentagram, diagonally to the upper left point, the leader cries out the names of each element as she touches their point with her athame:

I invoke air, water, and earth!

Participants shall cheer and welcome each of the elemental lords as he arrives.

And finally, as she seals the pentagram, she will invoke the spirit, and a hushed silence shall reign.

When all of the elemental lords are present, they will join the other participants in moving sun-wise in a circle around the altar. They will start off walking, but gradually increase their speed until they are jogging or skipping around the altar.

As they circle, participants shall chant:

Eko, eko, Azarak!
Eko, eko, Zamilak!
Eko, eko, Cernnunos!
Eko, eko, Aradia!

This chant shall continue until a protective circle of pale blue light has risen around the group and all present have let go of earthly concerns and worries, and entered into an altered state of consciousness.

Now the leader blesses the scented oil and carries the vial around the inside of the circle, dabbing a small amount of oil onto the outstretched palms of all participants, and putting some on her own palms before replacing the vial on the altar.

Remaining in the circle, facing sun-wise, each individual gently massages the oil into the back of the neck and between the shoulders of the person standing in front of him.

The leader says:

The god has toiled long in the sun to bring forth the fruits of this harvest, and now he will find relief in his demise. He looks forward to his sacrifice, for only in this way can he join his lover, the earth, and let the circle of life continue uninterrupted.

The leader now places the straw braid into the dish of salt or sand, and all present say:

So long, Sun God! Huzzah! Huzzah!

The leader lights the braid aflame.

Everyone remains silent, contemplating his or her own upcoming sacrifice this night, until the braid has burnt to ash.

At this point the leader pours some wine into the chalice. She lifts the chalice and exclaims, "I spill the sun god's blood upon the earth!"

She pours a little wine over the straw ash to fully extinguish it, and then refills the chalice.

"I now ask each of you present to sacrifice a little piece of your ego. Let us each name some unpleasant or unadmirable quality we would like to rid ourselves of. This shall be our personal sacrifice."

The leader will commence by saying, for example, "I shall sacrifice criticizing my husband's fashion sense," or "I shall sacrifice my gum chewing habit," or "I shall sacrifice gossiping about my neighbors," or whatever else seems fitting.

She takes a sip of the wine and passes the chalice to the person on her left, who does the same, until everyone present has sacrificed something.

After each person has had a sip of sacrificial wine, the chalice is refilled and the bread is sliced. The bread slices are passed around the circle so that everyone has one, and then the chalice, too, is passed around, whoever wishes taking a sip.

The leader says:

Sun God, we thank you for having sustained us, and for continuing to sustain us through your sacrifice. We are grateful for this first harvest, the grain harvest, which shall carry us through the dark part of the year.

Now the lords of the other three quarters are thanked, and all of them are revoked, and the circle is closed.

Everyone shall be free to mingle about, eating more bread, drinking more wine, and conversing, until they've had their fill.

Notes

Notes

Mabon

The Autumn Equinox: A Time for Action

Michael Furie

As THE HEAT OF summer begins to break and the first leaves turn from green to brown and fall from the trees, there is a subtle feeling that permeates the air—that shift into a different phase and a deeper focus. With the earth positioned at equinox, so that the sunlight is most directly overhead at the equator, we are once again at a time of balance. The hours of the day and night are almost equal on this day and we experience the liminal (threshold) time between the season of growth and the season of repose. This critical point is actually a period of immense potential that I feel should not be overlooked. The agricultural cycle is a most profound example (and can indeed be a template) for the prevailing energies astir in the world, and at this time of the year, we reach the point of harvest. Throughout the growth phase of the year, everything is (hopefully) increasing in strength and abundance, but the value of such treasure is limited at best if it is left to decay. That is why the autumn equinox is so crucial; it is the time to act, the moment when we claim the rewards of all the work conducted and achievements gained during the spring and summer seasons. Far from personal conjecture, the importance of this day has been expressed in both ancient and modern tales and religious texts. With the following few examples, we can only begin to comprehend the true (and often undervalued) power of the autumnal equinox, but they serve as wonderful starting places and important reminders of the inherent quality of this day.

Aspects of the Goddess

Though most easily labeled the "Witches' Thanksgiving" (and this moniker is certainly accurate) and left without much further explanation, this holiday holds an integral quality all its own. In the "Aspects of the Goddess" as presented in the book, *The Witches' Bible* by Janet and Stewart Farrar, the time of the autumnal equinox is seen as the station of repose; wherein the goddess presides over the time of rest and withdrawing of growth before the eventual station of death at Samhain. The Farrars drew upon the earlier works of Doreen Valiente and Robert Graves in presenting this framework of the Goddess's relationship to the year. They maintain that unlike the God who is viewed to actually experience the effects of the seasonal tides and shifts, she (the Goddess) presides over these shifts and remains eternal in her nature. The goddess creates the conditions of change and opportunity and these are reflected in the natural world. It is at key points like this equinox when these fundamental shifts are the most profound and we can take advantage of these thresholds and channel their energy into new avenues. While this approach focuses upon a singular goddess as the changer of seasons, another familiar mythos takes a different view.

Demeter and Persephone

In the most general sense, the Greek myth of how Persephone became Queen of the Underworld is a tale of seasonal significance. In older versions, she is already the goddess of the Underworld or becomes so of her own free will, but in the most widely told versions, such as in the Homeric Hymn to Demeter, she is taken there by Hades to become his bride. The daughter of Demeter (goddess of harvest, fertility, and agriculture), Persephone was the maiden goddess of spring. Hades, the god of the Underworld, fell instantly in love with her. Versions vary, but it is said that Persephone was lured away from her companions, a group of nymphs, by the powerful scent of a narcissus flower. She desired to give the flower to her mother and so plucked it out of the ground. This action sprang a trap concocted by Hades in which the earth opened and Persephone fell into his realm.

Demeter, panic stricken, searched for her daughter the world over (thus neglecting her duties in nature) to no avail until she came upon Hecate (goddess of witchcraft). Hecate advised her to inquire to Helios, the all-seeing sun god as to what happened to her daughter. Demeter did so and Helios told her what happened to Persephone. Demeter insisted upon the rescue of her daughter, and though Persephone was able to return to her mother and the upper-world, she was forever bound to Hades and the Underworld, for she had eaten a scant amount of pomegranate seeds while there, and to partake of any food or drink while in that realm was to leave one unable to return. A compromise was reached wherein Persephone was able to spend half the year with her mother and had to spend half the year with Hades as his wife and queen of the Underworld realm. When she was in this world, her mother was joyous and so the earth became fruitful and the seasons of plenty were underway. When Persephone returned to the Underworld, her mother was filled with upset and so allowed nature to wilt and decay, thus the earth was split into a period of growth and one of repose. The times of transition were the equinoxes, therefore the autumnal equinox can mark Persephone's yearly descent back into the Underworld. Her journey creates an incredibly profound shift in the natural world. Though this is probably one of the most dramatic representations of the seasonal shifts, the themes of descent and divine grief or panic as catalysts for change are more widespread than this single example.

Descent of the Goddess

In one of the foundational texts of modern witchcraft presented by Gerald Gardner (and published in such works as *Eight Sabbats for*

Witches by Janet and Stewart Farrar), the "Legend of the Descent of the Goddess," we are shown the goddess journeying into the Underworld to solve the mystery of death: why every created thing that she adored withered and died. As she traveled through the realm, the goddess was met by guardians of the portals who challenged her to strip free the garments and jewels of her station, and she was bound, "as are all who enter the Realms of Death, the Mighty One." When she finally met Death, he fell in love with her, but she loved him not. She asked why he caused all that lived to fade and die and he responded that the true cause was age and fate to which he was helpless; that his role is to offer rest and peace and also strength to return. He begged her to remain forever with him but she loved him not. Disappointed, he decided to give her the scourge of the realm, but he loved her too much to inflict pain or harm, so he only lightly scourged her and his gentleness kindled love within her heart. Joyfully, he then "taught her all the Mysteries and they loved and were one and he taught her all the magics." The teaching is that there are three great events in life: love, death, and resurrection in a new body, and that these are all controlled by magic. To be reborn, one must die, to die one must be born, and to be born there must be love.

Some have posited that this tale can be used to illustrate the unification of the anima (feminine) and animus (masculine) halves of ourselves and the resulting power this unification can bring forth. Some have suggested that this legend is in some ways related to the tales of Persephone and Hades (and also to tales of Inanna's and Ishtar's descents into the Underworld). We can also see an underlying theme of balance and how the light half and the dark half are intertwined and meet at critical points in time. Since the equinoxes are the only two moments of balance in the year, it becomes clear that these times can be seen as culminations of the power that came before and will soon be exchanged for a new paradigm. It is crucial to act before the moment passes or the energy will be lost; if we neglect to harvest, we will lose the fruit to age and fate (to which even death is helpless) and therefore fail to partake of the potential abundance.

Mabon ap Modron

Finally, in the Welsh tale of Mabon, we see the power of light needing to be nurtured and released from confinement. The word "Mabon" has, in modern times, come to be a name often used for the autumn equinox Sabbat. Though the association may be new, the tale of Mabon ap Modron (son of mother) is rather ancient and found in the *Mabinogion*. In the tale of *Culhwch ac Olwen*, we see that in order for Culhwch to be granted the hand of Olwen, her father demanded that he complete several impossible tasks. One of the tasks Culhwch must complete is to "enlist the houndsmanship of Mabon, son of Modron, who was abducted from his mother when he was three days old." Cuhlwch sets about his task and in the process questions the Ousel of Kilgrwri, an ancient bird. He asks, "Do you know anything of Mabon, son of Modron, who when three nights old was taken from between his mother and the wall?" The ousel had not heard anything but sent him to an even older creature for possible assistance. He went from creature to creature in turn: the Stag of Rhendevre, the Owl of Cwn Cawlwyd, the Eagle of Gwernabwy, and finally the Salmon of Llyn Llyw. With the salmon (the oldest creature and symbol of wisdom), Culhwch found success. The salmon told him that Mabon was imprisoned in Gloucester. A battle ensued in which Mabon was at last set free.

Mabon is seen as a god of youth and light, and his being taken from his mother could be viewed as light being pulled away from the world, held in repose, and then eventually returned in a revitalized form. If this is so, linking Mabon the deity with the autumn holiday follows a similar pattern as Persephone's return to the Underworld also occurring at this time. Both will later reemerge bringing the light and time of growth back to the world. This period of abundance grows steadily stronger until it is once again time to claim the rewards at this time of equinox, just before they are gone.

When the harvest is upon us, however we may choose to relate to it, the time for action has arrived. After the long journey through the cold of winter, the emergence of activity with the onset of spring, and the full force of nature's energy unleashed during summer, we reach the pinnacle. Though the peak of solar power has come and gone at the summer solstice, the fullness of growth has continued on and reached its zenith at the equinox. This same energy can be applied to our everyday lives. We can claim the power present at this time to reap the rewards of all our hard work throughout the year by using all forms of prosperity magic and also by taking the opportunity to empower ourselves now so that we may continue to thrive.

As the season of autumn unfolds, the hours of daylight begin to wane much more noticeably and the weather starts to cool; the energy shifts to the element of water and the likelihood of rain increases. Moving deeper into the season, we find that the atmosphere becomes ideally attuned to both introspection and divination, both of which are aided by a strong reserve of personal power. This being so, it is all the more important to gather our strength while we can so that we may enter boldly into the next phase of the year. We, much like the divinities discussed, must maintain our inner light so that we may survive through the dark time and emerge renewed, empowered, and ready to share our gifts with the world.

Cosmic Sway

Corrine Kenner

MABON, THE LAST SABBAT rung on the Wheel of the Year, symbolizes the cycle of life as it draws to a close. It marks the final harvest and a time of thanksgiving, as the bounty of summer is brought in for the dark days of winter.

We celebrate Mabon on the autumn equinox, when the Sun moves into airy Libra. Today, the hours of day and night are equal, balanced evenly on the scales that serve as the emblem of the sign.

Mythic Astrology: Jupiter

In astrology, the greatest rewards come from Jupiter, the king of the gods. Ancient astrologers called Jupiter the Great Benefic, the bringer of gifts. Like a cosmic Santa Claus, Jupiter bestows blessings, honors, and acclaim.

Jupiter was the ruler of Mount Olympus and the master of both mortal and immortal subjects. He had the ultimate power of life and death, and he's the cosmic ruler who put many of the constellations in their heavenly homes.

As the king of the gods, he made sure that all the other deities lived up to their responsibilities. He punished their misdeeds and settled their disputes.

He was also the father of Mars, the god of war, and Hebe, the Greek goddess of youth. His affair with Leto led to the birth of Apollo, the Sun god, and Artemis, the lunar goddess of the hunt. His affair with Themis, the goddess of justice, created the three Fates. And Athena, the goddess of wisdom, sprang full-grown from his head.

Jupiter, as you'll remember, was the god who freed his brothers and sisters from their father Saturn. The old god of time had swallowed each of them whole. Once he had liberated them, Jupiter claimed the heavens for himself, while his brother Neptune took the oceans and Pluto seized the realms of the dead.

History, however, repeats itself. As fate would have it, Jupiter would soon be threatened by his own child. After hearing a prophecy that his first wife, Metis, would give birth to a god "greater than he," Jupiter swallowed her. She was already pregnant with Athena, however. His undigested pregnant wife and unborn child made him miserable with a pounding headache until Athena eventually burst forth from his head—fully grown and dressed for war.

Jupiter had more children than most people can count. He had a number of famous dalliances with mortal women, whom he usually seduced in disguise.

He romanced Leda in the form of a swan. Her twin sons, Castor and Pollux, were ultimately enshrined in the constellation Gemini.

He assumed the shape of a bull for his tryst with Europa. As a result, she gave birth to Minos, who became king of Crete and keeper of the Minotaur.

Jupiter disguised himself as a huntress to woo Callisto, one of Artemis's maidens. His jealous wife, Juno, changed Callisto into a bear, and Artemis inadvertently killed her. Jupiter gave her new life as the constellation Arctos.

Jupiter disguised himself as Alcmene's fiancé to win her favors. Nine months later, she gave birth to Hercules.

He loved the princess Semele—but she also became the victim of Juno's wrath. Juno disguised herself as Semele's own nurse and tricked her into asking Jupiter for a favor. He agreed, but then she asked him to reveal his true form. The moment he did, thunder and lightning struck, and Semele was consumed by flames.

In at least one case, Jupiter tried to disguise one of his lovers. He transformed the beautiful priestess Io into a white cow. Juno wasn't fooled. She sent a gadfly to torment the unfortunate creature, who wandered the world in hopes of escaping from her tormentor. Eventually she reached Egypt. She resumed her original form on the banks of the Nile and gave birth to Epaphus, the king who built the city of Memphis.

Danae was the daughter of a king, and an oracle had foretold that her son would lead to the monarch's death. He locked Danae in a tower of brass, but Jupiter was able to descend in a shower of gold. When Danae's father discovered that Danae had given birth to a boy named Perseus, he locked them both in a trunk and had the trunk thrown into the sea. Jupiter rescued them, and eventually Perseus became one of the legendary heroes of Greece and Rome.

In astrology, Jupiter represents growth and expansion, as well as luck, opportunity, prosperity, and success.

Jupiter rules fiery Sagittarius, the sign of the archer. Jupiter also rules the expansive ninth house, where astrologers look for information about higher education, long-distance travel, and philosophy.

Reading the Signs

The Sun and Mars are in an easy trine, which means the two planets are in agreement on airy, intellectual concerns.

The Sun and Saturn, however, are squaring off. Saturn's earthy Capricorn energy will bring you down to earth, but it could feel unnecessarily heavy and burdensome. That's compounded by Saturn's sextile with the Moon.

You'll feel the need to express your concerns. Mercury, the planet of thought and communication, is trine antagonistic Mars and square that onerous Saturn.

The Moon is trine Venus, which should highlight romance and affection—but Venus is square Mars, which means the two lovers are simply annoying each other right now.

Mars and Uranus are also squared off and rubbing each other the wrong way. Uranus is getting a boost from a trine with Saturn, the ringed planet of boundaries and limitations.

You can still be social. Just agree to disagree on practical matters, and focus on the romantic aspects of Jupiter, the planet of good fortune, in a blissful trine with Neptune, the planet of dreams, and a sextile with Pluto.

Planetary Positions

- Sun in Libra
- Moon in Pisces
- Mercury in Libra
- Venus in Scorpio
- Mars in Aquarius
- Jupiter in Scorpio
- Saturn in Capricorn
- Uranus ℞ in Taurus
- Neptune ℞ in Pisces
- Pluto ℞ in Capricorn

Phases of the Moon

On September 25, a Full Moon in fiery Aries will reflect the full light of the Sun, which is in airy Libra. A fiery Aries Moon is bold, brave, and independent, and it fuels a desire for fresh starts and new beginnings.

On October 9, a New Moon in Libra will usher in an evening well suited to socializing or cultural events.

On October 24, a Full Moon in Taurus will lend itself to sensual pleasures. Go out to dinner if you can.

Practical Astrology

Astrology is a calendar-based study, and the twelve signs, just like the twelve months of the year, can be grouped into four seasons: spring, summer, fall, and winter. Each season is three months long, and each season has a beginning, middle, and end.

The signs fall into three corresponding modes: cardinal, fixed, and mutable. Loosely put, those modes conform to the beginning, middle, and end of each season. The modes are sometimes called quadruplicities, because there are four signs for each mode.

Cardinal signs correspond to new beginnings. The first day of Aries marks the first day of spring. The first day of Cancer is the first day of summer. The first day of Libra is the first day of fall, and the first day of Capricorn is the first day of winter.

Fixed signs mark the high point of each season. Just as you know that summer days are hot and winter nights are cold, the fixed signs —Taurus, Leo, Scorpio, and Aquarius—are clearly defined and dependable.

Mutable signs—Gemini, Virgo, Sagittarius, and Pisces—are flexible, adaptable, and changeable, because they correspond to the last month of each season. They pave the way for change.

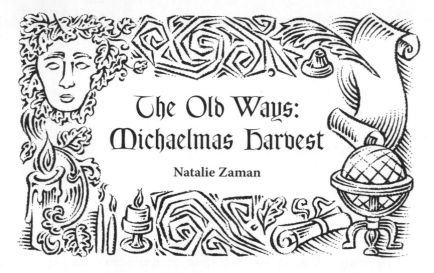

The Old Ways: Michaelmas Harvest

Natalie Zaman

IMAGINE FOR A MOMENT that you're living in the eleventh century, working with the seasons, going to church, and praying that you survive another year. September rolls around and it's time for Michaelmas—the feast day of that doughty warrior saint, Michael. It's such an important and solemn day that you'd spend three days prior to it fasting, going to confession, and then walking to church barefoot. That was the original plan when Michael's feast day—September 29—was established in the fifth century, but it fell too near the autumnal equinox, a time when folks were used to celebrating the last harvest of the year—not a time for austerity. There was only one thing for it: St. Michael would add another duty to his ecclesiastical résumé: he would oversee and bless the festivities of the autumnal equinox. He and his mythos would be inserted—opportunely in many cases—into already existing traditions.

Best known as the head of the army of God and ejector of Lucifer from heaven, Michael was, naturally, the patron saint of soldiers. He's also the patron of those who work with weights and measures. His feast day was determined by the dedication of his first church (built over a cave in Rome), but it is solidly (and perhaps, conveniently) positioned just after the autumnal equinox when the sun enters the astrological sign of Libra, represented by scales. His saintly skill set makes him the ideal candidate to invoke for strength, balance, and protection—the heart of the celebrations of both the autumnal equinox and Michaelmas.

The name Michaelmas is a bit of a misnomer as it suggests that the day belongs to Michael alone, when in fact the day also honored fellow archangels Gabriel, Uriel, and Raphael, all of whom undoubtedly helped Michael in the battle for Paradise. As the last of the harvest was brought in and folks started to look ahead to the dark days of winter, it was probably a comforting thought to know that Michael (whose name aptly means "Who is like God?" in Hebrew) and company, with their collective strength, would be present during the coming challenges.

The autumnal equinox was a traditional time for electing officials, paying debts, hiring servants, and, of course, bringing in the last harvest. Thanks to Michael and his deeds, September 29 became a kind of harvest "deadline." By the end of September, whatever crops were left had to be brought in lest the Devil—trapped on hell and earth and with an axe to grind—would ruin whatever was left on the vine by spitting or stamping on it. This was especially true of blackberries, which were at their peak in the month of September (and still are). Blackberrying—the foraging of this free and plentiful late summer fruit—is an ancient British tradition still enjoyed today.

Harvesting wild carrots also became a Michaelmas tradition. In Scotland, women would go out into the hills the Sunday before Michaelmas to dig up wild carrots. These were given in bunches of three tied with red ribbon or thread as tokens of prosperity and plenty in the coming year. Split roots were especially lucky, and given from a woman to a man, they held connotations of fertility. Michael's saintly touch can be seen in the tools that were used to free the carrots from the earth: a trident and triangular spade shaped like St. Michael's shield.

A traditional harvest festival meal in England, Scotland, and Ireland when it could be had was the Michaelmas goose, fed on the stubble that remained in the field after the harvest was brought in (but was already ideally plump having fed on fresh grass all summer). Eating goose at Michaelmas—sometimes called "Goose Day"—ensured good luck and plenty in the coming year. A case in point: Elizabeth I was enjoying a Michaelmas goose (served as if to look alive) when she was believed to have heard of the defeat of the Spanish Armada.

In the British Isles, the autumnal equinox, and then Michaelmas was considered a "quarter day," a time of reckoning. Rents were paid on quarter days, and remittance for this debt at Michalmas often took the form of a goose as can be seen in this bit of verse written by George Gascoyne in 1575:

And when the tenants come to pay their quarter's rent,
They bring some fowl at Midsummer, a dish of fish in Lent,
At Christmas a capon, at Michaelmas a goose,
And somewhat else at New Year's tide, for fear their lease fly loose.

The goose became associated with paying debts and balancing books; Michael's symbolic value as a figure of balance made it a natural transition to dedicate the meal and its connotations to his service.

A floral tribute to Michael's strength and the joy and merriment of the harvest lingers past both the equinox and his feast day, a bright aster that blooms from August into late October. A reminder that despite the darkening days, life continues and Michaelmas daisies, like their namesake saint, continue to thrive in the looming face of winter:

The Michaelmas daisies, among dede weeds
Bloom for St. Michael's valorous deeds.
And seems the last of the flowers that stood
Till the feast of St. Simon and St. Jude[1]

---

1   Medieval Michaelmas prayer as quoted in Historic UK

Michael is the champion of the autumnal equinox. Invoke him for strength and balance as the year tips into shadow. May your harvest be plentiful and your geese be fat!

Additional Reading

Bauld, Mary. "An Ancient Michaelmas Tradition." *True Highlands*, 2014. http://www.truehighlands.com/an-ancient-michaelmas -tradition-by-mary-bauld/

Johnson, Ben. "Michaelmas." *Historic UK: The Historic and Heritage Accommodation Guide*, 2013. http://www.historic-uk.com /CultureUK/michaelmas/

Walsh, William S. *Curiosities of Popular Customs and of Rites, Ceremonies, Observances and Miscellaneous Antiquities*. London: J. B. Lippincott and Company, 1898.

Warwicker, Michelle. "Are We Ready to Embrace the Michaelmas Goose Once Again?" *BBC Food*. September 29, 2012. http:// www.bbc.co.uk/food/0/19731413

Feasts and Treats

Laurel Reufner

The beautiful thing about a vegetable soup is that it's so customizable. If I've included anything in here that you really don't like, then leave it out. Did I forget your favorite garden treat? Add it in! And if you want this to be vegetarian, just leave out the beef.

Garden Harvest Soup

I'm honestly not sure how many this will feed, as we always hope for leftovers. A good guess would say it'll serve at least 8.

Prep time: 30 minutes
Cook time: 1 hour minimum
Servings: 8

Oil, for sautéing
1 medium onion, chopped
3 cloves garlic, minced, or 3 tablespoons
1 pound lean ground beef or stew meat, cubed
2 cups potatoes
1 cup carrots
8 cups vegetable stock
1½ cup green beans, fresh or frozen

1 cup celery
1 cup okra*
1 cup corn, fresh or frozen
½ cup barley
1 tablespoon summer savory, dried
1 tablespoon basil, dried
1 tablespoon thyme, dried
1 tablespoon marjoram or oregano, dried
Salt and pepper to taste

Add a small amount of oil or butter to the bottom of a large pot and let it heat. Add the onions and sauté until tender. Add the garlic and meat, if you're using it. While that is all browning up together, chop the potatoes and carrots.

Once the meat is browned, you'll want to pour in a little of the broth and scrape the bottom of the pan to loosen any stuck bits, which will provide some great added flavor to the soup. Once that's done, you can pour in the rest of the stock. Add the potatoes and carrots, which will take longer to cook than the other vegetables.

Finish chopping the rest of the vegetables that need it, adding them as you go along. Add enough stock or water to cover the top of the veggies and then bring the whole lot to a boil before reducing to a simmer. I like to let my soups cook for at least an hour, adding in the seasonings at about the half-hour mark. That's also when I'd add the barley.

*Okra is delicious in soups, but it will need a little prep work if you use fresh, otherwise it will become all slimey in the pot. If you don't want to bother with an added step, just use some frozen. To prepare the fresh okra, wash it well and trim off the tips and slice into about ½ inch thick slices. Finally sauté lightly in a pan until the cut ends are sealed.

Mr. Incredible's All-Around-the-Garden Salsa

A good soup is such a one-dish meal that I had a difficult time figuring out what else to offer for this sabbat meal. Other than the dessert, that is. And then my husband started making his own salsa. He kindly let me take notes while he made a batch.

Prep time: 20–30 minutes
Chill time: 1 hour, minimum
Servings: 14 (½ cup servings)

5–6 cups tomatoes, diced
2 jalapeños, seeded and minced
1 medium onion, diced
4 small ears sweet corn (about 2 cups) cooked and removed from the cob
1 tablespoon Rancher Steak Rub (see recipe below)

Combine all of the ingredients, except for the spice mix, and stir well. Sprinkle the spice mix on top and pour in about 4 cups of apple cider vinegar. Add enough water to top it off and let sit refrigerated for an hour or so for the flavors to get to know each other. Serve with either tortilla chips or maybe the cracker recipe offered in the Imbolc section.

Rancher Steak Rub

What follows is my take on the Rancher Steak Rub. I prefer my version in part because it contains much less salt. Feel free to adjust it even more to suit your tastes. This makes ¼ cup. Store leftovers in an airtight container for later use.

Prep time: 5 minutes

2 tablespoons sea salt
1 tablespoon pepper
1 tablespoon dried chopped garlic
2 teaspoons allspice, ground
2 teaspoons cinnamon, ground
1 teaspoons cloves, ground
1 teaspoon ginger, ground
Combine very well in a small dish. Shake well before using.

Handmade Tortilla Chips

You can always buy tortilla chips to go with your salsa or serve as crackers for your soup, but they are also very easy to make. If you're extra energetic, look up online how to make the tortillas from scratch, then follow the directions below. It makes 3 to 4½ dozen, depending on how you cut them.

Prep time: 5 minutes
Bake time: about an hour
Servings: at least 10

Non-stick cooking spray
9 corn tortillas 6"–8"
Spray bottle of water
Sea salt, if desired

Lightly spray your baking pan or rub it lightly with some olive or vegetable oil. Cut the tortillas into fourths or sixths according to your size preference. Lightly spritz them with water and then sprinkle with salt.

Bake by batches at 350 degrees F for about 18 minutes, carefully turning them halfway through baking. You'll know they're done when they change color. Allow to cool and then store in an airtight container.

Cranberry-Pecan Apple Crisp

Finally, maybe a little something for dessert? From salsa as an appetizer to an apple crisp as the ending, this meal covers a lot of territory. This particular dish was one of the most popular of the entire testing process—with both of my daughters requesting bowls of just the topping!

Prep time: 30 minutes
Cook time: 40 minutes
Servings: 8 easily

For the topping:

6 tablespoons butter, cold
1 cup flour
6 tablespoons brown sugar
⅛ cup sugar
¼ teaspoon cinnamon, ground
¼ teaspoon cloves, ground
1 cup rolled oats

For the filling:

½ cup maple syrup
¼ cup flour
1 teaspoon cinnamon, ground
8 large baking apples
¾ cup chopped pecans
½ cup dried cranberries

To make the topping, combine all of the ingredients in mixing bowl. Use a pair of knives, a pastry blender, heavy duty fork, or your hands to cut the cold butter into the rest of the mixture until it all resembles large crumbles.

Next peel the apples and cut them into slices about ½" thick. Place them in a bowl and mix in the rest of the filling ingredients, tossing to coat the apples. Place in the bottom of a glass baking dish. Spread the topping evenly across the top of the apples.

Bake at 375 degrees F for 30 minutes, and then cover the edges of the crust and bake another 10 minutes or until a fork poked into the apple slices doesn't meet any resistance.

This is best served warm, maybe with a scoop of vanilla bean ice cream drizzled with caramel sauce. However, it's also really good cold. If any of it survives that long.

Crafty Crafts

Linda Raedisch

WITCHES CALL IT MABON. Christians called it Michaelmas in honor of the Archangel Michael, a spirit who had his own shadowy beginnings in the ancient Near East.[1] Here in North America, few Christians have even heard of the Feast of St. Michael, though they might have heard of the Michaelmas daisy, a wild aster that dots the woodlands from late summer to early fall. Up until fairly recently, Michaelmas was an important spoke on the year's wheel. In 1680, an English colonist writing home from the remote wilderness of the colony of New Jersey listed all the berries he had gathered "from the time called May until Michaelmas."

If ever a season had a color, it's the Michaelmas season, and the color is purple from the lavender petals of those asters to the brighter, more pinkish hues produced by the pokeberries that are ripening at this very minute. (If you make your own pokeberry ink, wash your hands very carefully afterward and keep both the berries and the ink away from children and cats: it's highly poisonous to everyone but birds.) Blackberries leave a darker purple stain. At

---

1 Michael's deepest identity may be found in the asterism known as the Pleiades. The archangels Michael, Gabriel, Raphael, Raguel, Remiel, Sariel and Uriel from the Book of Enoch probably evolved from the Mesopotamian Sebittu, a tribe of axe-and-dagger-wielding gods who were often represented by two parallel rows of three dots each plus one dot at the end.

Michaelmas, they're having their last hurrah. In fact, in England it was considered bad luck to eat blackberries on or after Michaelmas. However, if you really have to have a blackberry on Michaelmas Day, it might be worth the risk: some say the bad luck doesn't kick in until Old Michaelmas which, since the switch from the Julian to the Gregorian calendar, now falls on October 10.

Medieval Window Leaves

Like my Candlemas snowflake, this design was pilfered from an inlaid medieval paving tile. In the original, the design would have been stamped into the leather hard clay tile. The veining in the leaves was then filled with a darker colored slip. Our process is more economical, for each leaf you cut out will yield not one but two leaf shapes.

If you're going out to buy some watercolor paper anyway, why not invest in a decent set of watercolor tubes? They work so much better than the dry little ovals of paint you can buy in the school supplies aisle of the grocery store. And when you use tubes, you don't have to worry about muddying the colors. Thin down some red to turn it pink, dab it on the wet paper, add orange and yellow, and let them bleed together. Yes, some leaves are still a little on the green side when they fall, but if you add green blotches to the mix, keep a buffer zone of yellow around them so they don't blend with the red and make brown. Brown leaves are for November.

And then again, you might want to tint your leaves in shades of lavender and mauve.

Time frittered: Just minutes per leaf.

Cost: About $20.00, less if you've already got a decent set of watercolors.

Supplies

A sheet of not too thick watercolor paper or not too thin drawing
   paper: in other words, paper that can get a little bit wet but is
   also easy to fold and cut through.
Clean sponge or paper towel

Watercolor paints
Palette, either store bought or a piece of wax paper
Small paint brush
Clear tape*

Dab your paper with a clean sponge or paper towel until it is just a little more than damp. You don't have to wet the whole paper at once; you can wet as you go.

Squeeze a little paint onto your palette and thin well with water. Dab onto wet paper with brush. If it neither spreads nor bleeds, you should either add more water to the paint or re-wet the paper.

Add more colors, but don't go overboard: a limited palette is best.

When the paper is all colored, set it aside to dry and prepare your leaf template. This can be cut from printer or other ordinary paper. I suppose you could cut it straight out of this book, but I really don't approve of cutting pages out of books.

The template represents half a leaf (or half of two leaves.) When your paper is dry, cut it into manageable, slightly larger than leaf-sized pieces that you can fold in half. Trace the template onto the colored paper, cut out, unfold, and there are your first two leaves. Make as many as your sheet of paper allows.

Now all that remains is to arrange the leaves artfully in the window, securing them with little rolls of tape. You might also consider gluing them to black or dark gray cardstock to make Michaelmas cards, an item that the stores these days just don't seem to carry.

Book Broom

If that early New Jersey colonist had occasion to sweep his New Jersey doorstep, he probably would have reached for a birch broom or "Indian broom." Birch brooms are not made like Witches' besoms; in fact, they were not made in the Old World at all. The colonists learned from the Algonquian tribes of the eastern woodlands how to score, peel back and bind the layers of birch wood into an effective cleaning tool.

My Book Broom is modeled after the birch broom. Because it's now September, and we're all feeling a little bookish, it's made from the page of a book, or, rather, a photocopy of a page from a book. (Because I don't approve of cutting pages out of books.) In true back-to-school spirit, I took mine from "Chapter Eleven: Quidditch" in *Harry Potter and the Sorcerer's Stone*.

In my younger daughter's beloved *Ever After High* series of books, the students play "Bookball," so when I'd finished the first prototype of my broom, I presented it to said daughter and announced, "It's a Book Broom!"

"What for?"

"For playing Bookball, of course."

She patiently explained to me that Bookball is not played with brooms; they just throw a book around like a football.

I'm sticking with Quidditch.

Time frittered: About 15 minutes

Cost: 15¢, assuming that you don't have to pay any library fines before you're allowed to use the photocopier.

Supplies

One 8½" × 11" sheet of paper on which you have photocopied a
   page from your favorite book
Ruler (optional)
White all-purpose glue*

Fold your sheet of paper in half like a book and cut along the fold. You only need one half to make one broom. (You will need one little strip from the extra half, so don't recycle it yet.)

Fold this half page in half again, again like a book, but don't cut.

Unfold and turn page print-side down.

Cut the left half of the page into vertical strips, but don't cut all the way to the top edge; stop about 1¾" from the edge. The strips

should be about ¼" wide. It's up to you if you want to measure; I prefer to eyeball.

When you have cut your row of strips all the way to the center crease, stop and turn the paper print-side up. Starting at the uncut side of the page, roll the whole thing up. Rolling it around a pencil or drinking straw will help to make it nice and tight which is what you want since this is going to be your broom handle. When you've rolled the whole page, strips and all, glue the seam securely.

It doesn't look much like a broom yet, does it? That's because it's not nearly finished. Pull the strips down one by one, revealing the text. Bind them with a narrow strip of that extra paper and secure with glue.

Speaking of books, as I was composing this year's "Crafty Crafts," books would regularly march themselves off their shelves in my living room and pile themselves on the kitchen table. They had come to help. And though our year-long paper trail of crafts ends here, if you suddenly find yourself wanting to know more about medieval tiles, Swedish manor houses, birch brooms, or even paper itself, the following books can be summoned to come and help you too.

Books

Bell, R. C. *Board and Table Games from Many Civilizations.* London: Oxford University Press, 1960.

Hughes, Sukey. *Washi: The World of Japanese Paper.* San Francisco: Kodansha International, 1978.

Jacobson, Dawn. *Chinoiserie.* New York: Phaidon Press, 2001.

Sjöberg, Lars and Ursula Sjöberg. *The Swedish Room.* New York: Pantheon Books, 1994.

Tolkien, J. R. R., and Baillie Tolkien, ed. *Letters from Father Christmas.* Boston: Houghton Mifflin, 1999.

Wilbur, C. Keith. *Indian Handcrafts.* Chester, Connecticut: Globe Pequot Press, 1990.

Plants in Practice: Sage

Charlie Rainbow Wolf

SAGE (*SALVIA OFFICINALIS*) IS another one of those herbs that is familiar to most people, whether they're into gardening or naturopathy or not. It's used in potpourri, cooking, and incense, and it also has magical rites. It's incredibly easy to grow, it has a nice flower and a pleasing scent, and it is a wildflower in many places of the world.

Sage is great for the beginning gardener. It's inexpensive from most garden centers, and if you know someone who has a parent plant, it can be easily split to provide you with a start. Give it some well drained soil and a lot of sunlight and then forget about it. It's pretty drought tolerant, and it will let you know if it needs water by wilting. Most of the common sages are perennial, anywhere from eighteen to twenty-four inches tall and up to thirty-six inches wide, and will come back again and again to bring their delights to your door. Older, woody plants benefit from a hard prune now and again. My husband's even inadvertently flattened a couple of mine with the lawnmower; they've just come back bright leaved and sweeter-smelling next year!

This herb is usually grown for its leaves, which come in dusty shades of green and have a very distinct, earthy aroma. Plant it near your cabbages and carrots to deter garden pests. It will help add flavor to your tomatoes if they're grown together, although keep it away from cucumbers. The flowers are pretty, but shouldn't be allowed to bloom as that will take the scent and taste away from the leaves. I keep one old sage that I do let flower though, because it attracts bees and butterflies and other pollinators into the garden.

Sage has a fairly long growing season and will tolerate mild frosts, but it's better to harvest the leaves before that point. Pick them in the morning after the dew is gone but before the sun gets too hot. Sprigs of sage can be dried and tied into bundles, or the individual leaves can be dried and stored for adding to recipes and loose incense. Finely chopped fresh leaves can be whipped into butter for a delicious herby spread, and this will keep in the freezer. Add fresh sage to honey, maple syrup, and herbal vinegars for added flavor, or add it to ice cubes to use in soups and stews at a later date. Sage can even be substituted for basil when making pesto for a different kind of flavor. Dried sage makes an excellent addition to salt rubs when cooking.

As a folk remedy, sage is popular and very beneficial. Sage tea is soothing for a cold or flu, helping to soothe the membranes, calm the nerves, and ease the stomach. It's a great mouthwash and helps to reduce swelling and bruising when applied as a poultice. As a massage oil, it's relaxing and helps to unknot tired muscles. It's said to assist the body's natural defenses against infections, and some herbal practitioners prescribe it to help with night sweats, menopause, and the end of lactation after pregnancy.

Magically, sage is cleansing and protective. It's the first herb that comes to mind when most people think about a smudging—or cleansing—ceremony. In addition to purification, it also aids in longevity, wisdom (as in "the wise old sage"), and in making wishes become reality. Sage is valuable in the grieving process, too, and for honoring the ones who no longer walk this earth.

A Mabon Cleansing Ritual

Whether you realize it or not, you're constantly being bombarded by the energy of other people and things as you move through your daily life. You can ground, center, and shield and help to deter most of this, but everyone has off days, or days when they feel more open than others. That's where this ritual comes in beautifully. It's done at Mabon to bring everything back into balance, but it's doable whenever you feel that the day has taken a bit out of you.

Like the other ceremonies, this can be done as a group, or worked alone. You'll need dried sage—bundles from an apothecary are best, but even the culinary spices will work, although if you go that route you should add a heatproof dish and a lump of charcoal. You'll want a flower pot or similar receptacle full of loose dirt or sand, a green candle and something with which to light it, and a broom—preferably a besom or one of the old fashioned brooms as opposed to something plastic. It's best to do this right on the equinox, but if you can't, that's okay, too. You don't necessarily need to cast a circle for this ceremony as it's one of protection and purging, anyway, but you may do so if you wish.

At the time of your ritual, light your sage and get it really smoking (temporarily remove the batteries from your smoke alarms—don't ask me how I know this one). Carry the sage through each area of your home or garden that you want to clean and protect. Make sure that you're surrounding yourself in the smoke, too. As you cleanse yourself and your environment, accompany the energy shift by singing or chanting. If you don't have a favorite, something similar to the following will do:

> *Spirits, sage, and those welcome here*
> *Purge and protect us from any fears*
> *Cleanse and calm all those whom we love*
> *With our prayers let the smoke rise above.*

Once you have saged every area, then it's time to sweep it. Place your sage onto the plant pot full of dirt so that it is safe, but don't extinguish it, not yet. Take your broom and go through the motions of sweeping out the unwanted energy and anything that is holding you back from being everything you be. Make your sweeping motions toward the door, and you can continue right outside. I've swept things through apartment complex halls and stairs and right down the path into the gutters before today!

When all the energy is swept out, and the area is clean, it's time to extinguish the sage. If you're using a bundle, plunge it into the plant pot of loose earth. If you've used the loose sage, put this in the earth and stir it around a bit to make sure that it's completely out. When it's extinguished and cool, take this soil or sand and tip it out of the plant pot somewhere that is not on your property—a ditch, or a hedgerow, for instance. You've now taken all the negative energy away from you and your home so that the balanced energy can return.

Sage asks you to pause and remember that challenges are a part of life; we have to have light and dark for there to be the equilibrium. What you've done is made way for the challenges with which you can cope and banished any residue that might overwhelm you. Keep this in mind, and call upon the wisdom of the lessons that sage has to teach the next time you start to feel anxious about something.

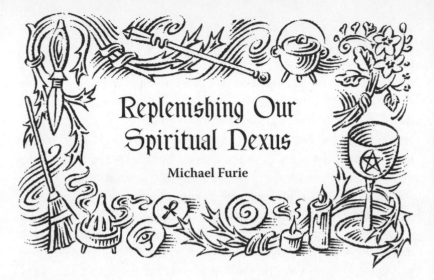

Replenishing Our Spiritual Dexus

Michael Furie

DURING THIS TIME OF the year as the weather begins to cool and the leaves turn from vivid greens to rich shades of yellows, oranges, browns, and even deep reds, the trees that bore them begin their shift into dormancy. The leaves fall from the trees, cascading to the ground in a colorful display of nature's efficiency. With their metabolism slowed to protect themselves through the potentially harsh conditions that winter may bring, the trees' focus has become that of preservation. We can learn from this example and attune our own rhythms to the prevailing tides. Gathering our strength at this time—as the power shifts away from growth and expansion—affords us an advantage during the fall and wintertime when our modern lives do not allow us to slow down. We can shore up our energetic reserves, so to speak, and this will help to reinvigorate our drive and power resulting in an improved ability to keep a steady pace even through the seasons of repose.

The autumn equinox is a time of balance and also the culmination of the growth phase of the year. Utilizing this energy to fortify ourselves and to help preserve the fruits of our labors is simply a matter of becoming an extension for the already present energy patterns of this seasonal shift. This ritual is written for a solitary person to perform, but it can be easily adapted to group use. The different tasks can be divided and someone can be assigned to guide the members through the meditation.

Items Needed

Bowl of beets
Bowl of hazelnuts (filberts)
Bowl of carrots
Bowl of grapes
Cauldron (or large bowl)
Dirt or sand (to fill the cauldron)
Athame
Wand
Bowl of salt
1 cup of water
Censer
Small plate of bread
Candles: dark red, orange, brown, gray
2 white candles
8 leaves (of varied color)
Incense charcoal
Sage incense
Candle snuffer (or spoon)

If possible, the area may be adorned with many more autumn leaves, as well as dried corn, gourds, and whole nuts such as pecans, walnuts, and almonds laid out in a circle to mark the ritual boundary. At the northern point of the circle, place the bowl of beets. To the east, set the bowl of hazelnuts, and to the south, place the bowl of carrots. The bowl of grapes is set in the west. Each of these foods align to one of the four elements: earth, air, fire, and water, respectively, and they are placed there to help draw in their power. Create an altar in the center of the circular boundary. On this altar place the cauldron filled with soil or sand in the center. To the right of the cauldron, set the athame and wand. To the left of the cauldron, set the bowl of salt and the cup of water. Behind the cauldron, set the censer. In front of the cauldron, set the plate of bread. Toward the back of the altar, place the dark red and orange candles to the left and the brown and gray candles to the right. These candles symbolize the waning strength of the sun and of entering into the time of decline. One white candle is set in each of the rear corners of the altar and lit prior to the rite for illumination. Set the eight leaves on the altar inbetween the tools in a pattern that pleases you.

After everything has been arranged and any other preparations have taken place, light the white altar candles and the incense. Pick up the athame and use it to cast a circle around the working area along the boundary, moving clockwise beginning and ending in the north. Next, stand facing east over the bowl of hazelnuts and call to the element of air saying:

Crisp autumn winds, blow in from the east, draw into my circle bringing wisdom and peace.

Turn to the south and the bowl of carrots and call to the element of fire saying:

Deep waning warmth of solar fire, draw into this circle bringing passion and power.

Turn to the west and the bowl of grapes and call to the element of water saying:

Gentle rains that quench and heal, draw into this circle bringing abundance and renewal.

Finally, turn to the north and the bowl of beets and call to the element of earth saying:

Holding the roots, earth nourish and bind, draw into this circle bringing love and strength combined.

Return to the altar and setting down the athame, light the autumn candles. As you light the dark red candle say:

The bright sun, whose power does wane [light orange candle].
The leaves that turn from orange to brown [light brown candle].
The clouds that turn the sky to gray; all the signs that autumn
has come [Light gray candle].

Pick up the wand. Close your eyes and envision a large tree with roots extending deep into the earth and branches that stretch up into the sky. This tree is connecting all three realms: the underworld, our world, and the heavenly realm. Visualize bright green leaves upon the tree gradually turning yellow, orange, brown, and red. See these leaves slowly falling off the tree and know that they represent that which no longer serves to nurture and so must be released. Mentally charge the wand with this energy and visualization so that the wand will carry some of the power of this tree into your circle.

Open your eyes and drive the handle of the wand into the soil in the cauldron, symbolically planting the tree into the earth, saying:

Ancient tree connecting all spheres, a beacon planted and pathway built; channeling power far and near, increased portion with abundance fulfilled; gathering energy, strength to the core; the magic is given and balance restored.

Visualize that the tip of the wand is glowing with power and that this energy is pouring into the circle and filling your solar plexus chakra (about three inches above your belly button) with pure white light. It is now time to reach out and call upon any deities with whom you would like to work, particularly those associated with the autumnal equinox such as Persephone, Demeter, the Horned God, Dionysus, etc. In your own words, ask them to bless and sustain you through the season. Pick up a piece of the bread and say:

In thanks for the gifts given to me, I freely share my bounty.

Take a bite of the bread and place the rest of the piece in the cauldron around the wand. Dip your finger into the salt and taste a bit of it saying:

Salt of the earth and of the sea, preserve abundance, blessed be.

Scatter a tiny pinch of salt in the cauldron over the bread. Pick up the cup of water, take a sip and say:

Waters of life, vital force, quench and renew, strength reinforce.

Sprinkle a few drops of the water into the cauldron over the bread and salt. By placing the offerings into the cauldron after they are charged with intent, their power is channeled through the wand and out to bring manifestation.

Now that the energy has been secured, it is time to pick up each of the eight leaves on the altar and hold them in your hands. These leaves represent the journey of the Sabbats, the past that we have experienced which has since fallen away leaving only the lessons gained. Giving thanks for the past opportunities and what you have been given throughout the year, reverently (and joyfully) toss the leaves up and away from you being careful that they don't fall on the candles.

Raise the athame aloft and say:

The time of the autumn equinox is that of harvest, when we reap the rewards of our hard work. In thanks and joy we guard and harness, our magical light, the divine spark.

Thank the deities for their presence and then release the elemental quarters. Move to the west and say:

Power of water, released and free, to fulfill the magic, so mote it be.

Repeat in the south, then east and finally, the north, substituting the proper element in each direction (fire, air, and earth respectively).

Finally, walk the circle one last time in a counterclockwise path, with the athame, pulling in the energy of the boundary and saying:

This circle is open, but shall never cease; the magic continues, the power released; the equinox has come to offer reward, abundance in measure and balance restored.

Extinguish the candles in reverse order of lighting: the gray, brown, orange, red, and then the two white ones with the candle snuffer (or the back of the spoon). Remove the wand from the cauldron and bury the offerings in the ground or a flower pot. The rest of the evening may be spent in feast. The foods most traditionally associated with the American Thanksgiving holiday are perfect for this sabbat. Blessings of the season to you.

Notes

Notes

The Witch's Tools Series

Notes